LALA LAJPAT RAI

LALA LAJPAT RAI:
THE MAN IN HIS WORD

Lala Lajpat Rai

GYAN

Published by

Gyan Publishing House
5, Ansari Road
Daryaganj, New Delhi-110002
Phone: 011-47034999, 9811692060
E-mail: books@gyanbooks.com

Distribution Network
gyanbooks.com
India, USA, Canada, UK, Australia, France

ISBN: 978-81-212-8734-0 (PB)
First Published, 1907

2nd Impression 2023

Printed at: Gyan Press, Delhi.

LALA LAJPAT RAI: THE MAN IN HIS WORD
Author: Lala Lajpat Rai

LALA LAJPAT RAI:

THE MAN IN HIS WORD.

MADRAS:

GANESH & Co.,

Thumbuchetty Street, E.

1907.

THE PUBLISHERS' NOTE.

In bringing out this little book the Publishers desire to express their obligation to the Editors of the *Hindustan Review*, the *Indian Review*, the *Modern Review*, the *D. A. V. College Magazine* and the *Punjabee* for permission to reprint articles which have appeared in their pages. Mr. Narayan Prasadarora, B.A., of Cawnpore, has also tendered valuable help in collecting the great Lala's writings and speeches.

TO

Our Mother.

"Struggle between truth and untruth, between vice and virtue, between honesty and dishonesty, between expediency and righteousness, between indolence and energy, between enterprise and spirit of lethargy and between time-serving selfishness and noble disinterestedness, without this struggle no nation can ever aspire to be great and influential. This struggle we have just entered upon."

(Lala Lajpat Rai, *On Hindu Nationalism.*)

VANDE MATARAM

Hail, Mother!
Sweet thy water, sweet thy fruits,
Cool blows the scented south wind,
Green waves thy corn,
Mother!
Land of the glad white moon-lit nights,
Land of trees with flowers in bloom,
Land of smiles, land of voices sweet,
Giver of joy, giver of desire.
VANDE MATARAM!
Millions and Millions of voices resounding
Millions and Millions of arms in resolve uplifting.
Dare any call Thee weak?
Obeisance to Thee! O Thou, mighty, with multiple might,
Redeemer thou, Repeller of the enemy's host,
Mother!
Thou art knowledge, Thou our religion,
Thou our heart, Thou the seat of life,
In this our frame Thou art the breath of life.
O Mother, the strength of this arm thine,
Thou the devotion in the heart!
Thine the image consecrate
From temple to temple!
VANDE MATARAM!
The wielder of ten arms, Dhurga, Thou,
Thou the Goddess of wealth, bower'd in the lotus.
Thou the Muse dispensing wisdom,
VANDE MATARAM!
Salutations to Thee! Holder of wealth,
Peerless,
With thy limpid water and luscious fruit,
Mother! Hail Mother!
Verdant, unsophisticated, sweet-smiling
Radiant, holding, nourishing,
Mother!
VANDE MATARAM.

CONTENTS.

INTRODUCTION.

"*People once awakened, and awakened rightly, cannot be put down*"—Lala Lajpat Rai.

The publishers of this book need offer no apology for bringing to public notice the life and teachings of a man whose name is at present on everybody's lips and whose sufferings in the cause of his country have "raised political agitation and the struggle for political liberty in India to the dignity of a Church." It is but proper that the meanest in the land no less than the highest should know Lala Lajpat Rai's claims to the people's good will and the Government's execration—how the Lala wanted to serve the Nation and how the bureaucratic Government came to think him at last so dangerous to its very existence, that it thought fit to kidnap him from his beloved country.

After all the controverseal writings which have appeared in the Indian Press about Lala Lajpat Rai's deportation it would be idle to dwell here on the merits and demerits of a measure whose only redeeming feature is that it is an Act of State. It is as idle now to expatiate on the retrograde and impolitic act of government as it is to dwell on the social and domestic virtues and also the political foresight of him whom Indians at all events believe in their heart of hearts to be a martyr. Ever since Mr. Morley condescended to recognise the belligerency existing between Educated India and Bureaucratic India by calling the former "enemies" in open Parliament, it is as foolish on the part of the people to pray for favours—even the favour of releasing Lajpat Rai, as it is on the part of the Goverment to expect more loyalty and less sedition from the people. For Belligerents never waste their breath in exchanging prayers and admonitions, but look to their own resources. "If you adopt a manly policy be prepared for the logical consequence" said the Lala to the Benares Congress delegates. Bureaucracy at least is arming itself with all the formidable weapons at its command to suppress a people's legitimate aspirations and, under the impression that all India is one great Kurukshetra, is bringing forth one by one its battallions of Acts and Ordinances to bind, gag and suppress all freedom of speech in the land—Yes, Bureaucracy is more earnest than the people in recognising the belligerency in India! What though guns and swords play no part in this great one sided war? In *their* place are hurled Edicts, Circulars, Ordinances and Acts—all in the perhaps sincere belief that the whole of India is seditious and on the verge of a civil war!

Bureaucracy is arming itself——meanwhile what is the Nation doing? The Nation at present appears like a house divided against itself. Its house is not in order—it is not prepared for the struggle. Some would fain give up the struggle for political rights in despair. They argue that a house divided against itself cannot stand.

Yes, it may not stand—still! It must march on! Let Lajpat Rai's noble words come to the rescue of those who are destitute of faith in the Nation's cause:—

"*Struggle, hard struggle is the law of progress. Yes, struggle we must, both* inter se *as well as against others. There must be a struggle between truth and untruth, between vice and virtue, between honesty and dishonesty, between expediency and righteousness, between indolence and energy, between enterprise and a spirit of lethargy and between time-serving selfishness and noble disinterestedness. Without this struggle no nation can ever aspire to be great and influential. This struggie we have just entered upon.*"

Yes, we have just entered upon this struggle both *inter se* as well as against outside forces. The so-called dissensions of the Congress on the one hand prove it; Mr. Morley's famous epithet proves it on the other. We have enemies in the camp as well as in Downing Street. "Shall we yield?" is the cry of many and many a wearied weakly soul, that expected Liberty to grow like a common Jack Fruit by the way side, that expected freedom to drop from above like a ripe mango all ready for the eating! Shall we yield and close this agitation of ours for more rights and more privileges and be content with the morsels thrown now and then from a lord's dining table as at a favourite dog?

No! "A people once awakened, and awakened rightly, cannot be put down." says the Lala!

It is impossible even for an all-powerful Bureaucracy

to put down an awakened nation, let it hurl its edicts ever so assiduously. The more such edicts, the more unpopular the Bureaucracy—the stronger becomes the Nation's cause. But the people need a warning not to commit political harry-carry in their premature despair. To such as are weak of heart and dull of political faith, a perusal of Lala Lajpat Rai's "Study of Hindu Nationalism" might be recommended as a wholesome tonic. "Let us not be impatient of what in my humble opinion seems to be a healthy sign of (political) growth. Let us not strangle it by drawing its undesirable (yet unavoidable) concomitants in high colours or by attaching undue importance to the same. * * * * * * * * *
Because there are some violent men, some bad tempered, some dishonest men, some traitors and some time-servers, it is no reason to record a wholesale condemnation of the same or to be disappointed with (or feel despair for) them." Like the deadly poison that arose at the Churning of the Ocean for making Heavenly Nectar, undesirable concomitants will always turn up when least expected. And in many instances they are unavoidable. But has not our religion taught us that even that Deadliest Poison may be rendered harmless to Iswara's children by His Heavenly Grace! The Lala's writings therefore call on the readers to have more faith in the political regeneration of the country. For "how can a Nation destitute of faith produce Martyrs?" He might well have said:—

Hold ye fast, the storm is coming!
Hold ye fast, brother to brother :—
The storm may come—the wind may rage,
But hold ye fast and brave the weather.

It requires all the nerve and all the strength of the Nation to brave and break the repressive fetters that are now being forged for the People's benefit by the Bureaucracy, and a proper study of the Lala's writings is sure to inspire the reader with the sanguine enthusiasm and robust faith in the Nation's glorious destiny with which every page of those writings is replete.

It has well and truly been said that Lala Lajpat Rai is the leader of the New Movement—the movement which recognises the limitations to the British Supremacy in India and emphasises the part which the Nation has still to play in the history of the world. The New Party's articles of faith need not be here explained—they are fully expounded in the speeches and writings of Babu Bepin Chandra Pal and Lala Lajpat Rai. The new party prefers to pursue a manly policy, and in the language of Lala Lajpat Rai, it is "prepared to follow the logical consequences of that policy." It craves no favours from Bureaucracy, it in fact recognises the state of belligerency darkly hinted at by Mr. Morley. Only Babu Bepin Chandra Pal called it a game of Chess instead of a game of War. And in that game, he said, "We do not know what shall be our next move until we know the move of our opponent." So the New Party and Mr. Morley seem to understand each other well enough ! The political atmosphere has thus been cleared and the fog of political dissimulation no longer clouds the scene of operations. Each side knows what it is about. The New Party wants thecomplete manhood of the Indians to assert itself in spite of every obstacle: the Bureaucracy wants to retain its hold as long as possible upon the country. The opposite parties have met face to face. The resources of Bureaucracy are matched against a people's determined will. There ought not to be any doubt as to the result of the contest. The bureaucracy will have to yield to the people what the latter have long been striving after, *viz.*—Popular Government.

And what form of Government will it be? We hear this query many a time put in the Indian Press; and in many ways has it been answered. The last Congress declared for "Swaraj"—and Swaraj will be either self-government under British Control or it will be absolute independence, according as the British are sympathetic or otherwise towards the manly aspirations of Indians. The well wishers of the British Raj indeed pray that it may be under the sympathetic guidance of Britain and they say it will be Britain's fault if she forces this foster child of hers to completely break away from her. One thing, however, is clear—the struggle for Political Progress must go on —whether with or without British sympathy, time alone can decide. In fact, *it cannot afford to wait* for British sympathy. A wise father retains the affection of his grown-up children—but what shall be said of him who stands in the way of his grown-up son setting up house for himself and feels peevish whenever a better arrangement in the house itself is suggested ?

The struggle is just begun. The arrest of Lala Lajpat Rai was the beginning of the struggle. The Bureaucracy with Mr. Morley at its head acknowledges it. The New Party with Mr. Lajpat Rai at its head recognises it. Of the two opponents, Bureaucracy and the People, the former is an organised entity with the traditions and heritage of over a century, the latter is a new growth, yet somewhat nebulous, its numbers yet uncertain, its resources yet untried, its heroes still in the making. The Bureaucracy is in its hoary age, the Nation is still in its youth, in its budding adolescence. All the good that Britain has till now done not only for India but for all humanity, the victories she has won, the arts and sciences she has developed, the education she has spread, the equality of man she has preached, the Christianity she has advocated—these and numberless other acts of benevolence and grace that characterised the greatness of Britain in her early days of conquest in India—all these stand as bulwarks in support of a jealous and timeworn Bureaucracy. There are many among Indians who gladly and sincerely forgive the present day haughty Englishmen all their sins on remembering the good deeds and qualities of their old-time predecessors. But with all their virtues and with all the benefits hitherto afforded to Indians by Engishmen—the fact still remains that Indians hanker after something more than a mother's milk, more in fact than even bread and butter. The tender care bestowed upon the infant by its father may have been angelic; but " there is a whisper rising in this country that loyalty is not a phrase, faith not a delusion, and popular liberty something more diffusive and substantial than the profane exercise of the sacred rights of sovereignty by political classes; that we live in an age when to be young and to be indifferent are no longer synonymous and that we must prepare for the coming hour." *

It is asked if the New Party desires immediate separation. This question has been repeatedly asked and been as repeatedly answered in the Press. The new party contemplates no such thing—it only keeps the goal clear in view—it may take decades and even centuries to reach the goal; but the goal is there and it is held aloft for public view in a serene atmosphere of open truth, unclouded by simulation, trickery or any paltering with conscience. For an Indian to deny that he has that goal in view is for a youth to deny that he will ever reach manhood. If all Indian parties were as clear in their statement of their ideals as this new party is, our political progress would be achieved much quicker. Does the new party then desire an immediate revolution as has only too often been alleged by the Anglo-Indian Press?

From what we have read and heard of the writings and speeches of the leaders of the New Party *we can emphatically say, No*! and why?

* " Sybil or the two Nations" by Disraeli.

"Recalling all the evil passions that a revolution arouses, all the ties it dissolves, all the blood it commands to flow, all the healthful industry it arrests, all the madmen that it arms, all the victims that it dupes —it is doubtful whether any man really honest, pure, and humane, would ever hazard it, *unless he was assured* that the victory was certain—ay, and the object for which he fights not to be wrested from his hands amidst the uproar of the elements that the battle has released."

No, the New Party contemplates no such thing as an immediate revolution! This should be clear to even a cursory reader of the writings and speeches of Lala Lajpat Rai. The Lala is conscious of the defects and weaknesses of the Indian Nationality, and like a sagacious politician his writings are mainly aimed at remedying those defects and removing those weaknesses. But he refuses to be overwhelmed by the difficulties in the way and asks his compatriots not to mind the thorns but to have the eye fixed on the divine rose of political freedom. His writings strengthen weak minds, while they encourage the timid and censure the indolently inclined. In these days of political activity —when the very air is surcharged with politics, nobody who follows the march of events with any pretentions to careful study can afford to miss a perusal of the speeches and writings of the first great martyr in the sphere of India's Politics.

G. ANNAJI RAO, M.A., B.L.,

LALA LAJPAT RAI.

Who is a great man? asks Lord Beaconsfield, and answers the question himself. It is he who 'affects the mind of his generation.' Judged by this test Lala Lajpat Rai is undoubtedly a great man. Whether one agrees with his views or not, no one who reads these pages will doubt the earnestness and sincerity of purpose with which he has worked for the National Cause, understanding by the term the development and enrichment of the people along all lines of activity, moral, social, intellectual, educational, spiritual, political and economical; nor will anybody think him capable of engaging in enterprises which cannot bear examination in broad daylight. Every one of the virtues which Mazzini attributes to Garibaldi—

a whole life devoted to one object—his country; consecrated by deeds of honour first abroad and then at home; Valour and constancy more than admirable; Simplicity of life and manners which recalls the man of antiquity; all the more mournful trials and losses manfully endured: Glory and Poverty! Every particular relating to such a man is precious—

finds a counterpart in the life of the great leader of the Punjab.

Lala Lajpat Rai was born in 1865 of humble but respectable parents in the small town Jagaran in the district of Ludhiana. He comes of an old Agarvara Baniya family. Lajpat never wearied of acknowledging his indebtedness to his mother. The Baniya caste is famous throughout India for its thrift—thrift practised as assiduously by the women who spend as the men who earn. In such a community Lajpat Rai's mother was remarkable for her skill in household management. None could excel her in the art of making a little go a long way. There was one uniform level of comfort maintained in the family whatever be the amount of income. The son testifies that when he was earning thousands his family was not more truly prosperous than when the family income was less than fifty—thanks to his mother's management. In the mother of Lajpat Rai was realised the noble Hindu ideal of a *grihaini*.

His father Munshi Radha Krishen Lala, who is fortunately living, has been a teacher of Persian and Urdu in a Government School. He is an excellent Urdu writer and the author of numerous pamphlets and books. Straightforward and honest, he is a great lover of knowledge. Among his works is a political pamphlet which attracted attention at the time of publication, written in reply to the famous monograph of the late Sir Syed Ahmed Khan in which the latter enunciated the policy which the Aligarh party is still pursuing. When again Sir Syed Ahmed Khan wrote an article against the principles and composition of the Indian National Congress, Lala Radha Krishen, surprised at the changed attitude of the leader of the Mussalman community, addressed an open letter to him which appeared in the Urdu paper 'Kohinoor'. Lala Lajpat Rai translated these letters into English and published them in 1888 when the Congress met at Allahabad under the

Presidency of Mr. George Yule. The veteran's pen is far from idle to-day. Munshi Radha Krishen's motto is plain living and high thinking. He would not on principle allow himself to be dependent on any of his sons and so he carries on a small business at Jagaran—his native town—which brings in enough to meet his modest requirements. Within the last few years he has suffered several grievious bereavements including the death of the second of his four sons—a promising graduate of the Punjab University—and of his noble wife. Now that Lala Lajpat Rai has been snatched away—not by death!—from his side, what a storm of mingled feelings must be raging in the breast of the venerable old gentleman: with the natural pang of sudden and forced separation from his first born, there must be mixed up a feeling of exultant pride at his belovod son having justified the training in public spirit and self-sacrifice which he had received from his father. The burden upon his heart must have no doubt been to a great extent lightened by the consciousness of sympathy demonstrated from end to end of this vast continent with the sufferings of Lala Lajpat Rai and his family. But those who wish to know what heoric stuff the old gentleman is made of and how bravely he has stood the shock of his son's deportation, cannot do better than read, mark and ponder over the following epistle which he thought fit to address to the public press just three weeks after the mournful event:—

" Scarcely 50 years ago the Hindus of the Punjab were a grossly ignorant and superstitious body. The religion consisted of silly fables and they could not face the attacks of Christianity and Islam. Conversions to these two religions were therefore somewhat common. Then arose Swami Dayanand, who nationalised Hinduism sweeping away the inventions of priests and charlatans, and striking at the root of image worship, The reconstructed Hindu mind of this Punjab now stood forth boldly to attack those before whom it had cowered so long. Conversions and deflection to other religions came to an end; and carrying the war into the enemy's country, the Arya Samajists began to take back into the folds of their neo-Hinduism people who had gone over to Christianity, or to Islam. Controversy raged furiously and very often courts of law had to be appealed to. Christians and Moslems who had been in the habit of having it all their own way when fighting Hinduism, began to feel a new pressure and, being worsted in controversy, gave out that the Aryas were a spiteful and contentious body. Christian Missionaries to whom each successive famine had been a veritable time of harvest, found their vocation gone; for, the Hindus led by Aryas began to look after their own orphans instead of handing them over to Christian propagandists. It was not seldom that English judges were appealed to, to decide who should be given the guardianship of Hindu widows and orphans and had to make the Christian Missionary hand over his future convert to his enemies? It became a common thing for a Missionary preaching in the bazaars to suddenly depart at the approach of an Arya!

"It was thus that the Arya Samaj became unpopular with certain very influential classes. As ill-luck would have it, the Editor of the *Punjabee* was an Arya Samajist. But it is difficult to find out why some orthodox Hindus in the Punjab have been rejoicing at Lajpat's deportation. They should know that the efforts of the Samaj, and of men like Lajpat Rai, have conferred great benefits on orthodox Hindus. Their children and destitute widows have been saved for Hindu Society. The thousands of souls rescued by Lajpat Rai, from famine and conversion were not the offspring of Arya Samajists, but belonged to orthodox Hindus. The chief sin of my son Lajpat consisted in this, that he stood forth a champion of his people and I rejoice that I had a son like him."

How many a father in similar circumstances would feel and think as the Munshi Radha Krishen has done! If ever India is to become a self-respecting member in the commonwealth of nations it can only be through such self-respecting fathers and self-respecting sons. Despite his advanced years Krishen Lala's step is as elastic, his frame is as erect and his brow as serene as in the happiest days of his youth.

Lajpat Rai had a brilliant career as a student. He distinguished himself at every stage, his weak health and narrow circumstances notwithstanding. His intellect was as strong as it was quick: he was regarded by his fellow students as an intellectual prodigy. He studied in the Government College at Lahore for two years being in receipt of a University scholarship. Having passed the first certificate examination of Law of the Punjab University he started practice in 1883, when he was hardly 18 years of age.

Two years later he passed the final examination standing second in a list of thirty condidates. This bare record of his student career does not however bring out clearly the influences amidst which he grew to be the man he is. In the evolution of character hereditary tendencies mark only the starting point of a man's career, the *direction* of which is however very considerably determined by the influence of environment. Endowed with a rich legacy of moral and intelletual attributes peculiar to the genius of the eastern Aryan, the good Lala had the benefit of an education in which the practical rationalism of Western science combined with the religious purity and moral elevation of Eastern literature put on him the hall-mark of true culture. He was naturally attracted towards some of the noblest spirits of his age of whom the most notable were Lala Hansraj, the late Guru Datta Vidyarthi and Chethanand. All these men, differently gifted as they were and differently circumstanced too, were moved by one common impulse—*viz.*, a keen desire to work for the regeneration and elevation of the Motherland which to them was no vague patriotic abstraction but was concretised in the land of the five rivers.

In their close association with one another were born those ideals of patriotism, of self-sacrifice, of untiring work and of unconquerable faith which have sustained Lala Lajpat Rai in later years of strain and stress and have also inspired the formation during the last two decades of enthusiatic bands of ardent young men who in their turn, each in his own way and in his own sphere, have been leading most of the progressive movements of north western India. Not a single movement started in recent times for the furtherance of educational, social religious or political reform but has had the benefit of Lajpat Rai's counsel or participation, and has received the impulse of his vivifying genius. While sympathising with and aiding every movement which made for progress, Lala Lajpat Rai early in his life identified himself with the Arya Samaj in which he found at first ample scope for the exercise of his patriotism, philanthrophy and religious zeal. The visit of Swami Dayanand in 1877 marked a turning point in the social and religious development of the Punjab. The Brahmo Samaj, while it emancipated the souls of men from the thraldom of superstition and blind alligeance to custom, was too eclectic for men who wanted a definite and tangible standard to rally round, and wandered too far afield in the region of belief and practice to satisfy the patriotic craving for a national heritage. Swami Dyanand, though assisted in his tour by the more liberal Brahmos especially of the Adi Samaj, noticed this tendency of the Brahmo movement and sought to supply a corrective by insisting on the authority of the Vedas as the revealed Word of God and proclaiming the social and religious ordinances of the Rishis as all sufficient for the social, moral and spiritual needs of the Hindu people.

This was just the sort of teaching for which the young Punjab was dimly yearning. By pointing to the prestine purity and simplicity of the Vedas, Swami Dyanand condemned on one hand the corruption and decay which had crept into popular Hinduism, and on the other satisfied the cravings of the National spirit which in those early days sought to realise itself in the field of social and religious reform. A gospel like the illustrious Swami's was a trumpet call for men to array themselves in opposite camps. Men had to declare themselves either foes or friends. No middle way was possible. The orthodox were pronounced in their opposition, while the Brahmos sought to take the life out of this rival reform movement by starting a number of associations in connection with their own Samaj which sought to supply the deficiency which the Swami pointed out. But it was too late. Swami Dayanand felt the need of an organization which would on one hand ensure healthy progress and on the other be a bulwark against denationalization. He conceived the formation of a grand National Vedic Church in which Patriotism and Reform went hand in hand and supplied the corrective one to the other. The opposition to Swami Dayanand's work was as determined as the zeal of his followers was fervent. The struggle between his followers whose number was rising by leaps and bounds and the ecletic and ultra-conservative Hindus was at its keenest between 1880 and

1885 when Lala Lajpat Rai was studying at Lahore. Lala Lajpat Rai and his friends were not the men in those stirring days to look on unconcerned as if they had no part to play in the fray. They determined to throw in their lot with the Dayanand party which was sorely in need of young men to defend its cause against the redoubtable champions of orthodoxy. Guru Dutt, Hansraj and Lajpat Rai were constituted Apostles of the new evangel. It was true they were students. But they did the work of grown up men,—preaching, debating and spreading the cause throughout the length and breadth of the Punjab. Their organizing capacity was truly marvellous. Hansraj being the eldest of the three counselled, Guru Datt inspired, and Lajpat Rai carried out the plan of missionary operations. In internal constructive work too, the three young men took a leading part. If the Arya Samaj of to-day may be said to be the creation, next to Swami Dayanand, of any particular men—those men were the three who fought its battle in their student days and nourished it with their earnings and their energy in adult age.

Having qualified as a pleader Lala Lajpat Rai elected to settle down to practice at Hissar in the Punjab. As in his early days, so now in his manhood good fortune followed him in the matter of genial associates and happy comrades. Among his new acquisitions were the noble hearted Pandit Lakpat Rai who has only recently given away all his life's earnings for philanthropic and educational undertakings; and Lala Churāmani, the founder of a famous Industrial School for waifs and strays, the father of Jaswant Rai, M.A., the proprietor of the *Punjabee.* Lajpat Rai practised down to 1892 at Hissar when he became the leader of the local bar. He also acted for three years as honorary secretary of the Hissar Municipal Board. It may be mentioned in passing that professional avocations did not take up the whole time and energy of Lala Lajpat Rai and his Hissar friends, the greater portion of their time being nobly and unselfishly spent in discussing questions concerning the welfare not only of their province but of India as a whole. Lajpat Rai's abilities and gift of speech earned for him an extensive practice, but his unambitious, unassuming and self-abnegating spirit, his plain simple mode of living combined with his profound and varied erudition in western and eastern literatures enabled him to attract a circle of friends and admirers to whom the Deportation has come as a personal calamity. In 1892 he transferred his practice to the wider field of Lahore, the nerve centre of the Punjab, whose Chief Court is practically the High Court of the Punjab.

Fortune's smile attended his advocacy, but since 1902 he has slackened his professional activity partly we believe on account of successive attacks of illness but mainly in order to devote himself more fully to the cause of his country. He has taken it upon himself to utilize his income from professional pursuits for the benefit of the Indian public.

In education, secular and religious, Lala Lajpat Rai has long taken a very active interest. He took part in the foundation of the Dayanand Anglo-Vedic College at Lahore, a First Grade college with an endowment of some five lacs which he was largely instrumental in collecting; it is, according to the Government Inspector's report in 1905, "the most numerously attended college in the province". He is a vice-president of the institution, and off and on for about a dozen years he has acted as its honorary secretary. He has taken an active part in teaching, having several times acted as honorary lecturer in History. He has made large donations to its funds. He is secretary also to the Anglo-Sanskrit College at Jalunder and a member of the managing committees of a number of Arya Samaj schools in the province."

It was chiefly his interest in education that took him to America in 1905, where he visited many educational institutions and took careful notes for future guidance. We may also mention that he gave important evidence before Lord Curzon's University Commission in 1902. After his return from the political mission on which he went to England as a colleague of the Hon'ble Mr. G. K. Gokhale, he organised a political society and collected funds for educating the patriotic sons of the Punjab in politics and economics with a view to send them out as political missionaries on the model, we believe, of the 'Servants of India Society' of Poona.

His attention was not confined to matters educational. In other departments of social service as well, the Lala's activity has been marked. His noble heart bled for the needy, the friendless, the houseless, the suffering and the starved. He organized relief works and orphanages, the outcome of his disinterested love for humanity in general and his community in particular. For several years he has been General Secretary of the Arya Samaj Orphanage at Ferozepur, by far the largest Hindu orphanage in Northern India, having several hundreds of orphans in its books. He is a member of the managing committee of the waifs' orphanage at Meerut, also a well endowed and flourishing institution. In 1897, and again in 1899—1900, he organised a Hindu Orphan Relief movement which succoured over 2,000 orphans, and he acted on both occasions as its General Secretary. The Government availed themselves of his experience in 1901, when he was invited to give evidence before the Famine Commission. His evidence was specially valuable as he had personally inspected the areas largely affected by famine. In April 1905, on the occasion of the great earth-quake in the Kangra District, he organised a relief committee on behalf of the Lahore Arya Samaj; and as Secretary of that committee he visited areas particularly afflicted, collected funds and himself supervised the administration of relief. The orphanages and relief works which Lala Lajpat Rai has organised and supervised with scrupulous care and pious devotion are standing monuments which bespeak the high and noble character of the Lala who in this respect followed faithfully the ideals of humanity and charity which are enshrined in the scriptures of India. A veritable *Darmaraj* of the Punjab, no earthly motive or ambition could deter him from the noble work of love and sacrifice into which he completely threw himself, heart and soul, despite tremendous difficulties in the way. The *Karnan* of his age, he has been the sunshine of many a gloomy and despondent heart. His philanthropic undertakings—living embodiments of his *Thyaga and Paropakara*—testify to his high capacity as financier and organizer.

Lala Lajpat Rai is also a man of extensive business connections. He is a Director of the Panjab National Bank, the first and the largest Indian Bank in Lahore. He is interested in several cotton mills and cotton presses in the Punjab, being in several cases on the Board of Directors.

Lala Lajpat Rai claims attention as a man of letters. As a journalist, he has for several years edited a vernacular magazine and a vernacular weekly journal, both conducted in the interests of religious and social reform and educatlonal progress; He has published in Urdu biographical monographs on Mazzini, Garibaldi, Sivaji, Swami Dayanand and Sri Krishna—books which have been widely read and greatly appreciated in the province. He has been in constant touch with several newspapers conducted in English, contributing to them frequently on the leading questions of the day. He has also written in English a life of Pandit Gurudatta Vidyarthi, M.A., the Indian reformer.

He has compiled a concise historical account of Hindu civilisation down to the commencement of the Musalman period. He has published various pamphlets and booklets of an occasional character.

Lala Lajpat Rai has always felt drawn towards politics : which indeed was a subject on which Hansraj and he could not look eye to eye. The elder patriot held that the work of the Arya Samaj was work enough for one life nay, for hundreds of lives. The younger and more forward leader's view, like Justice Ranade's was that the work of national regeneration was a larger and more comprehensive object than could be accomplished by any single agency however catholic it may be, and that it needed to be pursued along many lines of activity, moral, social, intellectual and political. He felt it his duty therefore, to promote, political activity first in his own province and through that in the whole country.

It was in 1888 A. D. that Lala Lajpat Rai joined the Indian National Congress movement when it met at Allahabad under the Presidency of Mr. Georgs Yule. Ever since his connection with this " un-official but National Parliament," to quote the words of Mr. Lal Mohan Ghose, his political activity has expressed itself in various shapes and forms, and in the political field, as in other fields, he has done all that a man could do with pen, tongue and purse.

In 1905, the Indian National Congress Committee having recognised in him an austere, sincere and selfless devotion to his country and her cause, selected him as one of its delegates to place before the British public the political greivances of the Indian people. The Indian Association of the Punjab voted Rs. 3,000 for the expenses of his tour in England: but he who had himself disbursed money for philanthropic and patriotic objects would have none of the money but gave it back to the support and benefit of students, and met his expenses out of his own pocket. The two Indian national delegates worked together for some time in England: but the Panjabee leader determined to visit America and study the working of institutions in the far western country—that latest born child of Modern Democracy. On his return he resumed his work in England with Mr. G. K. Gokhale; and in the political campaign carried on in several parts of England the Indian representatives brought home to the mind of the Britisher the evils of unsympathtic bureaucratic government under which India was labouring, and pleaded in eloquent language, adducing facts and figures in support of their contention, the cause of the half-starving and half-dying people of India. This political campaign, it may be confidently said, was a success, were it for nothing else but the message which as Lajpat Rai put it "the people of England wanted to send to you through me *viz.* the message that in our utterance, in our agitation, and in our fight and struggle for liberty, we ought to be more manly than we have been hithertofore"

After his return from England he has "been busy devising and organising ways and means for the political advancement and industrial emancipation of his country.

In the deliberations of the Indian National Congress which assembled in 1905 at the holy city of Benares under the presidency of Mr. G. K. Gokhale, he took a leading part, and supported a resolution on the "repressive measures in Bengal". His wit and humour, his thorough grasp of the situation, his warm appreciation of and eloquent tribute to the Bengali manliness, his sturdy patriotism, and above all, his unquestionable loyalty to the British Raj and his anxiety to befriend every popular measure of the Government, these are discernible in that short stirring speech (reproduced on page 149 of this book) which he delivered in the sacred hall of the National Congress.

The greatest fact in Lala Lajpat Rai's career and the one which has made his name a household word in every part of India is his Deportation. How this event has come to pass—though happily at the time of writing, the news of his release has caused joy in the heart of every Indian, be he Moderate or Nationalist—be he Mahomedan or Hindu—orthodox or Aryasamajist—how that unique event has come to take place, will not be fully and accurately known until official records supplemented by non-official testimony are in the hands of the public. But Lala Lajpat Rai, though perhaps surprised by the warrant of Deportation, was not quite unprepared for what has taken place. "Coming events cast their shadows before." Lala Lajpat Rai, true mariner that he is, read the signs of the coming storm ; and the letter (*vide* page 220) which he handed over to the editor of the *Punjabee* a few hours before his arrest, remains the most remarkable example of political prescience which has ever emanated from the pen of any Indian politician.

India was passing through stormy weather. The notorious Partition of Bengal was the precursor of a new political phenomenon in India—the birth of the nascent Nationalism. This infant political growth, the Anglo-Indian bureaucrats could not and would not tolerate. Of the ways and means they devised to strangle the national movement one was to strike a blow at the influence of popular leaders. Lajpat Rai was the first to thunder against Sir Bampfylde Fuller who insulted the *elite* of Bengal Society, including Babu Surendranath Banerji, on the occasion of the Barisal conference. He protested against the insinuations of Lord Minto in speaking of "*Honest Swadeshism.*" In his own province executive high-handedness reigned rampant, the Government of Sir D. Ibbetson had one rule for the *Punjabee* and another for the *Civil and Military Gazette.* Unpopular measures, like the Colonization Act which has since been wisely disallowed by the Viceroy, had stirred popular feeling which vented itself in public meetings. Of these meetings the Lala, according to Mr. John Morley himself, attended only two meetings, not on his own initiative but at the express request of the people. When the Lala who was sent for by the people to explain the object of the unpopular measures of the Government, was on his way to the meeting at Rawalpindi he was intercepted by Mr. Agnew—the Australian magistrate who was persecuting the leaders of the Rawalpindi Bar for their alleged championship of the cause of the people—and by the Superintendent of Police, and was advised not to deliver any lecture on pain of forcible dispersal of the meeting, and the loyal Lala Lajpat Rai accordingly informed the assembled people of the intentions of the magistrate and caused them to disperse peacefully. But the genius of Bureaucracy which little knows the feelings and thoughts of respectable citizens of India would not stop where it had during all these years stood, repressing the growth of full national life. The policy pursued by officers of Government is forcibly exposed in the *Hindustan Review*. :—

" You first drive a people into frenzy, to the point of desperation, by passing a number of highly unpopular and oppressive measures, without consulting them and without paying the slighest heed to their most reasonable objections urged in temperate language. If they keep their counsel to themselves and do not take the trouble to represent their opinions, you misconstrue their silence in to acquiescence in your doing. If they make known their views in respectable and mild language you pass by their representations in contumptuous silence. If they speak loudly and strongly, and seek to make themselves felt, you clap them into jail and go the length of banishing them from the land of their birth, without hearing, without trial, without consideration. Let this violent act of yours raise further loud-tongued protest, you set aside the legislature of the country and pass an executive ordinance withdrawing the indefeasible right of British citizens to meet in public for the ventilation of grievances."

When public affairs come to such a sad pass in this country, persons of unselfish motives, of noble intellect and of unswerving loyalty to the highest interests of their mother-land, *will* come forward and espouse the cause of the people even at risk to their own lives, and they will *not* surrender their conscience and patriotism to the dictatorial mandate of panic-stricken Bureaucrats, alien in race, complexion and habits, in thoughts and feelings, in ideas and ideals, in interests and ambitions. The frown of the authorities cannot in itself make an action bad or ignoble. The law is glorified when thieves and robbers, decoits and murderers, and persons of moral and spiritual depravity are visited with condign punishment. But when the flower of a nation are chosen for arbitrary punishment, the law degenerates into a savage weapon. Lala Lajpat Rai is undoubtedly among the choicest spirits of the age and of the race. Like Captain Dreyfus, he is an innocent victim of the rulers of the land.

"A man so open-hearted and straightforward, so genial and disposed to be friendly to one and all without distinction of class or creed; whose services were at the public command no matter from what quarter it came: of unsullied private character and spotless public career, his life was an open book that any one might pass and read; who loved light and worked in the light; to whom nothing was so abhorrent as the powers of darkness—of tyranny and treachery, of persecution and perfidy, of bad faith and low associations ; who shunned dark corners of dubious patriotism and always kept himself before the public gaze and in the sunlight of public criticism—how could, every one felt puzzled, such a man of open movements and open actions bring upon himself a blow aimed in the dark that in its terrible swiftness will not even allow him to lay bare his heart and show to all concerned how clean, how spotless, how devoid of mischievous thought and intent in any shape whatsoever it was." (*Punjabee*).

We wonder how a Government which had indented on the splendid, versatile services of the Lala on the occasion of the University and the Famine Commissions, can, in the name of consistency, policy or even expediency justify its conduct and character in inhumanly depriving one of the most intelligent and serviceable supporters of the British Raj of the elementary rights of liberty and self-vindication by banishing him from his native land on the beautifully vague pretext of "state reasons" under the sanction of a military, despotic Regulation which it does not blush to call a " law. ". His letter addressed to the *Punjabee* a few hours before his secret arrest and dark deportation seems *providential* ; but his appeal and warning to his Bengal friends assembled in the Benares Congress is *prophetic.* " If you have adopted this manly and vigorous policy, *be prepared for the logical consequence* (cheers). Don't conceal your heads, don't behave like cowards. Once having adopted that manly policy, stick to it till the last." The one reads like an unconscious autobiography, but the other fully lays bare the straightforwardness of a mind standing four square to all the winds that might blow. Questions without number were put in the British Parliament to the biographer of Gladstone and Burke, but these have been treated with scant courtesy. Under great pressure, Mr. Morley first tried diplomatic methods of persuasion to inspire confidence in the persistent members of Parliament who are interested in Indian progress, and these proved futile. It was only after his conference with Sir D. Ibbetson, "one of the ablest and most experinced Lieutenant-Governors," that he gave out the grounds on which he sanctioned this extreme and quite uncalled-for action. The Indian Parliamentary Committee met and denounced this high-handed measure and also passed a resolution that the Regulation of 1818 and other similar measures must be repealed: but why would Mr. Morley listen to their proposals, seeing that the Regulation comes so handy to an infuriated and frightened officialdom?

There is not a single Indian or unbiassed foreign journal that has not condemned this Military Act and the executive action of the Government of India. The most prominent politician, the Hon'ble Mr. G. K. Gokhale, has challenged the alleged conspiracy on the part of the Lala. Legally the action of Government has been questioned; and this aspect of the matter is ably handled in a letter which we reproduce at the end of the book from the pen of an Indian and originally published in the *Justice*, the organ of Social Democracy in England.

The Lala may have entertained very strong political views. But he is the last man to hatch a conspiracy in darkness and secrecy. In the deportation of the Lala—an idealist, enthusiast, *literateur*, practical philanthropist, bold politician, accomplished lawyer, cool-headed financier, cautious investor, earnest religious preacher and devout Arya Samajist, politics in India has entered upon a new phase and will, ere long, develop into a force which it will be impossible for any human power, armed though it be with the most drastic laws and a formidable array of soldiers and a magazine of shots and bullets, to change; and on the right evolution of the collective and mutually inter-dependent forces brought into play, the salvation of India depends.

It is a happy sign of the times that this fact is recognised even in the highest quarters. For what said Lord Minto a few weeks ago in his place at the head of the Viceregal Legislative Council? "I am well aware of the growing strength of political hopes and ambitions in this country and I welcome them as the natural result of the education British administrators have done so much to introduce and encourage. I have said so over and over again and I deny the accusation of want of regard for the growing influence of the educated classes of India. Far from wishing to check the growth of political thoughts, I have hoped that, with proper guidance, Indian capacity and Indian patriotism might earn for its people greater share in the Government of their country, They have proposals before them now which I trust will greatly contribute towards that end. The Government of India would be blind, indeed, to shut its eyes to the awakening wave which is sweeping over the Eastern world, overwhelming its old traditions and bearing on its front a flood of new ideas. We cannot check its flow, we can but endeavour to direct it into such channels as may benefit the generations that are to come. We may repress sedition—we will repress it with a strong hand—but the restlessness of new-born and advancing thoughts we cannot repress. We must be prepared to meet it with help and guidance. We must seek for its causes."

One wonders whether Lord Minto has realised all that his words signify in the shape of a conciliatory policy and a policy of encouraging, without stifling, the aspirations of the people after a self-respecting national existance. If Lord Minto and his adjutants in the Government of India had only sought the help of men like Lala Lajpat Rai in seeking for the causes of the unrest in the Punjab and in the whole country, they would have found in them friends and not " our enemies," such as they have imagined him and other popular Rawalpindi lawyers to be.

At any rate, it is a matter for rejoicing that the Government of India have at last thought fit to restore the spotless and illustrious Lala to his proper sphere. The Government of India, more than the happy Lala, deserve conrgatulation on an act of justice for which there should have been no occasion.

Long Live Lala Lajpat Rai.

"Come onward, come! Ye sons of Ind!
  The motherland your aid implores.
With dauntless hearts and ardent zeal,
  Enlist ye in your country's cause.
Let one resolve your actions guide,
  One spirit move your heart and soul:
Your feelings, efforts, hopes and aims,
  Let them all tend to the self-same goal.
Go, roam abroad in distant lands,
  And ever newer wisdom gain;
Awake, arise with ardour fresh.
  And chant a nobler—manlier strain.
Let not applause be your sole aim.
  Nor let abuse your soul subdue.
Devote your life to what is good,
  And what is great, and what is true.
Let all our party-strifes and feuds,
  Be scattered to the winds and skies!
Let Hindu clasp his Moslem friend
  For, all are one in Mother's eyes."

OPEN LETTERS

TO THE

HON'BLE SIR SYED AHMED KHAN BAHADUR, K. C. S. I.

No. I.

Sir,—Would you excuse me if I encroach upon your valuable time for a short while? Before I address you on my *matlab**, I think it advisable to state for your information that I have been a constant reader and admirer of your writings. From childhood, I was taught to respect the opinions and the teachings of the white-bearded Syed of Aligarh. Your *Social Reformer* was constantly read to me by my fond father, who looked upon you as no less than a prophet of the nineteenth century. Your writings in the *Aligarh Institute Gazette*, and your speeches in Council and other public meetings, were constantly studied by me and preserved as a sacred trust by my revered parent. It was thus that I came to know that you once approved of the contents of John Stuart Mill's book on "Liberty," and it was thus that I came to know (if my memory does not deceive me) that the present Chief Justice of Hyderabad, a staunch opponent of the National Movement, once translated Jeremy Bentham's book on "Utility" for the readers of your *Social Reformer*. Is it strange then that I have been astonished to read what you now speak and write about the "National

* *i.e.*, the subject-matter for discussion.

Congress"? Any person, in my circumstances, would shout out: Times have changed and with them convictions! Flattery and official cajoleries have blinded the eyes of the most far-seeing; cowardice has depressed the souls of the foremost of seekers after truth, and high sounding titles and the favours of worldly governors have extinguished the fire of truth burning in many a noble heart. Is it not a sad spectacle to see men whose days are numbered, whose feet are almost in the grave, trying to root out all the trees planted with their own hands!!!

Under these circumstances, Syed Sahib, it is, surely, not strange if I ask what has been the cause of this lamentable change in you. Old age and exhaustion of faculties may, perhaps, have some share in causing you to forget what you once wrote and spoke. Has your memory lost its retentiveness, or is it the blindness of dotage which has permitted you to stray into your present unhappy position?

If the former, I from amongst your old admirers will take upon myself the duty of reminding you of what, in moments of wisdom, was recorded and published by your pen and tongue, and this duty, I promise, I will fulfill with the utmost pleasure and with feelings of the highest satisfaction.

I will begin with your book on the "Causes of the Indian Revolt," which was written in 1858, though only translated and published in English in the year 1873. It may be worth while to note here that the translators of this were no others than Sir Auckland Colvin, the present Lieutenant-Governor of the North-Western Provinces, and Lieutenant-Colonel Graham, the writer of your biography. In this book, after having tried to prove that the mutiny of 1857 was no "religious war," nor the result of a preconcerted conspiracy, you say that "most men, I believe, agree in thinking that it is highly conducive to the welfare and prosperity of Government—indeed, that it is essential to its stability—that the people should have a voice in its Councils. It is from the voice of the people that Government can learn whether its projects are likely to be well received. The voice of the people can alone check errors in the bud and warn us of dangers before they burst upon and destroy us." To make the matter more clear you go on saying that "this voice, however, can never be heard, and this security never acquired, unless the people are allowed a share in the consultations of Government. * * * The security of a Government, it will be remembered, is founded on its knowledge of the character of the Governed as well as on its careful observance of their rights and privileges." These are noble words, nobly spoken; words of sterling honesty and independence of spirit. Can they bear any other meaning than that which attaches to that resolution of the National Congress which prays for the introduction of a representative element into the constitution of our Legislative Councils? Pray, tell me how can the people have a voice in the Councils of a Government if not by representation? How can the people of a country have their voice constantly heard if not through their representatives? But, to leave no doubts on the subject, I will go on giving quotations in proof of my assertion, that you have yourself in former times strongly advocated the introduction of a representative element into the Legislative Councils of India. After laying much stress upon the necessity of a Government respecting the opinions of the people it governs, you say: "The evils which resulted to India from the non-admission of natives into the Legislative Councils of India were various. * * * * It (*i.e.*, the Government) could never hear, as it ought to have heard, the voice of the people on the laws and regulations which it passed." Again you say: "But the greatest mischief lay in this, that the people misunderstood the views and the intentions of the Government. They misapprehended every act." After this you proceed to say that "if Hindustanis had been in the Legislative Councils, they would have explained everything to their countrymen, and thus these evils which have happened to us would have been averted." In your opinion, as expressed there, this non-representation of the voice of the governed in the Legislative Council of the realm was "the one great cause" and the "origin of all smaller causes of dissatisfaction." Nay, further, not to leave any doubts in the matter, and to prove that in your book you even go to the length of saying that your countrymen should be selected to form an assembly like the English Parliament (which demand, at the time you advanced it, was certainly more premature than it now is, though the National Congress, with all the advantages that the country has had in the way of education and enlightenment since that miserable year of 1858, only advocates the partial introduction of a representative element in the Legislative Councils), I shall give some more extracts from the same work.

There you say: "I do not wish to enter here into the

question as to how the ignorant and uneducated natives of Hindustan could be allowed a share in the deliberations of the Legislative Council, or as to how they should be selected to form an assembly like the English Parliament. These are knotty points. All I wish to prove here IS THAT SUCH A STEP IS NOT ONLY ADVISABLE BUT ABSOLUTELY NECESSARY,* and that the disturbances are due to the neglect of such a measure". Could clearer words be used than what have been quoted above? Is there any doubt as to their meaning? because, if so, I shall be obliged to quote the exact Hindustani words used by you to express the ideas propounded in the above lines. But no, I do not suppose you can feel any doubt on that point, because the English rendering was undertaken by no others than Sir Auckland Colvin and Lieutenant-Colonel Graham, the former of whom, at least, is now being proclaimed (whether rightly or wrongly, God knows) as an opponent of the National Congress.

Sir Syed, does it not sound strange that the writer of the words above quoted should put himself forward as the leader of the ANTI-CONGRESS movement? Is it not one more proof of India's misfortune that the writer of the above words should impute bad motives to the supporters of the National Congress, mainly because they advocate the introduction of some sort of representation in the Legislative Councils of India? Is not your charge of sedition against the promoters of the Congress, in the face of these, a mere mockery, a contradiction in terms? Thirty years ago, you advocated the institution of a Parliament, and yet you chide us saying that we want an Indian Parlia-

* The capitals are mine.

ment, notwithstanding that we protest that for the present, and for a long time to come, we do not claim any such thing? Mark the difference. India is no longer what it was 30 years ago. In the course of this period it has made a marked advance towards a higher civilization. The natives of India are no longer, with *very* few exceptions, ignorant or uneducated. The rays of education are penetrating and shedding their wholesome light inside most Indian homes; hundreds of thousands of Indians are as well educated as any average English gentleman, and we see scores of our countrymen every year crossing the "black waters" to witness with their own eyes the proceedings of the great British Parliament and personally familiarize themselves with the political institutions of the English nation. Can you in face of these facts still call us "SEDITIOUS"? According to your writings, we are the most loyal subjects of the Government, and if, notwithstanding what you have written, you still deserve to be called "the ablest of our loyal Mahomedan gentlemen," why, we deserve to be styled "the ablest of the most loyal subjects of the English Government."

To give a still more clear idea of what you thought about the fitness of India for this sort of Government, I give one more extract to the point, and then I will have done with your old writings for the present. After giving many arguments in proof of your position that the law which allowed the sales of land for arrears of Government revenue was also a cause of the outbreak of disturbances in 1858, you say: "A landed estate in Hindustan is very like a kingdom. It has always been the practice to elect one man as the head over all. By him matters requiring discussion are 'brought forward' (mind, not decided), and every shareholder, in proportion to his holding, has the power of speaking out his mind on the point." You are wrong when you say "in proportion to his holding." However, let it remain as it is. You proceed and say: "The cultivators and the choudhries of the villages attend on such an occasion and say whatever they have to say. * * * * You have here, in fact, in great perfection a miniature kingdom parliament." How is it that now you have changed your mind and have come to opine that these kingdoms, as you called them, should have no voice in the making of laws which materially affect the person, the property and the reputation of the people?

Some persons insinuate that these writtings which I have quoted came from an honest, uncorrupted mind, at a time when the writer had no prospect of being raised to the Legislative Council by mere favour. No, Sir Syed, no! I, on my own part, do not want to make such an insinuation againt the fearless writer of those noble words which have beeen quoted above.

Then the problem to be solved remains the same, *viz.*, why this change, why this inconsistency? I pause for a reply, with a promise of more in my next, and in the meanwhile beg to be allowed to subscribe myself,

27th October, 1888. THE SON OF AN OLD FOLLOWER OF YOURS.

——o——

No. II.

SIR,—It is more than two weeks now since my first letter was published, and I think, I have waited long enough for the reply which, it seems, you have no mind to send. However, in fulfilment of my promise, I am bound to go on giving quotation after quotation, bringing home to you your own former political teachings, and I hope I shall be able clearly to prove that you once believed in all the principles upon which the different Resolutions of the National Congress are based. This will leave you no alternative but either an open and unreserved confession of your apostacy or an unreserved retreat from politics.

Do not think, Sir Syed, that I shall rest satisfied with the publication of these letters in India. No, they will be duly published and distributed in free England, side by side with the pamphlets of your own pet Asssociation of yesterday.

In the book, already so often referred to, *i.e.*, "The Causes of the Indian Revolt," you say: "Government were but slightly acquainted with the unhappy state of the people. How could it well be otherwise? There was no real communication between the Government and the governed, no living together or near one another, as has always been the custom of Mahomedans in countries which they subjected to their rule. Government and its officials have never adopted the course without which no real knowledge of the people can be gained." Further on you say that "this cannot be expected from the English, as they almost all look forward to retirement in their native land, and seldom settle for good amongst the natives of India."

Now, I take the liberty of asking has there been any improvement of late in this direction ? Have the majority, or even one per cent, of the retired English officers, permanently settled in India ? On the contrary, we find that they are birds-of-passage just as much now as, or perhaps more than, they were when the above sentences were written. Then, have the Englishmen and the natives taken to living together or near one another ? Do you ever see Englishmen living in the Mahallas of your towns, however large the towns or however respectable the Mahallas may be ? None of the Englishmen have ever been seen doing that. In fact, their mode of living is so peculiar that they cannot. Or, do you think that the point has been gained by a few Anglicised natives like yourself having taken to living in Bungalows ? If that is what you argue, I assure you, you are sadly mistaken. Your living in Europeanized houses cannot be said to be a gain to native society. It is rather, if I may be allowed to say so, a very severe and deplorable loss. In the sentence quoted above, you admit that living together or near one another enhances our sympathies and gives us more occasions of seeing, mixing with, and obtaining a more intimate knowledge of each other. It is thus clear that Europeans can only really know us if they see us in our native homes, in our small thatched huts full of misery and sickness. How poor and miserable India is, they can feel only if they live amongst or near the houses of our agriculturists, and there see with there own eyes respectable native families sleeping in rooms into which an English beggar would scorn to step. Why is this? Is it because we Indians do not know how to live? Now, if you say that, go to those Indian residences which are occupied by our few rich or even well-to-do countrymen, and there you will find that our mode of living is quite on a par with that of Europeans. Does any one then ask how it is that I say that respectable natives live, everywhere, in buildings which can only properly be called hovels? The answer is, because they are miserably poor and cannot afford to build comfortable houses. Taxation is so high that they never feel themselves secure of their respectability. In fact, it is always in danger. The poor fellows are daily and nightly engaged in making the two ends meet. What I mean to say is that the fact of you or a few other natives having taken to live in Bungalows and imitating the English customs of eating and drinking and dressing cannot do any good either to India or to England. In fact, this will never help the English to realize the unhappy state of the people. Then the question is, how can the Government know the wants and wishes of its subjects? They cannot know them through official reports, because these reports are almost all prepared by persons who seldom see the real state of the people whom the reports concern. You yourself said: "But even these officials themselves were ignorant of the real thoughts and opinions of the people, because they had no means of getting at them" (*vide* your Biography by Colonel Graham, p. 49.) Then can the Government get this knowledge through the petitions of their subjects? I say, as you said—*no*. You said that these petitions "were," and I say they *are*, "seldom if ever attended to and sometimes never heard" (*vide* the same page of your Biography.) I add to this that even if they are ever attended to, enquiry into the allegations made in them is often entrusted to the same officials whose conduct forms the subject of complaint. Their reports are taken to be gospel truth and the petitions are thrown out.

Then, can the Government know the real opinion of the people through the Native press ? No, because the Government officials have always been hostile to it, and have ever asserted that these papers represent nobody but themselves.

Public meetings even are not effectual, because these are invariably declared to be the work of professional agitators, stump-orators and wire-pullers.

The question then is, that admitting as you do, that it is essential for the purpose of good administration that the people should have a voice in the consultations of the Government, how should that voice reach the Council Chambers, and how should the people be consulted before laws are passed ? You once said that "laws affecting the subject should be made after consultation with the representatives of the people"—ba salah wa mashwarah riyaya ke naibon ke—(*vide Social Reformer* of the 15th Shawwal, 1290, Hijri, equivalent to the 6th December, 1873, p. 163), and there cannot be any other answer to this question. Further on you said: "I am very sorry that this is not being done in India, and in not doing so Government is in error to a certain degree, but in a larger measure it is owing to the incompetency of the subjects, but I am confident that after a certain period—(baad chand roz)—sufficient education will remove both." (*Vide* the same Journal, same page.) It is fifteen years now, Sir, since the above lines were written, and it is, surely, time to ask, or, at least, to consider, whether that period, or "chand roz," to speak in your own words, has not expired yet. I am ready to concede, though it may be for argument's sake only, that the period has not expired, but are we not making steady progress towards the desired end? Your objections, unfortunately, are not based upon considerations of time, but are put forward as matters of principle. Then admitting, as you do, that this voice can only reach the Council Chamber through the representatives of the people, the only question to be solved is—who should be those representatives, or, in other words, how should they acquire that position? Can men, like Rajah Shiva Prashad and yourself, be properly considered as representatives of the people, and can the method of selection, by which you were sent to the Council Chamber, be accepted as of any value? I think no reasonable man would contend that it would have been possible, if Rajah Shiva Prashad had been an elected representative of the people of India, for him to have libelled the whole Indian nation, as he did, in his notorious speech on the Ilbert Bill. Could Rajah Peary Mohan Mukerjee and other native members have consented to the raising of the Salt tax if they had thought that their seats depended on the voices of the people, whose throats were, so to speak, to be cut by that obnoxious and inhumane measure? Then the correct solution is this and no other, that the people must be represented by delegates, elected by themselves; and subject of course to the restrictions to be imposed by the Government Co-sharers in the business of governing or legislating, these representatives must be such as to be totally independent of official favour or disfavour. If the selection of members for the Legislative Councils is to be entrusted to officials, I say it is a downright farce, and there can be no representation.

The majority of the quotations given above come from a book which was written about 30 years ago, and you may find an excuse by saying that the state of the people has since then undergone a mighty change, and that, in consequence of this, the remedies then suggested are no longer suitable. My dear Sir, this reply cannot stand a moment's examination. I am going to show that in 1881, which is only seven years ago, you held the same views and felt rather proud of them. When it was proposed to raise the old Punjab University College to the status of a University, you were one of the foremost opponents of the proposal. You, your admirers and followers, should not have forgotten that you wrote certain articles under the heading of "Our Vernacular," and got them published and circulated in a pamphlet form. These articles were published in almost all the leading vernacular papers of Northern India, and the educated community of the Punjab, who were strongly opposed to the establishment of a University on the lines suggested by Dr. Leitner, obtained effective support from these writings of "the ablest of the loyal Mahomedan gentlemen." In one of them (paper 2nd perhaps), which was published in your *Social Reformer* for 1297-98 Hijri (equivalent to 1881), at p. 135, you say: "National progress and National Government are both sisters born of the same mother. When a nation loses its independence, its progress only depends upon its learning the language and sciences of Conquerors and thus taking a part in the Government of the country. * * * * By way of flattery whatever may be said, and as a matter of policy whatever may be stated, the fact is that in *reality the relations of Hindustanis to their rulers are no better than those of slaves to their master.*" The italics are mine. I have tried to give a faithful translation of your Urdu sentence. If I have erred, I hope to be excused, and that my mistake may be pointed out. However, to satisfy the scruples of sceptical readers, I prefer to give the last portion of the sentence in Roman characters and leave them to judge for themselves whether the rendering is correct or not. The original words are: "Khushamad ki baten jo chahe kah le, aur political tariqe men jo kuchh beyan karna ho, keya jawe, magar Hindostanion ka hal apni fatahmand qaum ke sath gulami ki halat se kuchh ziyada nahin hai." In the same article, further on, you said that the "University College was being raised to the status of a University with the object of throwing obstacles in the way of our National advancement, and that the result of the clamour after Oriental studies could be nothing but that of keeping ourselves in the state of serfdom." (Iska natija yehi hai ki gulami ki halat men rakhne ke liye).

Sir Syed, would you still call *us* "seditious"? Remember that we are the product of that education which you so strongly recommended and which you have never been known to condemn. Our English education, the study of eminent European minds and European sciences—alas! that you cannot feel this!—has expanded our souls, and we can no longer be selfish "Sat Bachina" prodigies of your Oriental language. Sir, your fall seems to remind me of the fall of Adam. Just as Satan is said to be the cause of the fall of that progenitor of our race, this seeking after wordly honours seems to be the real explanation of your decline. It is nothing to you, because your term in this world must at no very distant period expire; but to us, who are yet, we hope, to live long and to fight out the bloodless battle of liberty, it is destined to remain a permanent disgrace. The line of argument against us would be that the races which produce such inconsistent philosophers are not fit to receive the boon of Local Self-Government. Sir Syed, if you have changed your political opinions, the sooner you announce it the better it will be, both for yourself and for us. It is simply childish to persist in your claim to consistency in the face of the above quotations. Better announce this change and explain why and how this took place. Again pausing for a reply, with a promise of more in my next, I beg to subscribe myself.

15th November, 1888. THE SON OF AN OLD FOLLOWER OF YOURS.

—o—

No. III.

SIR,—Well may we apply the opening sentence of Dickens's Tale of Two Cities to the present times in India. Well may we say that it is "the best of times" as well as "the worst of times." *Best*, as the country is on the point of having a *nätion*, *worst* as a particular section of the community wants to check the progress of the country and unfortunately is headed, or at least is said to be headed, by a man who has been a frequent advocate of representative Government in India. It is "the age of wisdom" as the country has risen from its deep lethargy and made up its mind to assist the Government by wise counsels. It is "the age of foolishness" as a particular party has the audacity to believe that their opposition will cause the national movement to die in its infancy. It is "the epoch of belief" because the different sectional interests have begun to believe in each other's sincerity: it is "the epoch of incredulity" because you, Sir, are said to be now-a-days against the introduction of a representative element into the Legislative Councils of India. It is the "spring of hope" when we see eminent English statesmen advocating the rights of the dumb millions of India. It is the "winter of despair" when we see her own sons deserting the cause of awakened India.

Sir Syed, I must remind you that it is the same India for the welfare of whose sons you established "The Siddors's Union Club" at Aligarh. Do you remember, Sir, that in that Club the alumni of the Mahomedan College were trained in the art of discussing public matters in public councils? I ask you, Sir, why you established that Club? Why did you formulate those rules of discussion which predict the establishment of representative institutions in the country? Oh, if we had only known that it was to end in *this!!* I feel that I have gone astray and must look to those extracts from your writings and sayings so dear to me, which foretold the establishment of representative Councils in India.

Will you please turn to page 49 of your Biography by Lieutenant-Colonel Graham where you are described as saying: "The people were isolated, they had no champion to stand up for their rights and to see justice done them, and they were constrained to weep in silence." Can you in the face of these words still say that the people never needed such champions, and that the Government has been doing and will go on doing without demand what it has thought and what it will think necessary for the welfare of the people? That it never needed the voice of such champions for the redress of grievances and the attainment of rights?

Having pointed out what the Government ought to have done to make itself popular (quotations as to which have been given in letters Nos. I and II) you said in the end of the same book, "The Causes of Indian Revolt," that "it was necessary for the Government to win the friendship and the goodfeeling of its subjects." Further on you said: "As yet, truth compels me to state, Government has not cultivated the friendship of its people as was its duty to do * * * * the father loves his child before the child loves him. * * * * If a man of low degree try to win the esteem of one in high position he is liable to be styled a flatterer and not a friend.

It was, therefore, for Government to try and win the friendship of its subjects, not for the subjects to try and win that of the Government. * * * * If Government say that what I say is untrue—that they have tried to cultivate friendship and have only been repaid with enmity—I can only say that if it had gone the right way to work, its subjects would most undoubtedly have been its friends and supporters instead of, as in many instances, rising up in arms against it. Now, friendship is a feeling which springs from the heart and which cannot be kindled by 'admonitions.' * * * * Government has hitherto kept itself as isolated from the people of India as if it had been the fire and they the dry grass—as if it thought that, were the two brought in contact the latter would be burnt up."

I have given this large quotation to recall to your mind some of the reasons upon which you formed the opinions which I have already quoted in my letters Nos. I and II. These reasons may also go to prove that the prayers of the National Congress as to the concession of volunteering to be allowed to the native subjects of Her Majesty are nothing but reasonable and consistent with the noble principles involved in the above lines. Now I have done with your book on "The Causes of Indian Revolt," so far as it concerned that resolution of the National Congress which prays for the introduction of a representative element in the Legislative Councils of India. Most of these extracts, except one or two here and there, were abstract, and perhaps you may, with your usual calmness, have the boldness to say that there is nothing in these quotations which goes to prove that you ever meant to say that these representatives to the Council of India should be elected by the subjects. Very good, I will search out quotations which will leave nothing doubtful. You may not have forgotten that two months after the opening of your Scientific Society you delivered* "a vigorous speech" at the laying of the foundation stone of the New Gazhipore, now the Victoria College. In the course of that address you said: "Bear in mind, gentlemen, that Her Most Gracious Majesty Queen Victoria has had proclaimed in this country that her servants and subjects, European and native, are to be considered as being on an equal footing; *and this assurance, gentlemen, is not a mere matter of form but a reality.*" The italics are mine. Now, Sir Syed Ahmed, will you still laugh at us because we believe this—this very proclamation—to be our Magna Charta?

Further on in the course of the same address you said: "THE APPOINTMENT OF NATIVES TO THE SUPREME COUNCIL WAS A MEMORABLE INCIDENT IN THE HISTORY OF INDIA. THE DAY IS NOT FAR DISTANT I TRUST, AND WHEN IT DOES COME YOU WILL REMEMBER MY WORDS WHEN THAT COUNCIL WILL BE COMPOSED OF REPRESENTATIVES FROM EVERY DIVISION OR DISTRICT, AND THAT THUS THE LAWS WHICH IT WILL PASS WILL BE LAWS ENACTED BY THE FEELINGS OF THE ENTIRE COUNTRY." †

"You will see that this cannot come to pass unless we strive to educate ourselves thoroughly. I once had a conversation with one in high authority on this very subject, and he said that Government would be only too glad if a scheme, such as I have sketched above, were

* On the 9th of January 1864. † The capitals are mine.

practicable, but he felt doubtful; if it were stated that there were qualified men in every DISTRICT, Government would gladly avail itself of their knowledge and give them seats in Council. I knew this only too well and felt ashamed that such was the case. What I have above stated is only to inculcate on your minds the great fact that Her Most Gracious Majesty wishes all her subjects to be treated alike; and let their religion, tribe, or colour be what it may, the only way to avail ourselves of the many roads to fame and usefulness is to cultivate our intellects and to conform ourselves to the age." Sir Syed, have the happiness to know that the day, which you in 1864 said was not far distant is coming nearer and nearer, and that you need no longer feel so much ashamed of your countrymen for not conforming to the age. Your prophecy is not fulfilled yet, but we are certain that sometime or other it is sure to be fulfilled, and then you will have the satisfaction of feeling that you did not prophesy in vain. Sir Syed, do you wish to withdraw this prophecy of yours, and if so why? Please explain—I and others like me are waiting in suspense. Only say that this prophecy was one of the hallucinations of a head which had been turned by the sudden inrush of Western ideas and we will be satisfied. Only say that with the return of sobriety and the calmness of old age you have come to know your own errors, and we will no more trouble you with these prophecies. Sir Syed, would you please point out what else could be the meaning of the above sentence except that, that India would some (in 1864, not far distant) day be governed by Councils composed of members elected by the people themselves? If not this, how can the laws be said to be "enacted by the feelings of the entire country."

Two months before you spoke the words quoted above, you, on the 9th January, 1864, started a Translation Society now known as the Scientific Society of Aligarh; and in the course of a speech then delivered pointing out the ignorance of your countrymen you said: "From their ignorance of the events of the past, and also of the events of the present—from their not being acquainted with the manner and means by which infant nations have grown into powerful and flourishing ones, and by which the present most advanced ones have beaten their competitors in the race for position among the magnates of the world—they are unable to take lessons and profit by their experience." Sir, we took your advice, and your countrymen have learnt the means and the manner by which they can advance the growth of their "infant nation" to the position of a "powerful" and a "flourishing" one. How is it that this growth which you so much desired in 1864 is an eyesore to you now? How is it that now at this period you cannot feel any pleasure in seeing a combination of all the different races and sects towards the accomplishment of the great end for which you have been until recently struggling so hard? How is it that you are going to prove that you did not deserve the distinctions so deservedly, as we thought, bestowed upon you? By your present attitude, by your present utterances, you mean to prove that all that you once said, all that you once did, for which you were rightly honoured both by the Government and the people, and for which you were said to be deserving of being "awarded a conspicuous place on the list of benefactors" of India, was, after all, but utter nonsense—because that is the phrase you now apply to the repetition of those same principles which you once so strenuously advocated by the supporters of the National Congress.

On the 10th of May, 1886, you addressed a large and influential meeting of the European and native residents of Aligarh on the necessity of Indian affairs being more prominently brought before Parliament and of forming an association for this purpose (at least so says your biographer on pp. 88 and 89). In the course of this speech you compared the British rule with that of the "former emperors and Rajas" of India. You said "it" (*i.e.*, the rule of the latter) "was based upon nothing but tyranny and oppression; the law of might was that of right; the voice of the people was not listened to; the strong and the turbulent, oppressed the feeble and the poor, and usurped all their privileges with impunity for their own selfish ends. It is only therefore by such usurpers and turbulent spirits that a despotism, such as flourished in Hindustan for many long centuries, is at all to be desired." Know, sir, that the National Congress wants nothing but that the voice of the people be listened to, and that the "strong and the turbulent" may not oppress "the feeble and the poor." The National Congress wants to achieve these ends by peaceful means and in fact by prayers; while it can only be the usurpers and the turbulent who desire to threaten, as you now do, the use of arms. It can only be the self-assumed "strong" who can threaten "the poor " with the use of the arms, by " the followers of the prophet." Further on you regretted the indifference, with which the affairs of India were treated in the Parliament, and laid the blame of it to a great extent upon the shoulders of your own countrymen. You said: " India, with that slowness to avail herself of that which would benefit her so characteristic of Eastern nations, has hitherto looked on Parliament with a dreamy apathetic eye, content to have her affairs, in the shape of her Budget, brought before it in an annual and generally inaudible speech by Her Majesty's Secretary of State for India." You entreated your countrymen to discontinue this apathy, and you asked them to exert themselves towards securing the proper representation of their interests in the governing body of the British Nation. You appealed to the " entire native community " " to co-operate " with the London Association established for the purpose. To your countrymen you continued to say: " You will have only yourselves to reproach when in after years you see the European section of the community enjoying their well-earned concessions whilst your wants remain still unmet." Sir Syed, the country then responded to your call, though imperfectly, and it is now that the country has felt the value of your words and begun to throw away the deep indifference which you so forcibly lamented. Pray will you tell me whether, prior to the movement of National Congress, there was no agitation for the redress of the grievances of Indians in India ? If so what was all this which you were doing ? Why did you establish and support all these associations? Why did you call upon the entire country to "*co-operate*" with these Associations if the Government had of its own accord been doing all that was needed for the welfare of India? In your criticism upon the Lucknow speech of the Hon'ble Pandit Ajudhia Nath of Allahabad you meant to ask (if I did not err in understanding and reproducing it from memory) the Congress-wallahs if any of their agitations had been existing when the Government granted all the boons which we enjoy. I have quoted largely from your own writings to show that such an agitation did exist, and that you yourself were one of the most prominent agitators. You even went the length of saying that no fear need be entertained of your (*i.e.*, of those who meant to take part in such associations, &c.,) being called discontented by the Government. To quote your own words you said: "I am afraid that a feeling of fear—fear that the Government or the district authorities would esteem you factious and discontented, were you to inaugurate a measure like this—deters you from coming forward for your country's good. * * * * Believe me that this moral cowardice is wrong—the apprehension unfounded, and that there is not an Englishman of a liberal turn of mind in India who would regard with feelings other than those of pleasure and hope, such a healthy sign of increased civilization on the part of its inhabitants. * * * * The natives have at present little or no voice in the management of the affairs of their country, and should any measure of Government prove obnoxious to them, they brood over it, appearing outwardly satisfied and happy while discontent is ranking in their mind." Further on you said that the natives were in the habit of inveighing against such measures in their homes, but to the Europeans they represented that they were satisfied with the justice and wisdom of these very measures. You loudly proclaimed "that such a state of affairs is inimical to the welfare of the country. Far better would it be for India were her people openly and honestly to express their opinions as to the justice or otherwise of the acts of Government." Would you pray tell me, Sir, why *we* are seditionmongers; is it because we speak "honestly" as to the justice or otherwise of the acts of the Governmet; is it because we have overcome the moral cawardice with which you charged us? Are we seditious because we do not want to keep "discontent rankling" within our hearts? Are we disloyal because we, according to your own teachings, have come forward to speak up for our country's good? If we deserve all these epithets on account of all these I must say, Sir, that you are the father of all this. You taught us to do exactly what we have begun doing now. You not only taught but encouraged us by your own example. Why do you now deprecate "this healthy sign of civilization" as you once called it on the part of Indians? If we, the followers of your old principles, have exceeded the proper dimension which, I humbly maintain, we have not, it is surely not advisable to root out these instincts from within us, but rather to point out the place and the occasion where we have exceeded. How have you come to oppose the principles themselves, the principles so lovingly promulgated by you? Say that the principles are not to be discarded, but the men abusing these principles are to be despised. We will then know how to love the principles and not the men. We loved you because you held these principles, because we thought you loved your country above everything, because we considered you to be one of the fathers of the present India, and if we have erred we must say we think that you should have pointed out our error in time. Truly has a poet said: "Khwab tha jo kuchh ki dekha tha afsana tha jo kuchh ke suna tha," *i.e.*, "what I saw was but a dream, what I heard an idle tale." Ah! human delusions are then destined to delude the human eye for ever!

Again with a pause, with a promise of more in my next,

I am yours, &c.,

22nd Nov., 1888. THE SON OF AN OLD FOLLOWER OF YOURS.

---o---

No. IV.

SIR,—The fourth meeting of the Indian National Congress is soon to be held at Allahabad, and so I think I must hasten to give some more of the most important quotations in this letter of mine. The less important ones I leave for some future occasion.

When this letter reaches you, you will be, possibly, smiling over the ex-Viceroy's speech delivered at the St. Andrew's Dinner, Calcutta. If you will only take the trouble of reading that speech with your eyes open, you will find that your uproar against the introduction of some representative element in the Legislative Councils of India is not liked even by those whom you have undertaken to flatter, and whose National traditions you try to belie.

Sir Syed, for God's sake, reconsider your position and do not disappoint us just when the morning of hope has begun to dawn over us and our mother-land.

Now to proceed with your old writings and sayings; please turn to pages 207 and 208 of your *Social Reformer* for 1298 Hijri, equivalent to the year 1881 A. D. There, while giving an account of your voyage to London, you said that on the way you happened to see Mr. D. Fitzpatrick, the former Deputy Commissioner of Delhi, with whom you talked about "the goodness or badness of the Punjab administration." Therein you profess to have said that the Government of the Punjab was a *Despotic* one, though a thousand times better than that of the Sikhs. Further on you say "the people of the Punjab may be happy and perhaps may like it because they have been just taken out of fire and made to sit in the *sun*. But we cannot like it. The goodness or badness of the Punjab Government, *i.e.*, of the Government of the non-Regulation Provinces, should be asked of the inhabitants of the Delhi, Panipat Rohtak, Hissar and Sirsa Districts, which once used to belong to Regulation Provinces and have now been subjected to a non-Regulation (or *beqánúni*) Punjab Administration. As far as I know people think that of many other punishments, which had been awarded to the inhabitants of Delhi and its adjacent districts in the Mutiny, this was also one that they were made over to the Government of the Punjab and thus made the subjects of non-Regulation Provinces." These lines were written at a time when the North-Western Provinces did not enjoy the blessing of having a Provincial Legislature of its own, and so the only superiority in the administration of the N.-W. P. over that of the Punjab *then*, was the existence of a High Court instead of the Chief Court in the Punjab, and the constitution of a Board of Revenue instead of a Financial Commissionership here. The word *Despotic* is your own, and is used in your Urdu style, and thus you cannot say that the word has been unwittingly thrust upon you by the translator. Even at the risk of unidiomatic English I have tried to give a literal translation of your Urdu sentences. If you think that this translation is incorrect, I trust you will not, for the sake of your own reputation, fail to publish a true translation of the sentences quoted. Now, will you please explain on what principles you designated the Government of the Punjab as Despotic, and how you distinguished it in that respect from the Government of India or that of N.-W. P.? I can venture to say that the Government of the Punjab was never more Despotic than the Governments of other sister Provinces. No doubt the merit of each Government to a considerable degree depends upon the personal character of its head. The Governments of Montgomery, Aitchison and even that of Sir James Lyall cannot be said to be more Despotic than that of any of the Governors of other Provinces. Can you, Sir, in the face of this broad accusation of yours, still designate us as reckless accusers of Government and its policy? Further on in the same article you go on saying: "In fact the present time is not one in which people may like a *Despotic* Government, nor are those virtues (which in ancient times used to be mixed with a thousand vices) of a Despotic Government, and by which the influence of the former were an antidote for the latter, to be found in these days. Now-a-days it is not possible for those virtues to exist in any Despotic Government, and the people who think that in India a *Despotic* Government, such as it used to be in by-gone times, would be more appropriate and useful than the constitutional form of Government, are greatly mistaken. They are just like one who judges a garden by its state in the autumn without caring to think what it will be in the spring." The word Despotic throughout this quotation is your own, Sir.

At another place, on page 132 of the same journal for the same year, under the heading of the Eastern Arts and Sciences, you exhort us not to devote ourselves to them but to the study of Western ones. You ask us even "to forget our mother-tongue" (an impossibility in itself) because you said our National advancement only "depended upon the spread of Western Sciences." You said: "Let us by all means remain loyal to the Government, let us always regard it to be our patron and well-wisher, and let us at the same time try to extricate ourselves from that servile and savage state in which we are." Nobly and truly did you say that this, and this only, should be the object of a generous kind-hearted Government who rules over a nation for the good of the latter, or, say, for the good of the human race. In the course of the same article on the same page of your "Tahzib-ul-Ikhlaq" you say "no nation can ever advance in parallel lines all travelling from one point to another. Nations always advance in the shape of a triangle, whose one corner projects in advance of the others. To think that we may not be divided in different sects is to pray that we may not be enlightened by the light of Western ideas." In contrast to this, please reconsider your Meerut speech, in which in fact you wanted to express that the whole nation must remain in the background because *you think* that the Mahomedan community has not sufficiently advanced to fully reap the benefits to be enjoyed by the granting of the boons prayed for by the National Congress. (*I* do not admit that the Mahomedan community is not sufficiently advanced.)

On page 136 of the same Journal you say: "I sincerely believe and wish to assure the Government that the same discontented educated critics" (meaning those educated gentlemen who severely criticize the Government measures and who are blamed for it) "yield to none in their appreciation of the British rule; hence it is not just to effect the ruin of our education on account of any apprehension of such criticism." These are the words which you addressed to those politicians who advocate the closing of Government Colleges and Schools, and who are of opinion that education in Western ideas and sciences has made the Indians disloyal. You would, I suppose, like to re-read those words also by which you encourage your own educated countrymen to fight out the battle of their national advancement bravely and without fear. You say; "Without doubt, there are many difficulties in the way of our doing so" (*i.e.*, promulgating those blessings of education, instruction and enlightenment which we acquire in those civilised countries to which we go or completing our education). "On one side we are to contend against the prejudices and ignorance of our own countrymen, and on the other side we are to bear the opposition of those narrow-minded men of the conquering race to whom our social and political advancement is an eyesore, and who dislike us because we have adopted English life, English politics and the manners of an English gentlemen; and change of dress even infuriates them to such a degree that they look at us with angry eyes as a pious man looks at a great criminal. But we should keep the good of our nation at heart and should bear all the difficulties and troubles which beset our way with the greatest possible forbearance and perserverance. I do not wish to conceal that Time, the Great Reformer, will let all these things be, and no opposition or discontent will be able to keep them back. But still there is no doubt that this narrow-mindedness is kindling the feelings of discontent, and is surely calculated to cause all sympathy and love between the governors and the governed to be banished." Sir Syed, have the happiness to learn that your countrymen took you to be a true prophet—that they are going to stick to every word which you wrote—are not to be daunted or baffled by any opposition,—no, not even by yours. How is it that you preached to us to perservere and yourself could not do this? (" Digran ra nafihat wa khud ra fazihat.") We have persevered, but the old man has fallen; what a pitiable spectacle of human weakness!

Next I will give an extract upon the great question

of native volunteers with which one of the Resolutions of the National Congress deals. On page 332 of your Biography, says your Biographer, that in March, 1883, when Mr. A. O. Hume (the beloved General Secretary of the National Congress) advocate the cause of native volunteers in India, and stated that in the *mutiny* he had a brigade of infantry, cavalry and artillery in the Etawah yeomanry levy—all Volunteers—he (*i.e.*, Lieutenant-Colonel Graham) addressed a letter to the Editor of the *Pioneer* in which he tried to rebut many of the arguments advanded by Mr. Hume, which letter he says brought you (Sir Syed Ahmed) down upon him in a letter which you wrote to him. He gives an extract from that letter on page 334, which runs thus: "I have perused your reply to Mr. Hume's letter advocating the volunteering of the Natives of India. In not allowing the natives to become Volunteers, the Government mean to say that they do not trust the Natives of India. Its consequences should be judged from the saying: 'If you want us to trust you, you should also trust us.' There yet exists a wide gulf between European and the Natives of India, and unless it be filled up *nothing can secure aud improve the prosperity of the country.*" The italics are mine. This you wrote in the middle of 1883, and now in 1887 and 1888, you say Indians do not want anything. On the same page Lieutenant-Colonel Graham writes as follows: "What I would advocate would be the selection by the local authorities in all large stations in India of a certain number of picked Native Volunteers—men of good family and well-known for their loatly—to be placed under the command of the Officer commanding the European Volunteers. I would let them select their own company officers, and once started I would also permit them to select their own recruits as vacancies occurred."

I say "give us this much and we will be satisfied for a long time to come."

A few important extracts more and I will have done with your old writings and sayings for the present. Contrast the meanings attached to the words "Nation" and "National" by you in your Meerut speech with those promulgated by yourself at Gurdaspur on the 27th of January, 1884. At Gurdaspur you said that "we (*i.e.*, the Hindus and Mahomedans) should try to become one heart and soul and act in unison; if united we can support each other. If not, the effect of one against the other would tend to the destruction and downfall of both (*Cheers.*) In old historical books and traditions you will have read and heard, and we see it even now, that all the people inhabiting one country are designated by the term one *nation.* The different tribes of Afghanistan are termed as one nation, and so are the miscellaneous hordes peopling Iran, distinguished by the term Europeans, though abounding in variety of thoughts and religions, are still known as members of one nation, though people of other countries also do come and settle with them, but being mixed together they are called members of one and the same nation. So that from the oldest times the word Nation is applied to the inhabitants of one country, though they differ in some peculiarities which are characteristic of their own. Hindu and Mahomedan brethren, do you people any country other than Hindustan ? do you not inhabit the same land ? are you not burned and buried on the same soil ? do you not tread the same ground and live upon the same soil ? Remember that the words Hindu and Mahomedan are only meant for religious distinction—otherwise all persons, whether Hindu or Mahomedan, even the Christians who reside in this country are all in this particular respect belonging to one and the same nation. (*Cheers.*) Then all these different sects can only be described as one nation ; they must each and all unite for the good of the country which is common to all."

Again in your Lahore speech, which was delivered in reply to the address of the Indian Association of Lahore, you, on the 3rd of February, 1884, said as follows "Even granting that the majority of those composing this Association are Hiudus, still I say that this light has been diffused by the same whom I call by the epithet of Bengalees. I assure you that Bengalees are the only people in our country whom we can properly be proud of, and it is only due to them that knowledge, liberty and patriotism have progressed in our country. I can truly say that really they are the head and crown of all the different communities of Hindustan. * * * I myself was fully cognizant of all those difficulties which obstructed my way, but notwithstanding these I heartily wished to serve my country and my nation faithfully. In the word NATION I include both Hindus and Mahomedans because that is the only meaning which I can attach to it (*i. e.,* NATION or *quam*)." Here in the end the word nation is originally used by yourself (see the account of your trip to the Punjab by Maulive Iqbal Ali, p. 167, line 18th). The capitals are mine. To resume : "With me it is not so much worth considering what is their religious faith, because we do not see anything of it. What we do see is that we inhabit the same land, are subject to the rule of the same Governers, the fountains of benefits for all are the same, and the pangs of famine also we suffer equally. These are the different grounds upon which I call both those races which inhabit India by one word, *i. e.*, *Hindu*, meaning to say that they are the inhabitants of Hindustan. While in the Legislative Council I was always anxious for the prosperity of *this nation.*" The italics are mine. This letter of mine has already exceeded its proper dimensions, and therefore I think I must not give more extracts, and must leave the rest to be commented upon by abler hands than mine.

Anybody reading these extracts will be once for all convinced of the former *loftiness* and present *lowness* of your *position*. Foreigners reading these extracts will not believe that your now famous Meerut and Lucknow speeches were in reality delivered by the same Sir Syed Ahmed Khan who was once proud (whether rightly or wrongly God knows) of his broadmindedness. This much seems certain : either you were not the author of those ideas reproduced in the above quotations, your recent utterances were inspired by some mind or other than your own.* Poor Sir Syed, you must feel sorry for all

* Can it be that your once massive, manly intellect has succumbed to the feeble, schoolgirl-like sophistries of your shallow-pated

this inconsistency, though you may not have the boldness to say so. Sir, I assure you that you should not despair; a small sacrifice at the alter of your country, a renewed profession of the faith that was once in you will suffice to regain for you the confidence of your countrymen. If you are not prepared to do so, I must think myself justified in impeaching you in the name of consistency, in the name of honesty and fair play, in the name of the great Mahomed whose decendant and follower you profess to be, in the name of Madhi Ali, your old devoted friend who once felt proud of showing to the world that the original Mahomedan rule was based upon democratic principles (see your *Social Reformer* for 1290 Hijri, p. 136, lines 8 to 23) ; and lastly in the name of the pupils of your own Mahomedan Anglo-Oriental College, Aligarh, whom you trained in the priniples which you now affect to detest. It is a year since you actually engaged yourself in creating and keeping up an opposition to the National Congress, but up to this time your countrymen have not been clearly enlightened as to what It is that you object to in the proceedings of the National Congress. You say we are not fit for a Republic and so do we say. You say we are not yet fit for a parliament and so do we say.

If you say that the introduction of some representative element even into the Government would be injurious to our community, we ask why and how, and

---

employe? That Merlin-like, the great heart that once beat true for India is now pulseless, and that you lie bound, inextricably, by the treacherous spells of a modern Vivient, even more despicable than his female prototype?

pray when did you receive that revelation, because up to 1884 you yourself acknowledged the necessity of these Legislative Councils being reconstituted upon some representative basis. Then, again, when were you inspired with the idea that the Hindu and the Mahomedan interests are sure to clash at least in this respect? Because up to 1884 you belived in the doctrine of Hindus and Mahomedans having one and the same political interests and being members of one and the same nation. To your friends Maulvies Mahdi Ali and Madhi Hussain, whose tergiversation is not less amazing than your own, I have only a few words to say. To the former that he had better now suppress his Lecture published in the *Social Reformer* for 1290 Hijri on pp. 136 and those preceding and following it. To the latter that he should now publicly recant the views set forth in his article under the heading of "Liberty" published in your *Social Reformer* for 1298 Hijri, 1881, from pp. 231 to 341. Until they do this I will ask them to abstain, if they desire any human being to credit them with common honesty, from abusing us and denouncing our principles, and to my other countrymen as well as to our rulers I have only to say further—

> "I know a maiden fair to see,
> Take care,
> She can both false and friendly be,
> Beware! Beware!
> Trust her not,
> She is fooling thee.
> She has two eyes so soft and brown,
> Take care.

She gives a side-glance and looks down,
Beware ! Beware !
Trust her not,
She is fooling thee !
And she has hair of a golden hue,
Take care !
And what she says *it is not true,*
Beware ! Beware !
Trust her not,
She is fooling thee.
She has a bosom as white as snow,
Take care !
She knows how much it is best to show,
Beware ! Beware !
Trust her not,
She is fooling thee."

With a promise to begin afresh in the year 1889,

I beg to subscribe myself, Sir,

Yours, &c., &c.,

20th December, 1888. THE SON OF AN OLD FOLLOWER OF YOURS.

[*N. B.—The extracts from your " Social Reformer " and the account of your trip to the Punjab by Maulvie Iqbal A'li have been translated into English for the purposes of these letters by myself.—L. R.*]

—o—

THE ECONOMIC AND INDUSRTIAL CAMPAIGN IN INDIA.

There can be no denial of the fact, that the industrial and economical future of our country mainly depends upon the introduction and successful working of the Joint Stock system. Gifted with vast natural resources, which can produce any amount of raw materials and with an enormous and ever increasing population which is always in want of employment, India could achieve wonders in the line of manufacturing industries, only, if it had the necessary capital and the still more necessary skill at its command. Of artistic skill it has plenty. What it lacks is the power and capacity of calling in the assistance of modern Science, and modern appliances in the refining of its arts, and the production of larger quantities, at lesser cost, of its articles of art. Precious little has up to this time been done in the way of enabling qualified Indians to acquire this skill. Beyond providing some facilities for acquiring an elementary and mainly theoretical knowledge of modern sciences in connection with the Arts Colleges, the Government has done practically nothing in the way of enabling or encouraging Indian youths to acquire mechanical skill with a view to the industrial development of the country. It was not perhaps to the interest of the British to take steps which might have eventually closed the Indian markets to English goods. If so, they probably did not foresee that the doctrine of free trade might drive even the English goods out of Indian markets in favour of countries better placed in their natural resources and in their populations than the British Isles. Thus their neglect has not only injured India, but brought no permanent benefit to Great Britain. Is it not a fact that English goods are being driven out of markets by the cheaper productions of Germany, United States, France and Japan? But in the absence of Government initiative in the matter, we, Indians, too have not done much to provide facilities for the acquisition of mechanical skill by our youths, because of want of foresight and of power of organisation in us. Instead of putting the horse before the cart we have been all this time busy in making the cart go with the horse behind. Instead of applying most of our humble resources in equipping our countrymen with mechanical skill in order to enable them to stop the exploitation of this country by foreigners, we have been spending lacs upon fruitless agitation for political enfranchisement. It never occured to us that in these days of science and machinery a nation poor in economics and skill could never be politically great or free. Thank God that after a lot of dissipation of energies we have been awakened to a sense of our duty in this direction and on all sides there is a demand for technical training and Industrial education. But few of those who cry for technical education and are even prepared to incur some amount of expenditure and sacrifice for the same know what technical education is, and how it can be introduced in this country.

The movement therefore is suffering for want of *expert* knowledge and no amount of agitation or enthusiasm can make up for that unless the latter is accompanied by earnest efforts to provide means to Indian youths to acquire this knowledge. Many an industry can be made to flourish if we had only technical knowledge to work it up. The first thing therefore to do is to send Indian youths to Europe and America to be trained as *experts*. Let each province send one youth every year to learn all that is required to start and successfully work up a particular industry. Japan has done the same through its Government, because there the Government represents the country. In India the case is different and the country will have to do this by itself what in Japan has been done by its Government.

Capital is the second important factor in the development of industries. Individual wealth is powerless before the accumulated wealth of millionaires who have joined together on the joint stock principles. Rich citizens can no doubt do a lot by investing their riches in manufactories and industries which can be run by them with their own resources. But *Joint Stock enterprise* must be met by similar combinations and these combinations, to be successful must be organised on sound principles and with perfect confidence in those who are at the helm of the affairs. This confidence can only be begotten by the promoters themselves being men of substance, having substantial risks in the enterprise and of acknowledged integrity and honesty of purpose. Joint Stock enterprise in India is yet an infant of very tender age, it is a foreign plant that has yet to grow and take root before it fructifies and as such it requires great care and caution to watch its growth and secure it a fruitful crop. The friends of Industrial development need not be told how suspicious and indolent the people of this country are.

Our lacking in enterprise is mainly due to want of faith in each other and unwillingness to co-operate for common good. It is therefore of the greatest importance that the business of company-promoting in this country should be entirely above suspicion. There seems to be no room for encouraging individual speculations under the sense of company-promoting. The English company-promoter, of whom we have of late read so much in British Journals, must not be allowed to abuse the confidence of those Indians who are disposed to give a fair trial to joint stock system and who if once deceived are not likely to enter the lists again. But equally vigilant must we be against the Indian company-promoter, if there are any, who may be disposed to copy their British co-adjutors and make a profession of company-promoting at the cost of those who might be willing to invest a portion or the whole of their hard earned savings, in a business or businesses which is or are likely to be of profit to themselves as well as to the country at large.

The Indian shareholder is generally a sleeping partner and prone to leave the business to those, relying upon whose name and fame, he signed his application for shares. He is no good for control or check and therefore gives *a carte-blanch* to the managers. If he is proved to have been unfortunate in placing his confidence all that he shall do will be to curse his stars and nothing further. He will not move an inch to see that those who have played fast and loose with his money, receive their deserts and thus deter others from similar acts of treachery and bad faith. Much less is he to be moved by considerations of public good or the good of the country. Under these circumstances the friends of industrial development can not be too vigilant against this class of company-promoters. In England itself a cry has already been raised to the effect that the existing laws do not sufficiently protect the shareholder from the devices of a cunning and sharp director. A writer in the *Contemporary Review* of June 1901, while reviewing the causes of the economic decay of Great Britain pens the dirge on the Company Laws of England. Says he, "Our company law is a most excellent law in favour of cunning company-promoters, financiers, stock-brokers and of every one who wishes to rob the nation of its accumulated saving." After giving a table of figures showing the amounts of capital involved in companies liquidated from 1892 to 1899 as ranging between 34 millions sterling and 77 millions he quotes the following remarks of the Inspector-General of Companies in liquidation:

"It appears that the total number of abortive and liquidating companies during 1899, were in proportion to the new companies registered, *60 per cent as against 56 per cent during the previous year.*" To explain it still more he is believed to have further said, "*About 37 per cent of the Capital belongs to the more or less solvent class while the remaining three-fourths in number or 63 per cent of capital wanted represent the insolvent class.*" The italics are ours. Upon this data the wrtier bases the following pregnant remarks of his own—"Whilst the thrifty part of our population has been robbed within a few years of several hundred pounds earned by millions of British toilers during a life-time of patient labour, none of the company-promoters who perpetrated these enormous frauds on the nation, nor their satellites have been imprisoned with hard labour. The new Company Law is not designed to protect the unsuspecting public but tc protect the company-promoter and his associates...........It is a law in favour of the strong against the weak. In consequence of this immunity from punishment for fraud, in consequence of the growing difficulty of making an honest living by productive industry and in consequence of the ease by which company frauds may be perpetrated under the shelter of our company law then popularity of promoting swindling companies is on the increase." The Indian Company Law is much the same as the English, in fact, almost a copy of it, and the rapidity with which companies here too are being floated and then *wound up* or sold at considerable loss to the shareholders raises an apprehension in our mind lest in a few years the state of affairs here might justify the same strictness as we have quoted above about the class of professional company-promoters in England. Let us hope at any rate that the occasion for such a complaint may not arise soon, although signs are already visible which excite our worst fears.

LAJPAT RAI.

——o——

FAMINE ORPHANS AND WAIFS.

That the last two famines have told very heavily upon the numerical strength of the Hindus is a fact which does not require to be established by any great array of facts and figures. The tracts mostly affected by these famines were mainly Hindu and consequently it was amongst the latter that the suffering was the most acute and the effects extremely disastrous. In these tracts the community not only lost lacs by death, but an immensely large number have so seriously deteriorated in physique, that though not totally incapable of bearing children, the offspring which they might bring forth must be small in number and extremely weakly in body. Besides actual losses by death many a family has been deprived of the means of continuity of line by the survival of women doomed to life-long widowhood. Even men who have survived their wives are not seen to be re-married. Add to this the loss by conversion to other religions, which have been sufficiently numerous to cause a gap which will not be easily filled up. However true it may be that people whom sheer want of food and drink forced to accept the protection of other religions in these periods of dire calamity can hardly be called converts, but it is a fact all the same that they are lost to Hinduism. The Hindu is conservative to the core, and loves his religion and nationality, above every thing else. To him the loss of religion is worse than death itself, but what is he to do when starvation and other privations following in the train of grinding poverty root out the very idea of religion from his mind. It was only in extreme agony, that they sacrificed their beliefs, to the necessity of keeping body and soul together. The choice lay between two agonies—one of starvation, the other of loss of every sentiment and connection that was dear and sacred—and it is no wonder that many succumbed to the second, though only after they had reached the last stage of suffering beyond which there was only the yawning abyss of annihilation. Many must have willingly preferred death to the acceptance of relief at such a heavy cost, but how can we blame even those who, fearing the pangs of slow dissolution, exchanged life or religion. Be what it may, it is a fact that in these calamitous scarcities which have held the country in their squeezing grip for the last five years consecutively, a very large number of men and women have been lost to Hinduism, which, otherwise would have been a source of strength and power generally as well as a source of increase to its numbers. Then again numerous families have been ruined and have practically (at least from a Hindu point of view) ended, by their young ones having been taken away to long distances from their homes, and kept in charge of organisation which are beyond the reach of their parents and relatives, if any living. These children though living, are for all purposes dead to their parents, their relatives, their caste and their community. We are talking not of orphans only but even of those who either deserted by their parents in the vicissitudes of famine or who strayed away from their homes either in search of food or in search of absent parents who had already left for labour, and who while thus straying were collected and relieved, as they say, by benevolent philanthropists belonging to other denominations. These children were principally the victims of that short sighted policy, which in the first instance, allowed very large number of relief seekers to accumulate on large works distant from their homes and their villages, and then allowed philanthropy to take charge of other people's children during the pendency of the famine, either from the Government poor-houses, and Government orphanages by the authority of Government Officers or from the streets etc., when they were straying in search of food or relatives. In plain words the truth is that the various missions engaged in the work of famine relief purchased so many converts to their faith at an awfully cheaper price per head than it ordinarily costs them to evangelise one non-Christian soul in India in years of normal rainfall. It is an open secret that even ordinary methods of sale and purchase were resorted to. Children, boys and girls, were sold and purchased at a few annas, or a few pices per head.

Don't you be thinking, gentle reader, that these are imaginary statements. We know what we state and we can prove it, if necessary, to the hilt. Why, quotations from Christian papers themselves, will bear out the truth of our statement. What, then does it amount to ? Briefly told it amounts to this, that a Christian Government, with its anti-slavery laws, allowed the missionaries of its own faith, to take charge of deserted children, in many cases with parents living, and in some cases to purchase them of parents themselves, with the ostensible object of converting them to Christianity in lieu of supporting them with food and water, in the time of famine. Ah ! but for fallen Hinduism, the state of things should have been the reverse. A Hindu would gladly feed and clothe any number of the poor of other religions, in times of famine, or no famine and would never think of taking advantage of other people's misfortunes and troubles and poverty, but when he requires the help of others he has to pay for it dearly. Neither a Muhammadan, nor a Christian will feed him except at the price of his religion. Even in this famine, if well-to-do Hindus had used some discrimination in the distribution of their charities they could have saved thousands of their people and their little ones from being sent out of the bosom of Hinduism for ever. Rich Hindus swelled the lists of famine Charitable Funds, a decent portion of which was spent through the Christian Missionary who used it in the Christian interest as effectively as he could. Broad-mindedness and charity to the poor, without any distinction of creed and caste is a noble trait of character of which Hinduism might be proud, *in the abstract*, but in this world of sects and creeds and in these days of struggle and competition between creed and creed, it does not pay. If over-rich, superfluously rich, resourceful Christianity cannot stand it how can poverty-stircken, slavery ridden, helples Hinduism afford to indulge in it? But we have digressed. It was not our object to read a sermon to the Hindus. We meant to state facts and to comment upon them a little.

To resume, in Rajputana alone, Hinduism lost seventy thousand of these unfortunate children, who were collected by Christian Mission of various denominations and despatched to distant places in various parts of India. The Arya Samajists took charge of about a 1,000 and sailed them of to the Punjab. There were some married girls amongst the latter who had been deserted by their husbands and who would have joined the seventy thousand mentioned above, but for their timely rescue by the Arya Samajists. The latter are now searching their husbands and using all possible means of restoring them to their families, but those whom the Christians took away, are gone for good, whether married, or unmarried, orphan or no orphan. The Arya Samajists removed these children to the Punjab because they could not maintain them on the spot. They depended entirely upon local support in their own province which they could not have got but by the removal of the children to the land of five rivers. No amount of descriptive rhetoric, short of the actual sight of misery, would have moved out people to the necessity of taxing their scanty means. The removal of the famine stricken children to the various districts in the Punjab was an effective appeal which touched more successfully the heart of every Hindu who could save even a little out of his own necessities. Then the question of maintaining and training them after the famine, was another difficulty in the way of providing relief on the spot. In the case of orphans at least, it was out of the question to give them temporary relief during the pendency of the famine, unless the relieving agencies were prepared to make permanent arrangements for bringing them up as useful members of society who could, in the course of time, earn their own livelihood. Of course all these ends could be achieved even in Rajaputana, if the Arya Samajists could command the same amount of funded help as was at the back of Christian Missions. Failing this, mere necessity forced them to remove the children to their province. But there was no such difficulty in the way of the *Padri*. He got his funds from

England, America or other parts of Europe. To him Rajaputana was as good as the Punjab, Bengal, Madras, Bombay, or any other place in India, still there might be some justification for those missions who had their permanent orphanages and buildings at the places to which they removed the famine stricken children of Rajaputana or the Central Provinces. But what possible justification could there be for the transfer of these children to distant places by those missions who had to keep them in hired buildings ? At Lahore, itself, two of the mission orphanages, one containing more than a 100 boys and the other more than a 100 girls are located in hired buildings. Is it not, then, reasonable to infer, that besides the avowed facilities of management and economy, there was another object too, which induced our philanthropic Missionaries to remove these children to places distant from their homes ? What ever be the object, however, there can be no denial of the fact that this action of theirs has resulted in the complete loss of those children to their families and homes, at least of such who have parents or other relatives living and willing to take them back. And this has taken place under the policy of neutrality followed by the Government. The truth is, that with these of recurring famines, which have become an almost permanent feature of this ill-fated country, this system of orphan relief is a standing menace to Hinduism, and it is therefore with great satisfaction that we have read the recommendations of the last Famine Commission on this subject. Our gratification enhances still more when we remember that in 1898 even a strong conscientious ruler like Sir Antony MacDonnell failed to carry into practice the principles now so clearly enunciated in this report. In 1898 Sir Antony allowed Christian missons to remove Hindu orphans of the N.-W. P. and Oudh to distant parts of India, while he had practically refused the same privilege to the Arya Samajists of the Panjab, a few months before. Consequently we are glad to find that the last Famine Commission have recognised the great importance" of this question and have recommended that the "policy of the Government in regard to orphans, should be formulated in Provincial Codes, *beyond risk of misconception either by its officers or by the public.*"* So far as the principles of this policy are concerned, we believe they have been the same all this time *on paper* at least. What we are thankful for, is the unambiguous and clear language which the Commissioners have used in making their recommendations. Should the Local Governments formulate their policy in the Provincial Codes in similar style, we feel sure, much of the misapprehension hitherto caused would be removed, and much unnecessary discontent would be stopped. The Hindus will know what they can do to keep children of their community within the pale of their religion. The following recommendations should therefore be hailed with delight by the whole Hindu community, as they are the persons principally affected by these rules, the Mahomedans being sufficiently powerful, united and influential to allow the destitute children of their community to be taken away with impunity by persons and Associations of other denominations.

---

* The italics are ours.

Para. 234 of the Report recommends that the following policy be adopted by Government with regard to orphans or destitute children *viz.* that "the State should be, in times of famine, the temporary guardian of children whom it finds deserted and should not, in our opinion divest itself of the care of them until a reasonable time has elapsed after the close of the famine, during which efforts should be made to discover the natural protectors of the children or, failing these, respectable persons of the same religion who are willing to adopt them." According to this recommendation it is the duty of the State henceforth to discover respectable persons of the same religion who may be willing to adopt children whose natural protectors have either died or cannot be found out. Failing such respectable persons the deserted children are not to be made over to persons or institutions of different religions "*until all efforts to find persons and institutions of their own religion willing to take charge of them have failed*"† This is a most substantial concession for which we are heartily thankful to Sir Antony and his colleagues on the Commission. The next important recommendation is contained in para 235, which proposes to place certain obligations upon private orphanages with a view to enable the District Magistrate to institute the enquiries contemplated by the 1st part of para 234 *i. e.*, the search for natural protectors, and also to enable the parents and relatives of lost children to trace out their children in such orphanages. This recommendation requires the private orphanages to maintain a register containing

† The italics are again ours.

full particulars regarding the children in these orphanages and also further that "a copy of the register should be periodically forwarded to the District Magistrate in order that he may make enquires for the parents or relatives of such children." But the most substantial part of these latter recommendations consists in recognising the right of the ostensible parents and relatives of the inmates of famine orphanages to free access to such institutions in order to reclaim their little ones. The hasty removal of the children to places distant from their homes is proposed to be stopped or checked by the rule "*that no unclaimed child be removed from the district in which it is found until a period of three months has elapsed after the close of relief operations in the district.*" *

Categorically put the Commissioners first admit:

(1).—That the action of European and native philanthropists in having taken charge of deserted children and in some instances in despatching them "to private orphanages" and homes in distant parts of the country has given rise to "misunderstanding."

2ndly.—That "it is of great importance that the policy of the Government in regard to orphans should be formulated in Provincial Codes, beyond risk of misconception either by its officers or by the public."

3rdly.—That "it is common experience that besides those children who are true orphans, others are deserted by their parents or relatives in the stress of famine, and reclaimed when it is over."

4rthly.—That "it is also common experience that re-

* The italics are ours.

latives and caste-fellows and sometimes co-religionists are ready to adopt children at the end of a famine."

And then they make the recommendations we have already referred to above. We hope Hindus all over India will profit by these recommendations and exert as they can to relieve and protect the orphans and other deserted children of their community in times of famine. Nay, we think, it is only fair that the recommendations contained in para 235, at least, should be given a retrospective effect and persons claiming as relatives and guardians should be allowed free access to all orphanages to find their lost children or the children of their deceased relatives. The Hindus of different provinces should combine and make a joined representation to Government to achieve this end.

In the end beyond thanking the Commission for their clear recommendation as far as they go, we have to express our disappointment at the absence of a suggestion that during the pendency of a famine all orphans or deserted children whether found by Government or other private charitable agencies be brought to Government orphanages, and be not allowed to be detained or admitted into private orphanages except after the requirements of para 234 had been complied with.

LAJPAT RAI.

——o——

A STUDY OF HINDU NATIONALISM.

I have read with considerable interest the article by a "Hindu Nationalist," on the "creation of a Hindu Nationality," in the June number of the *Samachar*, as also the contribution on the same subject, in the last number of this Journal, by my friend Pandit Madho Ram. While I heartily join in the "Hindu Nationalist's" appeal to the educated Hindus, yet I do not share his opinion that "the idea of Nationality is an essentially European and modern idea," nor can I agree with his reading of the facts of history relied upon by him in support of his assertion. In my humble opinion the ideas of "nationality" and "patriotism" are as old as the different countries into which the earth is divided, as ancient as the distinctions of race and religion that have been existing in this world from times immemorial and pre-historic. They may have been more phenomenal in one epoch than in another. Their hold on different races and nations may have varied in intensity or extent, but that the ideas have always been there, as fixed and immutable as those of truth and falsehood, is my firm belief. It is not, however, my intention to enter into a speculative or an historical controversy with the "Hindu Nationalist" on the origin of the sentiments of nationality and patriotism. Suffice it to say that I agree with most of his conclusions and am prepared to generally endorse the remedies suggested. In fact some of the thoughts expressed in his article were, as if, foreshadowed by me in my article on the Congress published in the *Samachar* for October 1901. This reference has been made not to suggest any borrowing on the part of the "Hindu Nationalist," but to show that these thoughts are just now uppermost in the minds of all such Hindus as claim to love their people and to think of the means of their progress.

The "Nationalist" begins by bemoaning the absence

of the idea of nationality amongst Hindus, and ascribes all our misfortunes past and present to the same fact. "The Hindus," he says, "offer a curious instance of a people without any feeling of nationality." Having thus laid down the proposition he appeals to the pages of history to support his conclusion and apparently seems to have made out a strong case. But he has evidently missed the fact that his own proposition assumes the existence of a people having a common name, who have made history by that name. Quite unconsciously he assumes the existence of a Hindu nationality when he talks of the unsuccessful efforts of the Rajaputs and the Mahrattas to throw off the foreign yoke and to found a Hindu empire. What he complains of is that these efforts were spasmodic, not supported by the general body of the people and therefore not quite national, but all the time he admits by implication that there was a na-ation which could and should have made a combined effort. Otherwise what can he possibly mean by saying that "the Mahratta were left to fight the last battle of the Hindus alone, unaided by the Sesodia or the Rahtore?" He admits that "if allowed to grow unchecked the Mahratta confederecy might have developed into a national empire." In the face of these facts we cannot deny the existence of a nation simply because all the members of that nation did not join in the struggle for defence, or that some of them suceeded, or proved traitors, or joined the enemy's camp. Nor can we deny the existence of the sentiment of nationality, because that sentiment was not sufficiently strong and marked to overcome all differences among the different members of that nation, to enable them to stand as one man in defence of national interests. In the next place, why ignore the united front presented by the Hindus of all classes to repel the fourth invasion of Mahmud of Ghazni, and why forget the empires of the Pandavas, of Asoka, of Siladittya, Vikram, Bhoja, and others? Even the ill-fated Prithwi Raj, the last of the Hindu Emperors, who paid the penalty of the empire in the battle of Thaneswar, could twice command the united services of almost the whole nation in his noble and valiant defence of the empire and the fatherland. Who knows that but for the treachery of that fratricide of a Jai Chand, history would have been made otherwise? But the treachery of Jai Chand and the defeat of Prithwi Raj do not detract from the character of the heroic stand which the nation made against the foreigner. Victories and defeats are not solely made by man but are regulated by many a cause some of which may be quite outside the control of the parties at war. If in 1193 Providence decreed the fall of the Hindus that alone is not sufficient to justify us in damning the Hindus of that period as men who were totally bereft of the sentiment of nationality. Then, as I have already hinted, the very fact of our people being known to other peoples by a distinctive name, is a proof of the existence of a Hindu nationality.

I am too old now to continue to believe that the name Hindu, was for the first time given to us as one involving abuse, contempt and reproach by our Mohammedan invaders. Rather, I believe that our fall and degradation helped the fall of the word also, and perhaps a peep into the philogical history of the word might prove that all the bad meanings that are now assigned to the word in the Persian lexicon were of a comparatively later origin, and an outcome of the fall of the Hindu nation. Long before the Mohammedan invasion, and perhaps long before the advent of the Prophet of Islam, we were known to the people of other countries as Hindus. If so, what did this name signify? Was it a tribal distinction? I say, no, because the Hindus were of many tribes. Was it a racial name? I again, say, no, because the Persians of Iran too, belonged to the same race. Was it then a religious designation? Yes, partly religious no doubt, but mainly national, and in evidence I can produce a number of quotations from the productions of early Greek Historians and Mohammedan writers. For example, in what other sense does the Homer of Persia, the gifted Firdousi, who has immortalised the struggles for supremacy between the Iranians and the Turanians, use the expression Hindu in the following verses, which I pick at random from his great work, the *Shahnam* : *

Then we find many references to our people as Hindus in the sacred books of the Parsis, the *Vindidad* and others. So far as the name is concerned, our only difficulty arises when we fail to find any trace of it in our own literature where our people are invariably styled as *Aryas*. But here again we find enough traces of the sentiment of nationality in the passages in which the Rishis ordained all Aryas to combine against the attacks of *Dasyus*, *Chandalas* and *Mlechhas*. Gods are often invoked

* The verses are in *urdu* characters which we reproduce at the end of the book.

for protection against these latter. As for indications of an imperial spirit amongst the Hindus, why the *Ramayana* and the *Mahabharat* are full of evidences of the same. What was King Yudhishthira's Rajsuya Yagna and by what name would you style the ambitious scheme of Jarasindhu ?

The fact is that the best and the most glorious period of Aryan supremacy is yet closed chapter to us. Almost the whole of the pre-Buddhistic period is shrouded in mystery. Even the literature that has reached us is so full of allusions, enigmas, signs, and names and is written in such an archaic language that the whole thing seems to be a mystery. According to the best of European authorities, the language of the Vedas is so full of obsolete and archaic forms and expressions that the whole seems to be a cipher which with the best of efforts might yet take years to decipher. Still we know and understand enough to be proud of, and to glory in the heritage which has descended to us from our " barbarien " (?) ancestors in the shape of a national literature. And this must be the fulcrum of the lever with which we are to rise as a nation. It will not do to be unjust to our forefathers and to deny the idea of national love in them. No, they were patriots according to the best of their own light. The history of our country, from the standpoint of a Hindu, has yet to be written and till that is done, let us suspend judgement, remembering that the men whom we desire to judge and whom we are sometimes inclined to hastily condemn (often unheard) were master minds, whose productions and teachings are of the loftiest in the whole range of written or known thoughts. We the English educated Hindus of the present day, who claim to have imbibed the new spirit of nationality and patriotism from the West would really do well to study a few chapters of the Vedic literature with care and thought, and I am confident that this study wiil open a panorama of new ideas to our view. Such a study will, I am sure, enable us to see that the key-note of the pre-Buddhistic Vedic religion was the *sacrifice of all for all.* True that the genius of a jealous and perverted, sometimes corrupt and selfish, priesthood built such a vast and stupendous superstructure of conventionalities and formalities, with an almost interminable labyrinth of rituals and ceremonials obscured by which the true spirit of the religion was practically lost and could no longer be the stay of the nation.

It is this submergence of the true spirit of the ancient Hindu faith under the load of conventional rituals and formal ceremonials, that has since been the bane of the Hindus and not the entire absence of the idea of nationality. But you might say, that we have been producing martyrs and no one can be a martyr except by the strength of faith. How can a nation destitude of faith produce martyrs ? Is there a nation who have shown more of faith in their religion, in their individuality, in their sacred laws than the Hindus ? How can you otherwise explain their tenacity in clinging to their forms of religion, their pertinacity to stick to their customs ? I purposely say, *forms of religion* became real religion—the religion that guides and moulds a man, or a nation, and that elevates and ennobles them, that raises them to high ideals, that evokes the highest of sacrifices, has long ago disappeared from us. In fact it was never in the post-Buddhistic period restored to its altar in the temple of hearts. True, martyrs we have certainly been producing, ever and anon, and sometimes in numbers, but when I accuse the Hindus of want of faith, I do not mean *individual faith*, but that *social faith* which is the parent of victory ; the faith that arouses the multitudes ; faith in their own destiny, in their own mission and in the mission of the epoch ; the faith that leades on to struggle; the faith that enlightens and bids men advance fearlessly in the ways of God and Humanity, with their religion in their heart and their future progress as their goal. It is such a faith that we have been wanting in since the time of Buddha and it is such a faith that we require to become a nation again.

I shall now discuss the observations of Mr. Madho Ram and I shall remark at the outset that even admitting for argument's sake, the absolute accuracy of all his statements and facts, and also the correctness of the inferences he draws therefrom I would beg to differ from him in a *matter of principle.* My esteemed friend seems to think that all these internecine quarrels, strifes and sectarian struggles which he records at such great length in the course of his article largely take away "the chance for the progress of Hindu Nationalism in our country," or to be more accurate in quoting his words, he questions the Hindu Nationalist, if in the face of circumstances stated by him "there is much chance for the progress of Hindu Nationalism in our country." I answer the question in the affirmative. What I am anxious to point out is, that the existence of these quarrels and strifes is neither a bar to the progress of Hindu Nationalism nor is it proof sufficient of the absence of the idea of Nationality amongst the Hindus. And this, for the simple reason that the idea of nationality does not necessarily imply a complete union amongst all its members on all matters, social, religious or political; nor does it suggest the existence of a state of perfect concord and harmony among its members or leaders, or the freedom of the latter from all human weaknesses such as lead to personalities or indulgences in strong or even abusive language amongst, and towards each other. Has there been any nation in the world in the past, or is there any nation now living, which has been or is free from these differences or quarrels? Surely, Roman, Grecian, and Mohammedan histories must be admitted to present splendid and noble types of nationality and nationalism, and the present times can not furnish better and nobler types of nationality than the English, the German, and the American and the French, not to speak of others equally noble though not so influential and powerful, such as the Swiss, the Italian, and the Dutch. Religious and social differences have played a prominent part in the histories of these nations and even now they are not free from the same. A mere glance at the English and Irish papers, a perusal of the speeches in Parliament and out of Parliament by political men, a study of the literature of different religious sects in the West and a perusal of the biographies of public men in these countries, will show that the incidents narrated by my friend, altogether lose in significance and weight in the presence of the more vituperative and sometimes highly abusive difference and quarrels of these magnates of the European world. The truth is that honest differences, controversial discussions, and criticisms of public men by public men, are absolutely necessary for the healthy growth and progress of nationality. Then we must he prepared to meet with human weaknesses, partialities, jealousies, personalities, insinuations, innuendoes, use of strong language etc., in these discussions, and controversies. Carried beyond a certain degree and limit, they might retard the growth of nationalism, or might bring down an already completed edifice of nationality. I am not however prepared to admit that the differences and the disputes amongst the different classes of educated Hindus at the present moment exceed that limit. It is wrong to suppose that the idea of nationalism or nationality requires a complete union in all details of religious, social, economical, or political life or that it requires a complete freedom from sectarian quarrels or disputes or jealousies. To expect so, is to expect what is an impossibility and what entirely ignores human nature. In my humble opinion it is sufficient for the growth of nationality, if the different parts that claim the shelter of its ways have a sense of unity, which is sufficient to make them combine against a common enemy and a common danger. Run on a few basal principles in religion, on the community of a sacred language, and on the community of interests, the Hindus ought to foster the growth of a national sentiment which should be sufficiently strong to enable them to work for the common good in the different ways and according to the lights vouchsafed to each. Let us keep ONE ideal before us.

Let our ideal be sufficiently high to cover all, sufficiently broad and extensive to include all, who take pride *in one common name*, a common ancestry, a common History, *a common religion*, a common language and a common future.

We will not advance the cause of nationality by one inch, if we decide to preserve an attitude of silent quietude, and non-disturbing peace in all matters religious and social. Such an attitude can only mean stagnation and gradual extinction. Struggle, hard struggle, is the law of progress. Yes struggle we must, both *inter se* as well others. There must be a struggle between truth and untruth, between vice and virtue, between honesty and dishonesty, betwen expediency and righteousness, between indolence and energy, between enterprise and a spirit of lethargy and between time-seeing selfishness and noble disinterestedness. Without this struggle no nation can ever aspire to be great and iufluential. This struggle we have just entered upon. We have just emerged out of stagnation, and it is no wonder that we are sometimes apt to exceed the limits of propriety, or to irresistibly throw in more of sectarianism and personality, where more or much less is needed. But national delinquencies or faults are not made up or remedied in a day. Let us not be impatient of what in my humble opinion seems to be a healthy sign of growth. Let us not strangle it by drawing its undesirable concomitants in high colours or by attaching undue importance to the same. Then there are men and men in all public bodies, religious and social. Because there are some violent men, some bad tempered, some dishonest men, some traitors, and timeservers in our public associations, it is no reason to record a wholesale condemnation of the same or to be disappointed with them. Public opinion in this country has yet to grow. It is a very feeble plant yet. Its growth must cause some unpleasant friction and struggle. Let us not be impatient of it. The country has yet to foster a cold spirit of disinterested, fearless criticism. Few people in this country are guided by purely public interests. Fewer still are those who can be moved to take interest in things which do not concern them exclusively and in which they have little at stake. The interests of others do not move them. What little criticism exists in the country, is at once dubbed as sectarian, as interested, or as the outcome of jealousy or personal animosity. This criticism, that potent weapon, which alone can effectually check the vicious or selfish tendencies of great and powerful men, is discouraged and strangled. What we should aim at is not the silencing of criticism but the purging it out of personalities, jealousies, abuse and vituperation. This will take time, but so long as this is not achieved, let us not discourage, run down and do away with criticism altogether. At any rate, in my humble opinion impatience at, or silencing of mutual, criticism, or absence of all controversy will not necessarily mean unity, or a healthy progress of nationalism. Having thus disposed to the best of my power the objections of the "Hindu Nationalist" based—to my mind—on a wrong view of our ancient history, and that of Pandit Madho Ram, who has, in my opinion, drawn erroneous inferences from the facts detailed by him and the accuracy of which I have assumed for the sake of argument, I conclude this article with a hope that I may be able to return to the subjects in a latter issue and discuss the present condition and prospects of Hindu Nationalism, the evidence of its progress and the chances of its future growth.

LAJPAT RAI.

THE SOCIAL GENIUS OF HINDUISM.

I.

An idea seems to be gaining ground amongst Hindus educated on Western lines that the genius of Hinduism is essentially individualistic and anti-social and that therefore no substantial reform in social life can come out of a revival of the past, and that we can only draw on the West and take light therefrom. They do not place much faith in reform on national lines and would rather go in for wholesale or bodily adoption of most at least, if not all, of the social institutions of the West. They would rather build a new social edifice on *rationality* as distinguished from *nationality*, in religion and in social life. Again there are a large number of Hindus who, although they are prepared to grant that there is much in our national religion as handed down to us in our sacred literature which may satisfy even the highest cravings of the human mind, whether in the sphere of the spirit, intellect or morals, cannot yet see the existence of a spirit of nationality among the old Hindus, or the old Aryans (as I will prefer to style the *pre-Pauranic* ancestors of the Hindus).

This current impression of the educated Hindus has very much been strengthened by the utterances of some eminent Hindus of the Western Presidency, whose learning, scholarship and devotion to the cause of the country entitle them to be heard with respect and admiration. They are supposed to say that Hinduism was wanting in the social principle, being ostensibly individualistic.

It is very unfortunate to have to differ in any point from men of such vast erudition, deep learning and great reputation. Ordinarily any man will shrink from such an unpleasant and risky task however strong and cogent his reasons may be for that difference of opinion. Still, what sometimes deters men of deep learning and great reputation, may not stand in the way of a man who, though possessed of lesser qualifications, is possessed of a stronger faith in the truth of his cause and believes that the question is of vital importance to the cause of progress and reform amongst his people. It is therefore upon the strength of this faith, though with the greatest possible diffidence and hesitation, that I venture to express an opinion on the question raised in the opening sentences of this paper. Let me however make it clear that I quite concur in the opinion expressed by so many eminent social reformers, that the question of social reform is one of *paramount national* importance. There can be no doubt that the whole future of the nation depends upon the amount of social efficiency we secure and display, but I do not at the same time share the general belief that socially, the ancient Hindus were a very inferior people and had no, or very poor, notion of social or national responsibilities. In one of my paper on a similar subject, I have already expressed an opinion, giving my reasons and proofs, that the old Hindus were not entirely void of the idea of nationality or patriotism. In this paper I propose to discuss their social ideals and standards. I am prepared to grant that the tendency of the prevailing Hindu beliefs (which are generally styled orthodox and *Pauranic*) has a greater leaning towards individualism and appeals more to the interest and well-being of the individual than to that of the society to which the believers belong. But beyond this I cannot go. I do not share the commonly accepted opinion that Hinduism as a whole is either essentially or even principally individualistic at the cost of the social obligations. No religion can be worth its name which does not take sufficient care of the individual. The development of the individual soul and its attainment of spiritual beatitude must be the goal of all religions. There can be no religion without this object. A religion without the teaching of spirituality is a misnomer and a lever without a fulcrum. All purely spiritual development must, from the very nature of things, be individualistic, and it should be the ambition of every human being to strive after the elevation and refinement of the spirit in him and thereby secure spiritual perfection resulting in perfect bliss, or (as some religions style it) salvation. No religion can, therefore, be condemned as individualistic, because it attaches great importance to the unfolding and developing of the spiritual side of men, nor can any religion be extolled as socialistic which either ignores the spirit altogether or gives it only a subordinate or secondary position. In judging of a religion or of a system of religious beliefs, what has to be seen is whether it gives sufficient importance to the different requirements and the different sides of human nature without sacrificing one for another. To be a perfect and sound religion, it must make adequate provision for the harmonious development of all those sides of human nature which are to form the basis of the upward progress of man. Such a religion cannot afford to neglect even the physical side, much less can it throw into the back-ground the social.

But before we proceed further we should like to clear the ground by first examining the social ideal which our English-educated friends have set up before themselves. The social ideal of Herbert Spencer is stated to be " a state of things in which the antagonism between societies having utterly ceased on the one hand and the conciliation between the interests of the individual and those of the social organism having been perfectly attained to, on the other, the individual also will have reached a stage of development in which it will afford him the highest pleasure to act in a manner conducive to the good of the social organism, and this even where such conduct is to all appearance directly antagonistic to his own material interests. Just as at present the highest happiness is often obtained in parental sacrifice." He expects that this altruistic instinct will, in course of time, " attain a level at which it will be like parental altruism in spontaneity" and so lead the individual to obtaining the highest of all satisfactions in voluntarily sacrificing himself in the interests of the social organism. In his *Data of Ethics*

Spencer professes to see in the process of social evolution going on around us, a reconciliation taking place "between the interests of each citizen and the interests of citizen at large, tending ever towards a state in which the two become merged in one and in which the feelings answering to them respectively fall into complete concord."

Leaving out of consideration for the present that social millennium of Spencer in which the antagonism between societies shall entirely cease, we are just now concerned with the internal social efficiency of our own social organism. The point to be seen is whether the religion and the laws that have guided the formation and development of that social organism do or do not contain the germ of that principle by which members may be required to sacrifice what to them appear to be their best interests as individuals for the interests of the organism to which they belong, or, to put it more accurately, whether Hinduism as a religion, in its teachings and in its system of laws contemplates that concord between the interests of its individual members and those of the community at large which, according to Spencer, is the key-note of the process of social evolution going on around us, and which he so admiringly holds up as affording prospects of that social millennium which, according to him, will soon be established on earth.

In the opinion of Mr. Benjamin Kidd the Darwinian science of evolution as it is now understood, does not afford " any warrant for anticipating the arrival of that state of society contemplated by Mr. Herbert Spencer." Further he rejects his conception of the process of social evolution (quoted above from his *Data of Ethics*) " as being inconsistent with the teachings of evolutionary science."

Admitting that " the forces which are at work in the evolution of society, are certainly, on the whole, working out the greatest good of the greatest number in a progressive community ; he takes care to point out that the earlier utilitarian conception of the greatest number being related merely to the majority of the existing members of society at any time, has now given way to the greatest number being " *comprised of the number of generations yet unborn or unthought of, to whose interests* the existing individuals are absolutely indifferent." And in the process of social evolution which the race is undergoing, says he, " it is these latter interests which are always in the ascendent." Applying the principle to the limited sphere of a particular social organism it comes to this, that the social efficiency of the latter depends not only on the subordination or merging of the individual interests of its members to or in the intersts of the whole, but also in looking forward to and guarding the interests of the generations yet unborn. A Social organism can therefore be considered as efficient, only if, beyond requiring its members to sacrifice what to them seems to tend to their individual good, happiness or prosperity ; if the same clashes or is inconsistent with the good of the whole, it also takes sufficient care of the interests of the generations yet unborn so as to guarantee the continuance of that state of efficiency in the future. The social system of a nation is perfect or imperfect, complete or incomplete, natural or unnatural, progressive or retrogressive, according as it does or does not fulfil the requirements set forth above. But before we proceed to examine the social system of the ancient Hindus in the light of these considerations, we prefer to clear two more points. The first is that there must surely be something wrong in a social system from which has developed the modern civilization of Europe, which has evoked strong and sweeping condemnation from so eminent a scholar and scientist as Professor Huxley.

" Even the best of modern civilizations," he says "appears to me to exhibit a condition of mankind which neither embodies any further ideal nor even possesses the merit of stability. I do not hesitate to express the opinion that, if there is no hope of a large improvement of the condition of the greater part of the human family if it is true that the increase of knowledge, the winning of a greater dominion over nature which is its consequence, and the wealth which follows upon that dominion are to make no difference in the extent and the intensity of the want with its concomitant physical and moral degradation amongst the masses of the people, I should hail the advent of some kindly comet which would sweep the whole affair away as a desirable consummation."

What Professor Huxley says about the whole human family can more or less be said of the internal state of every great nation of Europe.

The solution of the social problem of India therefore does not necessarily lie in the wholesale imitation of the West to the entire neglect of its past, with its glorious heredity of laws and principles which might shine even with greater splendour if studied in the light of modern history. We do not mean to say that we should decline to take any light from the West or be prejudiced against it because it is of the West. But what I do maintain is that social reform should only proceed on safe and, as far as possible, on reasonable and national lines. The best and safest social reformer will be he who can read the ancient system of the Hindus in the light of the modern knowledge thrown upon it and who out of this joint study can recommend the line of action which he considers to be likely to lead to true social progress (felicity). I may at once say that I do not believe in the possibility of a wholesale bringing back or revival of the past such as perhaps some of the Theosophists and also some of the Arya Samajists contemplate. Such a thing is impossible and it will be a waste of energy to try to achieve what is impossible. It is very important that my co-religionists should realize the impossibility and also the futility of this attempt, and should desist from doing or sying anything which may tend to lead the Hindus astray and make them direct their energies into unprofitable or doubtful channels. I have already said that the *first* necessity of the Hindus of to-day is the acquistion of that degree of social efficiency which alone can enable them to hold their own in the stress and strife of this world of competition. No nation can as such be spiritually high or pure which is socially corrupt, degraded or *inefficient*.

What I aim at in the present paper is to show that there is a great deal in our past which can rightly inspire or guide us in the building up of our future social edifice, or in the mending of the existing one and that we should be going equally astray if in our anxiety to copy the West we ignore or neglect our own laws and lessons which a study of our past alone can impress upon us.

The second point which I want to clear up is that it is not by reliance on unguided and uncontrolled reason that we can get at the true principles of social progress. Reason when uncontrolled, is styled by Kidd to be "the most profoundly individualistic, anti-social and anti-evolutionary of all human qualities." In this opinion the central feature of our evolution has always been the supreme struggle in which the control of this disintegrating influence is being continually effected in the intersts of society first and of the race in the next place; and that the function of the immense and characteristic class of social phenomena which we have in our religious system is to secure the necessary subordination of the present interests of the process of evolution that is in progress. "It would be impossible," adds he, "to conceive any altruistic feeling of this kind which could exceed in strength the parental instinct. *Yet one of the plainest facts of our time and of past history is the perversion of this instinct under the influence of rationalism* and the suspension of its operation in furthering the evolution the race is undergoing. We have discussions proceeding in the literature of the time in which rationalism, with reiterated emphasis, points out, to use the phrase already quoted, that "there is something pathetically absurd in this sacrifice to their children of generation after generation of grown people." No observant person, who has watched the signs of the times, can have the least doubt that *in a state of unrestricted rationalism, the institution of marriage and the family would undergo modifications incompatible with the continuance of that process of simple self-sacrifice with which the interests of the race are bound up.* We have unmistakable evidence of the perversion of the parental feelings amongst the Greeks and Romans under. such rationalistic influences. Speaking of the decay of the Athenian people, Mr. Francis Galton says, "We know, and may guess something more, of the reason why this marvellously gifted race declined. Social morality grew exceedingly lax; marriage became unfashionable and was avoided; many of the more ambitious and accomplished women were avowed courtesans, and consequently infertile, and the mothers of the incoming population were of a heterogeneous class." The same state of popular feeling with respect to marriage prevailed during the decline of the Roman Empire. "The courtesans," says Mr. Lecky, "were raised in popular estimation to an unexampled elevation, and aversion to marriage became very general." And we have at the present day that striking example, ..., of the perversion, under similiar circumstances, of the parental feelings amongst the most brilliant and able race amongst the European peoples and the consequent failure of that race to maintain its place amongst others in the evolution which is proceeding under our eyes in the civilization in which we are living.

It will, I hope, be now clearly seen how dangerous it is to give under prominence to "rationalism" in any programme of social reform and to divorce it from religion

We are, in any case, in a position now to judge of the wisdom of the ancient Aryans in developing all the social laws on the basis of religion and in making the latter so comprehensive as to include everything that is necessary for the right progress of man, as a member of a family, as a member of a social organism and last but not least as a member of his race.

II.

With these introductory remarks I proceed to produce evidences of the social conception of the Hindus, showing the idea of social unity in their religion and in their rules of life. *Firstly*, in my opinion one could hardly come across a more beautiful, a more comprehensive and a truer view of the unity of the social organism than is expressed in the idea of the division of castes,—the much abused, much maligned and much misunderstood idea of the four castes representing the different parts of the creator's body—*the Sharir of the Purusha.* To take the earliest and the highest authority, first, *Rig Veda* X. 90, verses 11 and 12, literally translated into English by Dr. Griffiths, run as follows :—

'11. When they divided *Purusha* how many portions did they make ? What do they call his mouth, his arm ? What do they call his thighs and feet ?

'12. The *Brahman* was his mouth, of both his arms was the *Rajanya* made. His thighs became the *Vaishya*, from his feet the *Shudra* was produced.'

These Verses give expression to two of the sublimest truths about the social relations of man with man as an individual and with mankind as a whole. They establish the oneness of humanity in the body of the Lord and they explain away the phenomena of differences in the capacities, powers and faculties of individuals. As parts of the same whole, they are to sustain, support, supplement, help and co-operate with each other. As individual units of one organism they have, each of them, their own separate functions to perform. Applying this to a particular social organism as distinguished from general humanity, they form the basis of a complete system of social duties. In no other way could one better express the mutual inter-dependence of all parts of society upon one another, be they high or low, and also the essential oneness of the whole.

Taking it in another and a higher sense, it is a better and more effectual representation of collective Humanity representing God himself, than any put forward by the Prophets of the Religion of Humanity from Augustus Comte downwards. Read in that light, the verses standing by themselves explain only a partial or a relative truth. For the whole truth, you must read the whole hymn together. It was our misfortune that such a grand exposition of the greatest of social truths should have so degenerated in the hands of an interested priesthood as to be made the basis of the present-day inhumanly, ingenious, corrupt, invidious, and demoralising distinctions between man and man. But this experience is not so very exceptionally confined to Hinduism only. The evil genius of man has in this and other countries, and in this and other systems of religion, more than occasionally subverted and distorted some of the sublimest truths taught to him by God and nature with a view to advance the interests of particular individuals or of particular classes and to oppress others. Take the history of any great religion, be it the humility-professing Christianity, militant Islam, or Buddhism, you will find similiar distortions in abundance, thus showing that the tendencies of priesthood have been almost the same everywhere. The same idea of the good of the whole runs through the various duties that the Hindu Shastras assign to the four orders. *Manu Smriti* (a treatise on laws, the compilation of which the European scholars fix at about 200 B. C.) is one of those books which lay great stress on caste distinctions, and advocate vast and rather astounding inequalities of treatment between the Brahmans and Shudras, verging in some places almost on inhumanity and cruelty. It is a book held in universal esteem by the orthodox Hindus be they of any sect or school. As such we shall be on the safe side in giving quotations from it, supporting the original social conception of the caste system. Verses 88-91 prescribe the duties of the different Varnas :—

88. " To Brahmans he assigned teaching and studying (the Veda), sacrificing for their own benefit and for others, giving and accepting (of alms).

89. The Kshatriya he commanded to protect the people, to bestow gifts, to offer sacrifices, to study (the Veda), and to abstain from attaching himself to worldly pleasures.

90. The Vaishya to tend cattle, to bestow gifts, to offer sacrifices, to study (the Veda), to trade, to lend money, and to cultivate land.

91. One occupation only the Lord prescribed to the Shudra, to serve meekly even these (other) three castes."

The one note that runs throughout these rules is the *service of others* and the social good and the prosperity of the whole community. The Brahmana is enjoined to study not for the benefit of his soul only, but to *teach others*, a purely social duty. In the same way, it was the duty of the Kshatriyas *to protect the people*.

Mark, please, the distinction between *ruling* and *protecting*. The same may be said about the duties assigned to the Vishyas and the Shudras. We may, here, for a moment take the liberty of drawing the attention of the promoters of the different caste conferences and caste-organisations to these rules of Manu. These rules show that each of these castes was understood to exist and work for the benefit of all, and not for the benefit of their own caste-people only. If it was the duty of a Brahmana to teach *all*, a Kshatriya to protect *all*, similarly the duty of a Vaishya was to produce and to trade for *all* and that of a Shudra to labour for *all*.

From the division into *varnas* (castes) we might proceed to the division of an Aryan life into the four Ashramas and there also you will find the same idea running through the duties and obligations assigned to each. For instance, wherein can you find such a system of free and compulsory education deeply interwoven with religious merit as amongst the Hindus? Every twice-born Hindu was bound to educate his children unless he intended to degrade them to the level of a Shudra, and every Aryan householder was threatened with severe religious demerit if he refused food or alms to a *Vidyarthi*. The various rules laying down the respect that it was the privilege of the teacher to command, show the great importance which the old Aryans attached to the position and the professionof a teacher. Shloka II, 165, lays down the obligation of studying the Veda, for all Aryans:—"An Arya must study the whole Veda together with the Rahasyas, performing at the same time various kinds of austerities and the vows prescribed by the rules of the Veda."

Shloka 154 gives precedence to one who has learnt the Veda, over all those whose claim to respect lies either "through years," *i.e.*, age or "through white hair," *i.e.*, old age, or "through wealth" or "through powerful kinsmen."

A householder destitute of the knowldege of the Veda was looked down upon as unfit for social intercourse with the twiceborn. A student was not to accept food from the house of any one who was deficient in the knowledge of the Veda or in performing sacrifices or who were not known as earning their livelihood by lawful means. Similarly at the time of the selection of a wife, a good man was ordained to "avoid the ten following families, *be they ever so great or rich* in kine, horses, grain or (other) property." "(Viz.) One which neglects the sacred rites, one in which no male children (are born), *one in which the Veda is not studied*, one (the members of) which have thick hair on the body, those which are subject to hemorrhoids, phthisis, weakness of digestion, epilepsy, or white and black leprosy," The same idea is again prominent in III. 63 :—"By low marriages, by omitting (the performance of) sacred rites, *by neglecting the study of the Veda*, and by irreverence towards Brahmanas, (great) families sink low."

In the case of Brahmana it is so very pronounced in

the following verses :—" II, 197. The oblations to gods and manes, made by men ignorant (of the law of gifts), are lost, if the givers in their folly present (shares of them) to *Brahmanas who are mere ashes*.

" III, 168. As a fire of dry grass is (unable to consume the offerings and is quickly) extinguished, even so (is it with) an unlearned Brahmana; sacrificial food must not be given to him, *since it (would be) offered to ashes*. "

See also 133 and 142.

Texts to this effect, full of similar sentiments and breathing the same spirit, can be multiplied by hundreds, not only from the Manu Smriti but from the other *Sutras* and Smritis as well.

Looking to the life of a Hindu *Grihasta* (householder), what ideals of altruistic sentiments are set forth by the texts that describe his daily duties ? Where, on earth, will you find rules such as those which are so explicitly laid down by the epics, the Puranas, and other books containing pictures of ancient Aryan life, and which rules were so scrupulously observed in olden times? The five great daily duties of the Hindus are well-known. In English phraseology they are styled 'sacrifices'. In Sanscrit they are called *Maha* (great) *Yajnas*. Tracing back their origin you find the germs and the ideals in the Veda Mantras, but in the *Shatapatha Brahmana*, one of the most ancient Hindu Shastras, whose place in antiquity is, by common consent, only next to the Vedas themselves, you see them in a more organised shape. We quote from the translations of Julius Eggling, published in the Sacred Books of the East series, Vol. XII, pp. 190 and 191.

" 1. Verily, whoever exists, he, in being born, is born as (owing) a debt to the gods, to the *Rishis*, to the fathers and to men.

2. For, inasmuch as he is bound to sacrifice, for that reason he is born (owing) a debt to the gods ; hence when he sacrifices to them, when he makes offerings to them, he does this (in discharge of his debt) to them.

3. And further, inasmuch as he is bound to study (the Vedas), for that reason he is born as (owing) a debt to the *Rishis* ; hence it is to them that he does this ; for one who has studied (the Vedas) they call ' the *Rishis* ' " treasure-warden."

4. And further, inasmuch as he is bound to wish for offspring, for that reason he is born (owing) a debt to the fathers ; hence when there is (provided by him) a continued, uninterrupted lineage, it is for them that he does this.

5. And further, inasmuch as he is bound to practise hospitality, for that reason he is born as (owing) a debt to men ; hence when he harbours them, when he offers food to them, it is (in discharge of his debt) to them that he does so. Whoever does all these things has discharged his duties ; by him all is obtained, all is conquered.

6. And, accordingly, in that he is born as owing a debt to the gods, in regard to that he satisfies (*ava—day*) them by sacrificing ; and when he makes offering in the fire, he thereby satisfies them in regard to that (debt) : hence, whatever they offer up in the fire, is called *avadanam* (sacrificial portion)."

This quotation speaks only of the four *yajnas*. But

the Sutras and the Smrities which are mostly of later date, speak of five, adding as fifth the debt which man owes to the animals and plants, &c. The Smriti which goes after the name of Manu and is by European scholars believed to be a compilation of about 200 B C., also speaks of five and ascribes the rule to the necessity of expiating the sins committed by each householder, in the use of hearth, the grinding stone, the broom, the pestle and mortar.

Below I give all the verses bearing on the subject, a comparison of which with the quotation given from the *Satapatha* will give the reader a very clear idea of the difference between the ideals of the pre-Buddhistic and post-Buddhistic periods of Aryan civilization.

" III.—67. With the sacred fire, kindled at the wedding, a householder shall perform according to the law the domestic ceremonies and the five (great) sacrifices and (with that) he shall daily cook his food.

68. A householder *has five slaughter-houses* (as it were), *viz.*, the hearth, the grinding stone, the broom, the pestle and mortar, the water vessel, by using which he is bound (with the fetters of sin.)

69. *In order to successively expiate* (*the offences committed by means of all these* (*five*) the great sages have prescribed for householders the daily (performance of the five) great sacrifices.

70. Teaching (and studying) is the sacrifice (offered) to Brahmana, the (offerings of water and food called) Tarpana the sacrifice to the manes, the burnt oblation, the sacrifice offered to the gods, the bali offering that offered to the Bhutas, and the hospitable reception of

guests the offering to men.

71. He who neglects not these five great sacrifices, while he is able (to perform them), is not tainted by the sins (committed) in the five places of slaughter, though he constantly lives in the (order of house-holders).

72. But he who does not feed these five, the gods, his guests, those whom he is bound to maintain, the manes, and himself, *lives not, though he breathes.*"

The idea expressed in 68, 69 and 71 is peculiar to this Smriti and other later books and is entirely foreign to the spirit as well as the letter of the earlier law books. It seems to be essentially *Jainist.* The truth and sentiment expressed in 72 is both lofty and beautiful.

The same idea pervades the whole chapter which lays down the duties of the order of house-holders Shloka 76 explains how the sacrifice to gods (*i. e.* the Agnihotra) is also based on an altruistic conception of man's duty towards all other living creatures;—

" 76. An oblation duly thrown into the fire reaches the sun ; from the sun comes rain, from rain food, therefrom the living creatures (derive their subsistence)."

In the same way Shlokas 77 and 78 proceed to show the prime importance of the order of the householders, thereby expressing a very high standard of the social conception of the Aryas :—

" 77. As all living creatures subsist by receiving support from air, even so (the members of) all orders subsist by receiving support from the householder.

78. Because men of the three (other) orders are daily supported by the householder with (gifts of) sacred knowledge and food, therefore the (order of) househol-

ders is the most excellent order."

Shloka 79 promises a noble reward for the due performance of these duties and lays particular stress on the necessity of the householder cultivating strength :—

79. *(The duties of) this order, which cannot be practised by men with weak organs,* must be carefully observed by him who desires imperishable (bliss in) heaven, and constant happiness in this (life)." Could there be a higher conception and could it be more forcibly expressed than in III. 118? The idea is common to most Hindu Shastras. In the Bhagavat Gita, Sri Krishna gives expression to the same in IV. 31,

" 118. He who prepares food for himself (alone), eats nothing but sin; for it is ordained that the food which remains after (the performance of) the sacrifices shall be the meal of virtuous men." Then look at the following detailed rules about the entertainment of guests and the distribution of food to dependents and you will be at once in a position to know why the Hindus (the bulk of them) have been proverbially hospitable.

" III. 105—A guest who is sent by the (setting) sun in the evening, must not be driven away by a householder; whether he has come at supper time or at an inopportune moment, *he must not stay in the house without entertainment (i. e.*, without being fed and looked after).

114. Without hesitation he may give food, even before his guests, to the following persons, (viz)., to newly married women, to the infants, to the sick, and to the pregnant women.

115. But the foolish man who eats without having given food to these (persons) does, while he crams, not

know that (after death) he himself will be devoured by dogs and vultures.

116. After the Brahmanas, the kinsmen, and the servants have dined, the householder and his wife may afterwards eat what remains.

IV, 32. A householder may give (as much food) as he is able (to spare)* *to those who do not cook for themselves*, and to all beings one must distribute (food) without detriment (to one's own interest)."

Even now every Hindu of the twice-born caste thinks it obligatory to give a part of his cooked food in charity, be it only one cake, to a Brahmana. It was these rules which when practised left no room for public poor houses, orphanages, &c., &c.,

The following shlokas lay down a high standard of regard for women, which it was the duty of every Arya to maintain and respect.

" III, 55. Women must be honoured and adorned by their fathers, brothers, husbands, and brothers-in-law who desire their own welfare.

56. Where women are honoured, there the gods are pleased ; but where they are not honoured, no sacred rite yields rewards.

57: Where the female relations live in grief the family soon wholly perishes ; but that family where they are not unhappy, ever prospers.

58. The houses in which female relations, not being duly honoured, pronounce a curse, perish completely, as destroyed by magic.

---

* This would include ascetics, sanyasis, vidyarthis, orphans, and other destitute people.

59. Hence men, who seek (their own welfare), should always honour women on holidays and festivals with (gifts of) ornaments, cloths, and (dainty) food.

60. In that family, where the husband is pleased with his wife, and the wife with her husband, happiness will as surely be lasting.

61. For, if the wife is not radiant with beauty, she will not attract her husband; but if she has no attractions for him, no children will be born.

62. If the wife is radiant with beauty, the whole house is bright; but if she is destitue of beauty, all will appear dismal."

The following shloka lays down the consequences of a householder's (a married man) neglect to earn his livelihood and of his dependence upon others for the same:—

" III. 104. " Those foolish householders who constantly seek (to live on) the food of others, become, in consequence of that (baseness), after death the cattle of those who give them food."

The following prayer is a fitting sequel to the Shastraic life of a " *Grihastha* " as explained above and shows the high standard of altruistic morality that prevailed amongst the Aryas :—

" III. 259. *May liberal men abound with us!* May (our knowledge of) the Vedas and (our) progeny increase! May faith not forsake us! MAY WE HAVE MUCH TO GIVE TO THE NEEDY!"

The following are the principles in accordance with which Brahmanas and other twice-born people were ordained to control the great and inevitable struggle for life. They represent a high state of national righteousness.

"IV. 2. A Brahmana must seek a means of subsistence which either causes no, or at least little, pain (to others), and live by that except in times of distress."

"IV. 17. Let him avoid all (means of acquiring) wealth which impede the study of the Veda; (let him maintain himself anyhow, but study (because that) devotion to the Veda-study secures the realisation of his aims."

"IV. 18. Let him walk here (on earth), bringing his dress, speech, and thought to a conformity with his age, his occupation, his wealth, his sacred learning and HIS RACE."

"IV. 170-174. Neither a man who (lives) unrighteously nor he who (acquires) wealth (by telling) falsehoods, nor he who always delights in doing injury ever attains happiness in this world. Let him, though suffering in consequence of his righteousness, never turn his heart to unrighteousness; for he will see the speedy overthrow of the unrighteous, wicked men.

Unrighteousness, practised in this world, does not at once produce its fruit, like a cow; but advancing slowly, it cuts off the roots of him who committed it.

If (the punishment falls) not on (the offender) himself, (it falls) on his sons, if not on sons, (at least) on his grandsons, but an iniquity once committed never fails to produce fruit to him who wrought it.

He prospers for a while through unrighteousness, then he gains great good fortune, next he conquers his enemies, but (at last) he perishes (branch and) root."

" IV. 176. Let him avoid the acquisition of wealth and the gratification of his desires if they are opposed to the sacred law, and even lawful acts which may cause pain in the future or are offensive to men."

The following lay down a perfect standard of charity :—

" IV. 120. A Brahmana who neither performs austerities nor studies the Veda, yet delights in accepting the gifts, sinks (with the donor) into hell just as (he who attempts to cross over in) a boat made of stones (is submerged) in the water.

191. Hence an ignorant (man) should be afraid of accepting any presents ; for by reason of a very small (gift) even a fool sinks (into hell) as low into a morass.

192. (A man) who knows the law should not offer even water to a Brahmana who acts like a cat, nor to a Brahmana who acts like a heron, nor to one who is unacquainted with the Veda." (For a definition of cats and herons see 195 and 196).

" 193. For property, though earned in accordance with prescribed rules, which is given to these three (persons), CAUSES IN THE NEXT WORLD MISERY BOTH TO THE GIVER AND THE RECIPIENT.

194. *As he who (attempts to) cross water in a boat of stone sinks (to the bottom), even so* AN IGNORANT DONOR AND AN IGNORANT DONEE SINK LOW.

195. (A man) who, ever covetous, displays the flag of virtue, (who is) a hypocrite, a deceiver of the people, intent on doing injury, (and) a detractor (from the merits) of all men, one must know to be one who acts like a cat.

196. That Brahmana, who with downcast look, of a cruel disposition, is solely intent on attaining his own ends, dishonest and falsely gentle, is one who acts like a heron.

197. Those Bramans who act like herons, and those who display the characteristics of cats, fall in consequence of that wicked mode of acting into (the hell called) *Andhatamisra*."

The following *shlokas* will show how the social and national interests of the community were guarded against an undue and unseasoned desire towards abnegation and ascetic life.

" VI. 35-37. When he has paid the three debts, let him apply his mind to the attainment of final liberation; HE WHO SEEKS IT WITHOUT HAVING PAID (HIS DEBTS) SINKS DOWNWARDS.

36. Having studied the Vedas in accordance with the rule, having begat sons according to the sacred law, and having offered sacrifices according to his ability, he may direct his mind to (the attainment of) final liberation.

37. A TWICE BORN MAN WHO SEEKS LIBERATION WITHOUT HAVING STUDIED THE VEDAS, WITHOUT HAVING BEGOTTEN SONS, AND WITHOUT HAVING OFFERED SACRIFICES SINKS DOWNWARDS."

The following extracts will show how strongly the ancient Aryas felt and believed in the unity of a political or social organism.

In their opinion the safety and welfare of all consisted in the righteousness of all. Any failure of duty by individuals operated to corrupt the whole society, and if ever the number of those who failed to fulfil their obligations or act in accordance with law, increased, it was considered a sure sign of the decay of the national power, strength and virtue. The king representing the commonwealth was required to protect his people, always to keep their interests in view, to see that all orders and classes and individuals performed their respective obligations properly. His neglect or failure to secure the due performance of every one's duty was calculated to result in disaster to the whole community.

There are numerous texts in Manu and other Shastras which can be quoted in support of the above position, but I am afraid, I will be only increasing the length and size of the paper if I did so. I will therefore confine myself only to a few, by way of example, in which the idea stated by me seems to be sufficiently prominent.

VIII. 22. Foretells the ruin of a commonwealth by *famine and disease* in which the number of the twice-born decreases and which principally consists of Shudras (*i. e.* labourers and menial classes). How can a nation continue to exist which has no brain to guide the organism, no arms to protect it, and no traders and manufacturers to maintain and increase its wealth ? No one can conceive of a self-governed community consisting of labourers only. An increase of the labouring classes with a corresponding decrease of the learned, the fighting and the producing classes, is a sure index of decay and *coming ruin.*

" That Kingdom" says Manu, " where Shudras are very numerous, which is infested by atheists, and *destitute* of twice-born (inhabitants), soon ENTIRELY perishes, affected by famine and disease."

Being "destitute of twice-born" is equivalent to being destitute of knowledge, power and wealth. A nation not possessing these cannot exist as a nation and is bound to lose its position as such. Famine and disease are sure to follow in the train of ignorance, weakness and poverty. Let my countrymen ponder over the sublime truth preached in this verse and it shall at once dawn on them as to why they are such frequent victims of famine and disease. The true course then to be followed in order to uproot them is to increase the stock of national knowledge, national strength and national wealth. That is the best, the safest, the most effective, and the only cure of these national afflictions of ours. Here is a remedy, an unfailing remedy, pointed out by the son of "Swayambhuva" himself, the great Manu. Let us apply it with faith, and it is sure to drive away the diseases with which we, each and all of us (both individually and socially), are at the present moment afflicted.

The idea of the ruling class being only a part of the whole social organism and of its earning merit or demerit by the actions of the whole is beautifully and with characteristic force expressed in the following four *shlokas* which we quote from chapter VIII :—

304. A king who (duly) protects (his subjects), receives from each and all the sixth part of their spiritual merit, if he does not protect them, the sixth part of their demerit also (will fall on him).

305. Whatever (merit a man gains by) reading the Vedas by sacrificing, by charitable gifts, (or by) worshipping (Gurus and Gods), the king obtains a sixth part of

that in consequence of his duly protecting (his kingdom).

306. A king who protects the created beings in accordance with the sacred law and smites those worthy of corporal punishment, daily offers (as it were) sacrifices at which hundred-thousands (are given as) fees.

307. A king who does not afford protection, yet takes his share in kind, in taxes, tolls and duties, daily presents and fines, will after death, soon sink into hell."

There are many more texts which similarly tell us of an advanced political science including political economy, having been developed by the Hindus. Elaborate rules and provisions are laid down for the appointment of state officials, the imposition of taxes, tolls and fines, the regulating of state expenditure, the administration of civil and criminal justice, the control of Revenues, the necessity of paying special attention to agriculture, trade, commerce and manufactures, &c., &c.

These all give one an idea of the social position of the Hindus. There are among them some rules which undoubtedly appear to be very invidious, childish, and grotesque but they form only the exceptions even if we were to grant that they are not subsequent interpolations or additions by interested priests. That they are later interpolations can be proved in many ways and by the testimony of the best scholars. However, this is only by the way.

Before I have done with the laws of Manu, I should like to point out that there are various texts in Manu which bespeak an anxiety for the welfare of the unborn generations. Amongst Hindus, marriage is a sacred duty and a sacrament, and as such it is regulated very strictly and with the greatest regard for the interests of the unborn generations. The rules as to Brahmacharya, marriage, and its consummation are all framed with that express object in view. It is the procreation of good, virtuous and strong progeny whch is the object of an Aryan marriage according to the Aryan laws. Hence all marriages are regulated accordingly. "Let him," says Manu, "who desires TO RAISE HIS RACE, even form connections with the most excellent (men) and shun all low ones."

With these laws before us, it is surely unjust to say that the genius of Hinduism is essentially individualistic.

I have given these quotations from Manu-Smriti alone, although most of these rules and many more similar to these are also to be found in other books on the laws of the Aryas. Some of the rules are to be found expressed in almost the same language in every book on Hindu law.

III

From the laws of Manu, we proceed to examine the Vedic literature for traces of the social idea therein. Taking the Rigveda first, which is (according to European scholars) the most ancient of all the Vedas or for the matter of that, the oldest book in the Library of the Aryan race, we find the following exhortations in the 10th Mandala, Hymn CXCI.

"2. Assemble, speak together: let your minds be all of one accord. As ancient Gods unanimous sit down to their appointed share.

3. The place is common, common the assembly, common the mind; be so their thoughts united. A com-

mon purpose do I lay before you, and worship with your general oblation.

4. One and the same be your resolve, and be your minds of one accord.

United be the thoughts of all that may happily agree."

The translation is that by Dr. Griffiths, but that there is a mistake or a misprint is clear from a comparison of the third stanza as given above with the original Sanscrit. *

The word (mantrah) means scripture or vedic hymns, --" A portion of the Veda including the Samhita and distinguished from the Brahmana,"--a charm, a prayer, a revolution or plan or policy (see Dr. Apte's Dictionary, p. 842). I fail to find any authority for its being translated by "*place.*"

The 1st stanza, which we have not reproduced, is a prayer to God (Agni) in which the Lord is asked to bring about the gathering of all friendly creatures round the common altar.

The translation of the second stanza, 2nd line, seems to imply that none should encroach upon other's rights and all should peaceably enjoy their shares.

In the second line of the third stanza again, the original gives the idea of a common worship.

The teaching of the hymn is reproduced in Atharva Veda, Book VI. 64, which Dr. Griffiths translates as below :--

" 1. Agree and be united: let your minds be all of one accord.

* We reproduce the stanzas at the end of the book.

Even as the Gods of ancient days, unanimous, await their share.

2. The rede is common, common the assembly, common the law, so be their thoughts united.

I offer up your general oblation: together entertain one common purpose.

3. One and the same be your resolve, be all your hearts in harmony: one and the same be all your minds that all may happily consent."

In this translation the word "*mantrah*" is rendered into "rede" and the idea of a "common law" is expressly given out.

In my opinion these two Mantras inculcate the conditions of an effective social organisation which is thus made to depend upon—(*a*) community of language. "Speak together or speak alike."

(*b*) Respect for individual rights.

(*c*) Common scriptures, common social life and common laws.

(*d*) A common (national) purpose or mission.

The same idea is more clearly and still more beautifully expressed in Atharva Veda, III. 30, which, as translated by Dr. Griffiths, runs as follows:—

"1. Freedom from hate I bring to you, concord and unanimity. Love one another as the cow loveth the calf that she hath borne.

2. One-minded with his mother, let the son be loyal to his sire.

Let the wife, calm and gentle, speak words sweet as honey to her lord.

3. No brother hate his brother, no sister to sister

be unkind. Unanimous, with one intent, speak ye your speech in friendliness.

4. That spell through which Gods sever not, nor ever hear each other hate, that spell we lay upon your home, a bond of union for the men.

5. Intelligent, submissive, rest united, friendly and kind, bearing the yoke together. Come, speaking sweetly each one to the other, I make you one-intentioned and one-minded.*

6. Let what you drink, your share of food be common: together, with one common bond I bind you.

Serve Agni, gathered round him like the spokes about the chariot nave.

7. With binding charm I make you all united, obeying one sole leader and one-minded even as the Gods who watch and guard the Amrita, at morn and ever may ye be kindly-hearted."

The same spirit runs through Atharva, VI, 73 and 74.

"1. Let Varun come hither, Soma, Agni, Brihaspati come hither with the Vasus. Unanimous, ye kinsmen, come united, come to the glory of this mighty guardian.

2. The inclination, which your hearts have harboured, the purpose which hath occupied your spirits,

---

* Bloomfield's translation (Sacred Books of the East, Vol. XVII, P. 134): stanza 5 is translated as follows:

"Following your leader, of (the same) mind, do ye not hold yourselves apart. Do ye come here, co-operating, going along the same waggon-pole, speaking agreeably to one another: render you of the same aim, of the same mind."

7

This annul with sacrifice and butter. In me be your sweet resting place, O kinsmen.

3. Stand even here ; forsake me not. Before us may Pushan make your path unfit to travel.

Vastoshpati incessantly recall you ! In me be your sweet resting place, O kinsmen !"

" I. Close gathered be your bodies : be your minds and vows in union !

Here present Brahmanspati and Bhoga have assembled you.

2. Let there be union of your minds, let there be union of your hearts :

All that is troubled in your lot, with this I mend and harmonise.

3. As, free from jealousy, the strong Adityas have been the Vishnu's and the Rudra's fellows. So free from jealousy, Lord of three titles ! cause thou these people here to be one-minded."

Passages like these are to be found in abundance in the Vedic literature (Sacred Books of the East, Vol. XIII., P. 360) and can be multiplied at pleasure. For the actual working of this spirit of unity you may study the Ramayana and the Mahabharata. In the latter you find a Devayani being appealed to sacrifice all her kshatriya pride, anger and dignity for the welfare of all of her race with success.

In its pages you find many interesting and instructive sermons on political science, the most noteworthy of which are those given by Bhisma on his death-bed.

Then the celebrated *Chanakya* also says in his *Niti-Shastra* :

" Sacrifice a member for the sake of the family, a family for the sake of a village, a village for the sake of a district, and even the earth for the welfare of the soul."

There are other treatises on political science which promulgate the same truth. These quotations are only relied on to show that the sacred books of the Hindus contain the germs and the foundations of the highest social ideals and testify to the prevalence of a very high standard of social life amongst them with all the duties and obligations that such a life involves and implies.

It is not my intention to suggest that we can or need learn nothing from the Europeans, but my object is only to show that there is sufficient in our sacred books round which we can rally for social strength and reform, and that with all our eagerness to sit at the feet of European savants and scholars we need neither des-credit our ancestors nor indulge in general lamentations for want of social ideals in our past.*

LAJPAT RAI.

—o—

THE RELIGIOUS UNITY OF HINDUISM.

(a). *THE ARYAN SCRIPTURES.*

It is often said that Hinduism is not the name of a particular religion, nor that of a religious nationality, and that it does not represent one set of beliefs, common to

* In the above article I have relied upon the English translation of Sanskrit Texts by European scholars so that there may be no occasion for a charge of straining the words or of extorting meanings or of inventing theories of my own ; although I do not believe that these translations are the best that could be done.

all who call themselves Hindus, and that therefore it is perfectly idle to appeal to the Hindus in the name of a common nationality. It has become almost a fashion to insist that the term Hinduism is too vague to be properly defined, and that there is hardly anything substantially common which binds one Hindu to another in the ties of national brotherhood. Hinduism, in short, is said to be more of a congeries of different religions, sects holding diverse and not unoften diametrically opposite views on matters of faith and doctrine. Hinduism is said to include and cover almost every form of religious faith known to or practised by mankind, from the purest monotheism to the lowest form of animism, polytheism, heno-theism, pantheism, in fact all sorts of *isms*. There is a fairly large class of Hindus who suffer from want of faith in the potentialities of their religion to unite them or to inspire them to the lofty ideals of a great religions platform whereupon to bring together a Hindu union. To many the idea of a Hindu union seems to be nothing more than an unrealizable dream. In their opinion, the talk of a Hindu nationality is a senseless talk, and the attempt to bring about a union amongst Hindus on the basis of religion is extremely impracticable. Some even go further and opine that the religious difficulties of the Hindus cannot be met with, removed or solved by an appeal to the Shastras, and that amongst Hindus religious reform, too, must proceed on lines and ideas borrowed from the West. We confess we are unable to subscribe to these views, and are rather inclined to hold just the otherwise. We have substantial reasons to maintain that Hinduism is at least as much a religious nationality as its sister faiths, Christianity or Islam. These two latter contain as many varieties and shades of religious beliefs and doctrines in themselves, if not more, as Hinduism does, of course giving due consideration to the ages of these three religions. If Hindus have got their Vedantists, the Muhammadans have their Sufis and the Christians have those who have raised the banner of higher Christianity. If Hindus have their Trinity in Brahma, Vishnu and Shiva, the Christians have theirs in Father, Son and Holy ghost. If the Hindus have got their *Avatars*, the Christians have (besides the great incarnation of God in the body of Christ) their Popes and saints. If the Hindus believe in different deities, there are Muhammadans and Christians who believe in saints, *Walis*, Mahdis, &c., &c., If the Hindus have their sacrifices, the Muhammadans and Christians have theirs also. If there are Hindus who are steeped in superstitious beliefs and observe many gross forms of worship, there are millions and millions of Muhammadans and Christians also, particularly the latter, whose religious practices are as gross as those of the multitude of Hindus. If there are fables in the Puranas, there are equally ridiculous stories in the Quran and the Bible. What is, then, that deprives Hinduism of that binding force which knits together the different discordant elements in Islam and Christianity? What are the special features of the latter that are absent in the former? Is Hinduism entirely devoid of any basal principles on which the foundations of a church national could be laid? It is these latter, that, we, at first propose to take in hand and examine touching upon the former whenever it is relevant to do so. Our first contention is, that, like the general mass of Muhammadans and Christians, the Hindus, likewise, directly or indirectly profess to accept the Vedas as their religious scripture. The great bulk of the latter, like the great bulk of the former, believe that their scriptures are the word of God, and are infallible. There are learned Muhammadans and Christians who cannot go so far and do not believe that the Quran and the Bible are the word of God. On the question of the exact authority of the scriptures in these great religions of the world there are as many schools and shades of thought with all their varieties and niceties in one as in the other. There are scoffers, agnostics and sceptics everywhere. Everywhere there are men who do not care a jot for the scripture, make no secret of their views, but still cling to the outer form of the religion, the very essence of which they take pleasure in decrying. The number of such Christians is legion who do not believe that Christ was the Son of God or the son of the virgin, or that the Bible is the revealed word of God, but who do not still care to go out of the pale of outward Christianity. For the purpose of religious rites and ceremonies, for the purposes of baptism, marriage, etc., they are as much Christians as those who believe that every letter of the Bible was spoken by God Himself.

We have said all this not with the intention of disparaging either Islam or Christianity but only in support of our contention that in these respects the religious difficulties of the Hindus are in no way greater in extent, or larger in volume, than those of their fellow subjects, the

Muhammadans and the Christians. We know there are some people who are so hepeless of Hindu unity, or who are so much perplexed with the endless variety of religious belief in Hinduism, that in moments of despondency they have been heard to apostrophize if it would not be better for India if all Hindus were to accept Christianity. But irrespective of spiritual efficiency or inefficiency of Christianity, we are afraid even from the unity point of view we will not thereby be nearer the desired millennium. That such is the opinion of all impartial and disinterested observers will be amply borne out by the following quotations which we cull from a paper written by the late Professor Theodore Goldstucker on the "*R*eligious Difficulties of India." In the paper under reference were noticed certain (then) recent publications* by two learned Hindu converts to Christianity, criticising Hindu religion and philosophy and exhorting their late co-religionists to solve their religious problem by embracing Christianity.

After giving copious extracts from these publications containing the views of these learned Padries on the inconsistencies and anomalies of Hindu religion and Hindu philosophy, with his own comments thereupon, the learned Professor says :—"There is another serious perplexity into which our learned authors must be aware that they will throw even those Hindus

---

* (1) Dialogues on Hindu Philosophy comprising the Niyaya, Sankhya and the Vedanta to which is added a discussion on the authority of the Veda by K. M. Bannerjee of Bishop College, Calcutta.

(2) A Rational Refutation of Hindu Philosophical Systems by Nilkanth Shastri Gore.

who may be clever enough to overcome all these difficulties, but it has as little been removed by them as indeed any difficulty which besets the solution of the religious problem in India. Their object as we have seen, is to persuade their countrymen to embrace the Christian religion, but they have neither explained to them what the Christian religion is, nor where it may be found. Any Hindu, who follows the deductions of Mr. Bannerjee, would simply infer that there is but one Christian religion, which a devout student of the Bible might easily acquire from a perusal of the sacred book. Let him descend, however, from the region of abstraction into that of reality, and he will soon discover the endless variety of opinions which may be founded on the apparently so intelligible scriptural text, and he will soon learn that, so far from this being a mere possibility, hundreds of creeds have sprung up from this same scriptural soil, every one of which claims to be in exclusive possession of Christanity. *And if he be disposed to investigate historically the mutual relation of all these creeds he will find that their difference is so essential that it was strong enough to perpetuate the most inveterate animosities and to result in wars the like of which cannot be traced in the history of any other creed.*

" We have no desire to enlarge upon this theme, for we have said enough to explain why we hold the solution proposed by Mr. Bannerjee to be an impossibility. Attempts of conversion are too frequently made without examining the limits within which they are possible and the result in which their momentary success may end. If a man derives his religious views from his own individual information or from sources which are void of authoritative influence, he may yield them to the views which are of a higher range without causing injury to the nobler part of himself. *But if the creed of an individual is founded on texts held sacred and authoritative, it is a national creed; no individual can abandon it without severing himself from the national stem; no nation can surrender it without laying the axe to its own root. For religion based on texts believed sacred, embodies the whole history of the nation which professes it; it is the shortest abbreviation of all that ennobles nation's mind, is most dear to its memory and most essential to its life.* No religion has better illustrated this truth than the religion founded on the Bible. It could be, and was successfully, introduced amongst all nations which possess no texts supposed to be divinely inspired, and therefore of general authority, and whenever a nation possessing merely the semblance of such a text, adopted it, it thereby decreed its own end. The Romans and Greeks, when becoming Christians, ceased to be the continuation of the classical Romans and Greeks, in history, in literature, in character. Their political importance based on the conditions of the past, was brought to a close, and they had to grow into another nationality. The conditions under which this religion introduced itself into the countries of Europe was always the absence of a book ascribed to divine authorship. When Mr. Bannerjee speaks of the Jews, he has chosen an exact counter instance which goes far to prove that even a people without land, without any history which can be called their own—that a people exposed to all the horrors of persecution and all the allurements of seduction did not and does not espouse that very religion which exercises the most powerful influence on its actual destinies and which it even supports and favours amongst those who profess it. The Jews do not become Christians, simply because they believe that their Testament is a sacred book."

Having expressed these views as to the undesirability and impossibility of converting Hindus to Christianity, Professor Goldstucker further addresses the Hindus themselves, and lays down what, in his opinion, is the true key to the solution of their religious difficulty. We cannot do better than once more quote his words which are full of significance and pregnant with great meaning to all educated Hindus:—

"We have been carried, however, with these remarks to the point where we cannot shrink from expressing the views which we entertain of the duties of the Brahmanical Hindus of our own days. We need not emphasise more than we have already done, that we reject as unwise and unpractical any attempt to persuade them to become Christians or to adopt the Biblical scriptures as their spiritual code. We want them to become a nation worthy of their ancestors and worthy of the great role, which in ancient times they have acted in the history of the human race, and we are satisfied that they cannot regain that position by breaking the *spring ties* of their life, and by exchanging their own religious uncertainty for that of any other creed. It is necessary, however, that they should realise the condition in which they are. We need not prove to them that the minds of the enlightened portion ef their nation are estranged from the sectarian worship as it is practised now, but who could satisfy them that they are utterly remiss in examining where the root of the evil lies. Every Brahmanical believer, if asked, will tell that the mode of his worship is founded on the Vedas. He refers us, it is true, occasionally to the Puranas and Tantras, but he himself admits that these works have no authoritative powers unless they can prove that the tenets they contain are drawn from the Vedic source. The pivot, then, on which all religious questicns of India turn, is and remains—the Veda. Philosophers and non-Philosophers, Vishnuits and Sivaits, all echo the word Veda; * * * * * "

Forty years have elapsed since these words were written by one of the profoundest Sanskrit scholars and one of the most competent and shrewd students of comparative religions, which Europe produced, but the words hold as good, as true and as forcible to-day as they were ever. In fact, the events of these forty years have, instead of showing any flaw either in the arguments or in the sentiments of the learned Professor, proved, if any further proof was needed, how accurately did he grasp the real situation and how truly did he lay down the solution.

We repeat, therefore, before we close, for the present, that the pivot on which all religious questions of Hindu India turn is, and remains—the Veda. To the Veda, therefore, we must go for light and guidance in our religious troubles, and in the Veda we shall find our solace.

LAJPAT RAI.

THE ONE PRESSING NEED OF INDIA.

(A SENSE OF PUBLIC DUTY AND A HIGH STANDARD OF PUBLIC MORALITY)

A question has often haunted us, asleep or awake, as to why is it that notwithstanding the presence amongst us of great vigorous and elevating religious truths, and of the very highest conception of morality, we have been a subject race, held down for so many centuries by sets of people who were neither physically nor spritually nor even intellectually so superior to us as *a fortiori* to demand our subjection.

We do not require a Herbert Spencer to tell us that the social efficiency of a social organism as such, depends upon the sense of social responsibility amongst the members of such an organism. The greater and the intenser the sense of responsibility amongst the individual members, regarding the safety and the welfare of the whole, the greater and the stronger the efficiency of the organism.

It is precisely this sense which is wanting in us and which stands in our way as a nation. Physically we are the equals of any people on earth. Barring those high class Hindus who think their glory consists in weak constitutions, delicate limbs and womanly features or who are given to determine their position in society by the amount of fat on their body and by the amount of physical inactivity which attends their business in life, the majority of our countrymen possess fine physiques and are able to withstand any amount of hardship and struggle. Even with the little they get to satisfy their animal wants, with their coarse food, scanty clothing and ill-ventilated and excessively crowded homesteads they produce a soldiery which ranks amongst the best in the world. Whether it be the Rajput, the Jat, the Sikh, the Gurkha, the Purbia, the Marahtta, or the Punjabi Mussulman the view expressed above holds equally good in the case of all. All of them have by turns, earned the highest praises of military experts under whom they had occasion to serve beneath the British flag. Whatever may be said of the many mistakes of head and heart by which they lost their own battles before the advent of the British, no one can question their bravery and valour. History is full of their deeds. Intellectually too, given the opportunities, the sons of India have given no occasion to shame their mother country. The Hindu civilization, the Budhistic achievements are standing monuments of their high intellectual calibre. Under Mohammadan rule as well, when according to the celebrated Alberuni, the elite of the Hindu community sought the safety of the remotest and the farthest parts of the country to be secure from the molestation of the fanatically disposed Mohammadans, the country continued to produce intellectual giants whose names still shed luster on the country of their birth. Under the British, too, with the few opportunities that are possessed by the Indian scholar to distinguish himself, the country has produced a Bose, a Ramchandra, a Paranjpe, a Ranade, and many others whose names are the common property of all Indians. Then if we look to the domain of religion we stand almost unequalled. What other country in Europe can show the equals of the unknown authors of the Upanishads, Budha, and Shankracharya ? From religion if we come down to tbe regions of philosophy, where in one country could we find such a galaxy of truth loving, honest and bold thinkers, as the immortal authors of the six Darshanas, and some of their commentators and elucidators ? Again, glancing at the history of chivalry and noble deeds, does not the history of the Rajputs raed like a romance ? Why then, are we so low in the scale of nations? What is it that keeps us down and does not allow us to raise our head above the waters ? We are not wanting in flexibility or adaptability. Where on earth will you find another case parallel to Hinduism ? Notwithstanding 12 centuries of Islamic propaganda backed by all the forces of political ascendancy and of that moral superiority which is the ancher sheet of a virgin religion and a conquering creed ; notwithstanding again of 100 years of active evangelical work done in the name of Christ by devoted Missionaries, Hinduism still reigns supreme in the land and baffles all attempts made from time to time, to displace and overthrow it. How is it then, that with all the education we have received during the one century of British rule, with frantic professions of patriotism that are the natural result of a knowledge of our degradation and helplessness, with wild cries of nationality in danger, with pathetic appeals for reforms in the administration of the country, we have so far failed to gain anything substantial in our quest after national liberty ? How is it that our cries make no impression, our appeals go unheeded and our professions turn to be of no avail ? While sparing no occasion or means of criticising Government measures, very often offering right and sensible criticism, with that amount of persistency which sometimes we show, we are yet powerless to obtain even the smallest measure of reform either in constitution or in administration, or even of remedial justice? Why leaving the political sphere aside, how is it that even in matters of social reform which being in our hands no Government prevents us from giving effect to, we have so far failed to achieve that amount of success which the Herculean efforts of men like Ram Mohan Rai, Dayaeand Saraswati, Ishwar Chandra Vidyasagar and Madadeva Gobind Ranade deserved? The reply is the same as we have already given above. We are individually wanting in that sense of social responsibility which requires each and every member of the organism to place the interests of the community or the nation over and above those of his own. Amongst us selfishness, greed and calculation reign supreme. Most of us cannot even think of the society or the community or the nation. But even those who can think and do profess to care for them do not care a farthing for the same, when their own individual interests seem to clash with the interests of the society. Most of us, including some of the very highly educated men, who do not fail to exhibit often an unpardonable pride in the amount of learning locked in their brains who very readily spend hours in finding fault with the commas and semi-colons of less gifted brethren, who do not fail to parade their knowledge of the philosophy of Herbert Spencer, of the Science of Huxley or of the fine poetic genuis of a Shelley or a Tennyson are utterly dovoid of a sense of social responsibility.

We know that men who denounced the institution of child marriagé in the vehement language they could command, where at the same time conscious of the fact that they had themselves already fixed a date for the marriage of their seven years aged girl with a boy of a similarly tender age. We have known men whose professions of patriotism were often the most profuse giving a point blank refusal to any demand of help for any national institution. We have known of great *patriots* rolling in wealth, possessing palatial residences, enjoying the blessing of a good fixed income, never moving their finger to reduce misery that was next door to them· Wa have seen great *patriotic* Indians passing by in a spirit of perfect indifference, when another countryman of theirs was being cruelly beaten by a European. No Indian is supposed to make any move unless such move pays or benefits him in cash or in kind in any way. If you go to a gentleman to ask him to join such and such an association or to do such and such a thing, the question that he puts to you or if he has not the courage to do so openly, to himself, is what shall he gain thereby? We know that people give subscriptions, attend meetings, join Associations and Samajes and do a lot of other things that have the look of public spirit or national help but how many of them, may we ask except when moved by religion, do so by a sense of public duty and individual rosponsibility for the national cause? It is very unpleasant to speak ill of one's own countrymen or to appear to be ungrateful to those estimable gentlemen who do keep public movements going but to be truthful we shall be failing in our duty if we were to pretend a belief in their patriotism. It is our firm belief that if the country could have claimed the one tenth part of that patriotism which is often paraded and assumed, the state of things would have been different and no Government could have ignored the existence or the demands of such patriotism. But the facts are otherwise ; not that the social ideals taught by our religion are low and mean, not that this rank selfishness and base calculation of self interest is countenanced by the teachings of our greatmen, not that this sense of national and public duty is entirely absent from the teachings of our Shastras. No. Political degradation for so long as practically extinguished the very germs of this noble sentiment from our blood. Our immediate ancestors did not possess it, so we could not inherit it from them. As for its inculcation from without we are sorry that the advantages of Western culture have not been unmixed. While very few have imbibed its noble sentiments, a large number have taken and adopted in life its materialistic tendencics. We know that we require the latter, too, rather badly but we cannot forget, that, if we once allow ourselves to be possessed of these only without the other necessary and counteracting tendncies, we are done for. The country may grow rich, it may extend its commerce, it might even begin to manufacture for other countries ; but unless all this is accompanied by a sense of public duty in the people of this country, all this will not avail us, nay, might be the very foundation of future fall, if further fail is yet possible. Yes, we want all this, but first and foremost of all we want the habit and sense of subordinating our individual interests to end before the interests of the community at large. In short, what we pre-eminently want is that every Indian may be sufficiently patriotic and dutiful to believe and act up to the belief that the interests of the country are paramount and must override all private considerations. We want this to be regularly taught as the highest religion that will bring about the salvation of India. To promulgate this we want faithful and true preachers who may be living examples of the truth of their propaganda and who can show the power of their faith in their own persons. Let each province produce a number of such preachers and we are convinced that patriotism will gain firm ground in the country and the cause of nationality will advance with leaps and bounds. Without this we may go on crying for decades and decades but we shall not advance an inch.

—o—

REFORM OR REVIVAL?

We thought that with the fall of the old class of Pandits we had done with those wars of words which were formerly carried on with all the weight of great learning and accompanied by a demonstrative show of deep erudition, but we had evidently counted without our hosts the great body of Indian reformers that are the products of English education, who owe nothing to the old school of Pandits and for whom the old school of Pandits have incurred no responsibility whatever. Before the spread of English education in this country there were only two classes of public literary or intellectual entertainments to which the people were treated now and then and which supplied some diversion from the otherwise dull monotonous or in some places extremely hazardous lives which they generally led. The one was the most popular and useful practice of reciting the *kathas* to mixed and general audiences consisting of all classes of people from old men to boys and from old ladies to young girls. The ancient epics of the land—the chornicles of the life of Rama and his consort, and the great Mahabhart—were very often the books that were thus recited.

These *kathas* were greatly instrumental in keeping the national spark alive through so many vicissitudes of national fortune, when on occasions it had almost reached the point of total extinction. The second were the periodical religious discussions, which in most instances originated with the advent of a learned Pandit from the outside.

Very often the new Pandit's discourses had caught the popular ears and the local Pandit or Pandits thought their dignity, presitige and even emoluments were in danger, to prevent which calamity they considered it their duty to come out and give a challenge to the newly arrived, to prove his superiority in the knowledge of the shastras by an open discussion. Or it might be that the new-comer thought his success depended on drawing out the local theologian and giving him a defeat. Be it as it may, the invariable result was that the discussion began with words, the accuracy of certain expressions used by one or the other, the applicability or the non- applicability of certain rules of grammar and ended often if not always in words and sometimes in blows. I am sorry to observe that the present quarrel over "reform or revival" between the reformers seems to me to resemble, at least in parts, the above mentioned wordy polemics between the Pandits. The reformers claim to be the leaders of the community. They have occupied the place of the Pandits and divines of former times. They profess to lay down rules for the guidance of the general mass of people. They are agreed that the state of Hindu society is bad and rotten, that it needs great and radical changes and that without these changes the whole social fabric stands in danger of giving way and burying the nation down in its debris. They have remedies ready, patent and infallible. On most of these they agree, only to differ on the name by which the same is to be styled. Their agreement as to the remedy disappears in their differences about the wordy habitat to be given to the proposed and contemplated changes. One class of people who have already established a name for themselves do not like to give up the name they have patented and by which they have gained distinction. These latter gentlemen call themselves reformers and insist upon certain social changes being introduced in the name of "reform" and reform only. The other class who have lately come into prominence call themselves "revivalists", and they swear, that any change in the social customs and institutions of the community can only be introduced under the shadow of revival. They think they cannot tolerate reform. The result is that while the former taunt the latter as "revivalists and reactionaries", the latter mock the former as "reformers and revolutionists". Both classes contain amongst them great and good men, men with pure motives and noble intentions. They are generally prominent men—well read and deep in the lore of history. Both classes are to all appearances sincere in their convictions and efforts, but to the great misfortune of the country and the nation they cannot join their heads and work amicably. The wordy weapons are sometimes changed, and while the reformers take their stand on "reform on rational lines" the revivalists plead for "reform on national lines." Here for once at least they seem to agree on reform, as the force of the difference is centred on the words "rational" and "national". The result is that much ink and paper are uselessly spent in dilating upon the necessary soundness of reform and the danger and risk of revival, and *vice versa*. Unfortunately no one ever sees and deplores the great waste of valuable time and precious energy which this quarrel involves—time and energy which could be usefully employed in, nay, which is imperatively demanded, by so many other things that are the *sine qua non* of national progress and that should be done but are not done from want of working hands. On both sides are arrayed tough warriors armed with the knowledge and experience which is gathered by deep study and growing years. On both sides are arrayed sturdy and stout soldiers possessed of and carried by the enthusiasm of youth, full of ambition, and proud of credentials gained by academical successes and literary achievements. On both sides the pen and the tongue are being used with strength and vigour not totally devoid of grace. It is very perilous to come between such daring, bold, and determined fights specially for a comparatively ill-provided and poorly circumstanced man like myself who can wield neither the pen with the dexterity that comes of practice, nor the tongue with that skill which is the outcome of discipline. In fact I am rather inclined to think that it is positively dangerous for recruits who have not had the advantage of regular lessons in drill or of the discipline that comes out of exercises at the manouevres, to interfere between such veteran combatants. But the interests at stake are so great, the field is so vast, the workers in the field are so few and far between, the amount of energy available is so little and the resources are so limited, that on better thought I have decided to take the risk and raise my voice against what to me looks sheer waste of opportunities and misapplication of energy.

I will begin by examining into the respective programmes of reformers and the revivalists and see if there are any vital and real differences which justify so much contemptuous talk of each other. On both sides, I believe that the social reform programme begins and very rightly too, with the question of early marriage. I confess I am unaware of any radical difference between the views of the reformers and the revivalists on the point. In provinces other than the Panjab Mrs. Besant is believed to be the leader of the latter. Now, who does not know that she is opposed to early marriages and denounces them as unshastraic and disastrous? She has in fact taken pains not only to definitely pronounce against this evil custom, but to give force to her utterances, has shut the doors of a department of her school at Benares against those who might have been or might be by the improvidence have their guardians married at a tender age. The Arya-samajists also may to a certain extent be called revivalists, but in this matter of early marriage and the marriageable ages of boys and girls they go to a step further than even the most radical reformer is prepared to go just now. They say and preach, and try to enforce their precept, that no girl be married under 16 and no boy under 25. Now let us ask if there is anything irrational in saying that the institution of child-marriage is not only condemnable by reason, but is actually opposed to the letter as well as the spirit of the Shastras. From the question of child-marriage we may proceed to the great evil of the present divisions and sub-divisions of caste. Mrs. Besant and her school have already pronounced against the sub-divisions in the main castes. Her defence of the original Hindu conception of four castes principally coincides with the views of the Arya-samajists in the matter and practically knocks the present caste system on the head, though in theory only. In practice neither the Arya-samajists nor the reformers can go further than denunciation. All of them agree that a beginning should be made with the sub-divisions. The sub-divisions having been swept away (which is not likely to be achieved very soon or very easily) the time will then come to think of the remoulding or the fusion of the main castes on shastraic or rational lines. For the present we are all agreed that the existing arrangement is an unmixed evil, and the sooner it is done away with the better. From castes let us proceed to the question of foreign travel, and here again we find a practical unanimity. Of course, there are and there shall continue to be ultra-orthodox people who will not give up their opposition to any of these measures and will continue to say that they are un-Hindus; but just now we are not concerned with them, as we dare say there is no one who can justly or even contemptuously be called a revivalist who condemns foreign travel on the plea of revival and no reform. Then let us take up the great question of female education. I know of no sensible man in the country, not to speak of the revivalists only, who is a man of culture and education, who is opposed to it. The school of Mrs. Besant, the Arya-smajists, and the reformers are all pledged to it. There may be and there are practical difficulties in the way of educating our girls and sisters and wives, but nobody questions the desirability, nay the necessity, of giving, if possible, the very highest education to girls. People may differ on the *modus operandi* or may have different views about schemes of education to be enforced in the case of females, but there are no two opinions on the question of principle. There may be some among the so-called revivalists who are not favourably disposed to an exact copy of European customs and usuges relating to females being adopted by the Hindus, but surely there is none who can in the name of revival defend the existing Purdah system or the universal ignorance of women. Similarly we do not think there is much difference of opinion at least so far as practical measures feasible at present are concerned, on the necessity of raising the social status and bettering the condition of low castes, if Hinduism is not bent upon social indifference and mad neglect of vital interests which might result in disastrous consequences. With the exception of some apparently spurious passages in Manu and other Smritis, there is absolutely nothing in the more ancient literature to justify the inhuman and cruel treatment to which the low castes are at present or were till lately subjected. We think we have almost exhausted the list of prominent subjects comprised in the list of reforms advocated by the social reformers, having reserved one important matter to be discussed last, viz. the question of widow remarriege.

On this question there exists undoubtedly real difference of opinion between the so-called reformers and the so-called revivalists. We grant that the question is a very important one; but still we are not prepared to admit that a difference on this single question justifies all that bitterness which characterises the writings of these two classes about one another. The real and important differences are on questions of religion and worship which the social reformers profess to exclude from their curriculum of school and college education. Here in the Punjab, fortunately we have been spared that bitter fight over these words which is going on in the Western and Soutnern Presidencies, although we are not unware that of late attempts have not been wanting to introduce it in collegiate and inter-collegiate debates. We cannot but deprecate these unwise attempts and will warn our young men from throwing themselves into the vortex of this absolutely unnecessary and uncalled for fight over words. We may be pardoned for pointing out that to us the fight seems to be generally on the same lines and on the same grounds which marked the polemics of the old class of Pandits. The real truth is that the so-called reformers are mostly in faith and in religion Brahmos. They were the earliest in the field and fought for reform when the revivalists had not yet come into existence. The revivalists are the products of a wider diffusion of Sanskrit literature whcih has taken place principally within the last quarter of a century. This study has afforded them sufficient and strong evidence of their ancestors having enjoyed a great and glorious civilization from which most of the present evil practices and customs that are the bane of modern Hinduism were absent. They therefore naturally look to the past for light and guidance and plead that a revival might lead them into that haven of progress which is the object of all. They have found that most of the social evils existing in their society were not to be found in ancient Hindu race and they have therefore begun to appeal to the authority of the past and the shastras for the introductions of these very reforms for which reformers had been pleading with much force though with scanty success on grounds of utility and natural justice. The revivalists are naturally popular in Hindu society as they take their stand on the authority of the Hindu Shastras and thus threaten to oust the reformers from their hard earned position. Then to add insult to injury, their exposition of the popular religious beliefs of the Hindus is so injurious and cunning as to justify a reasonable fear in the minds of the reformers that they are taking the nation back to superstitions and low and debased forms of worship from which English education, contract with Western religion, and a study of the master-minds of the West was just extracting them with so desirable a success. The reformers had thus based their religious propaganda on the same basis on which their social programme rested, viz., grounds of rationality. The revivalists having taken to the defence of the so-called national, have extended the same base to the removal of social evils and thus the fight began between "reform on national lines" and "reform on rational lines." But, as I have pointed out above, so far as real social reform is considered, both lines of work lead to a common conclusion. It is not therefore fair to entangle social reform in this quarrel which is really based on differences in religious views. Let "the reformers" by all means if they like, ridicule the religious views of "the revivalists"; and criticise or hold them to derision, but it is not, to say the least, graceful and fair to talk of them contemptuously in matters of social reform. The same should we say to the revivalists. Happily here in the Punjab, as we have already said, there is not much difference between reform and revival. By far the strongest reforming agency in the Panjab appears to accept both. To them reform is revival and revival is reform. It is true they attach much importance to nationality or to national lines, but subject to the important proviso *that they are not irrational.* The Aryasamajists shall have nothing *irrational* though it may even have the look of being national. They want everything national which is rational as well. They even go

in for things *national* if only they are not irrational; but no further. According to them nothing can be either national or rational which is against the letter or the spirit of the Vedas. So far there seems to be no danger of the Panjab being involved in this meaningless distinction between reform and revival, but we think it is better to take time by the forelock and sound this note of warning to guard against any contemplated or impending mischief. But over and above that, it is our earnest request to the leaders of the Hindu community in the Western and the Southern provinces to abjure this absurd distinction and to work harmoniously for social reform, at least so far as all are agreed upon. Lately I had occasion to listen to an address on social progress by an esteemed friend of mine who is a pronounced social reformer. In the course of his remarks he treated the revivalists with scant respect, and in support of his views read the following quotation from the Amraoti speech of that great reformer—the late Mr. Justice Ranade:—
"On the other side, some of our orthodox friends find fault with us, not because of the particular roforms we have in view, but on account of the methods we follow. While the new religious sects condemn us for being too orthodox, the extreme orthodox section denounce us for being too revolutionary in our methods. According to these last, our efforts should be directed to revive and not to reform. I have many friends in this camp of extreme orthodoxy, and their watchword is that revival and not reform should be our motto. They advocate a return to the old ways, and appeal to the old authorities and the old sanctions. Here also, as in the instance

quoted above, people speak without realising the full significance of their own words. When we are asked to revive our institutions and customs, people seem to be very much at sea as to what it is they want to revive. What purticular period of our history is to be taken as the old? Whether the period of the Vedas, of the Smritis, of the Puranas, or of the Mahomedan or modern Hindu times? Our usages have been changed from time to time by a slow process of growth, and, in some cases, of decay and corruption, and we cannot stop at a particular period without breaking the continuity of the whole. When my revivalist friend presses his argument upon me, he has to seek recourse in some subterfuge which really furnishes no reply to the question. What shall we revive? Shall we revive the old habits of our people when the most sacred of our caste indulge in all the abominations, as we now understand them, animal food and drink which exhausted every section of our country's zoology and botany? The men and gods of those old days ate and drank forbidden things to excess in a way no revivalist will now venture to recommend. Shall we revive the twelve forms of sons, or eight forms of marriage which included capture, and recognised mixed and illegitimate intercourse? Shall we revive the Niyoga system of procreating sons on our brother's wives when widowed? Shall we revive the old liberties taken by the Rishis and by the wives of the Rishis with the marital tie? Shall we revive the hecatombs of animals sacrifieed from year's end to year's end, and which human beings were not spared as propitiatory offerings? Shall we revive the *shakti* worship of the left hand with its indecenies and practical debaucheries ? Shall we revive the sati and infanticide customs, or the flinging of living men into the rivers. or over rocks, or hook-swinging, or the crushing beneath Jagannath car ? Shall we revive the internecine wars of the Brahmans and Kshatriyas or the cruel persecution and degradation of the aboriginal population ? Shall we revive the custom of many husbands to one wife or of many wives to one husband ? Shall we require our Brahmans to cease to be landlords and gentlemen, and turn into beggars and dependants upon the king as in olden times ? These instances will suffice to show that the plan of reviving the ancient usages and customs will not work our salvation, and is not practicable. If these usages were good and beneficial, why were they altered by our wise ancestors ? If they were bad and injurious, how can any claim be put forward for their restoration after so many ages ? Besides, it seems to be forgotten that in a living organism as society is, no revival is possible. The dead and the buried or burnt are dead, buried. and burnt once for all, and the dead past cannot therefore be revived except by a reformation of the old materials into new organised being-" Now, if it be permissible for a comparatively young and inexperienced man without laying himself open to a charge of disrespect for one of our revered leaders whose great wisdom, deep learning, and general judicial-mindedness are accepted all around, I will, with due deference to the late Mr. Ranade, beg to point out the injustice of the observations quoted above. Cannot a revivalist, arguing in the same strain, ask the reformers into what they wish to reform us ? Whether they want us to be reformed on the pattern of the English or the French? Whether they want us to accept the Divorce laws of Christian society or the temporary marriages that are now so much in favour in France or America? Whether they want to make men of our women by putting them into those avocations for which nature never meant them? Whether they want us to substitute the legal *niyoga* of the Mahabarat period with the illegal and immoral *niyoga* that is nowadays rampant in European society? Whether they want us to reform into Sunday drinkers of brandy and promiscuous eaters of beef? In short, whether they want to revolutionise our society by an outlandish imitation of European customs and manners and an undiminished adoption of European vices? The revivalists do not admit that the institutions which they want to revive are dead, burnt and gone. The very fact that they wish to revive them goes to show that they believe that there is still some life left in them and that given the proper remedy, their present unhealthy and abnormal state is sure to disappear and result in the bringing about of the normal and healthy condition of affairs. In fact, in an earlier part of the same address, Mr. Ranade summed up the position of the revivalists in a few well chosen and apt words when he admitted that, "In the case of our society especially, the usages which at present prevail amongst us are admittedly not those which obtained in the most glorious periods of our history. On most of the points which are included in our programme, our own record of the past shows that there has been a decided change for the worse and it is surely within the range of practical possibilities for us to hope that we may work up our way back to a better state of things without stirring up the rancorous hostilities which religious differences have a tendency to create and foster." It is exactly this working up our way back which the revivalists aim at. No revivalist has ever pleaded for the institutions selected by Mr. Justice Ranade as the butt end of his attack against them.

The real significance of these words,—"reform" and "revival"—if any, seems to be in the authority or authorities from which the reformers and the revivalists respectively seek their inspiration for guidance in matters social. The former are bent on relying more upon reason and the experience of European society, while the latter are disposed to primarily look at their shastras and the past history, and the traditions of their people and the ancient institutions of the land which were in vogue when the nation was in the zenith of its glory. On our part we here in the Panjab are prepared to take our inspiration from both these sources, though we prefer to begin with the latter and call in the assistence of the former mainly to understand and explain what is not clear and ambiguous in the latter. But so long as our conclusions are principally the same, I think the fight is not worth being continued and may be dropped for good.

LAJPAT RAI.

-——o——

RELIGION AS DEFINED IN THE WEST.

A consideration of the religious problem must be begun with a consideration of the primary question, *viz.*, "what is religion?" One would think that, universal as the idea of religion is, there must not be any differences about its meaning and conception and that everybody, all over the world, must have the same notion about it. But, strange to say, there is no other subject upon which there exists a greater want of unanimity than that of religion. There are great, important, wide and extensive differences in men's conceptions of religion. No two communities understand quite the same thing from it. Professor Max Muller says, "If there is a word that has changed from century to century and has a different aspect in every country in which it is used—nay which conveys peculiar shades of meaning as it is used by every man, woman or child—it is religion." Still a comparative study of religions will disclose a fair amount of agreement or at least some salient points which form the fundamental basis of most of the great religions of the world. Before we come to these common salient points we think we might profitably consider the various definitions of religion, that have from time to time been attempted by those who have discussed the subject and thrown light upon the same. We might begin with the root-meaning of the word and its etymological derivation, though perhaps we may not gain much therefrom. Unfortunately even here we fail to find a unanimity. Some amongst them whose derivation has been accepted by Max Muller, derive it from Latin *relegere*, to gather up again, to take up, to consider, to ponder—opposed to nec-legere, to neglect. According to this derivation religion originally meant attention regard, reverence and awe and was not restricted to reverence for the gods. Very soon, however, it became more and more restricted to reverence for the gods and divine beings. People began to speak of a man's religion, meaning his piety, his faith in the gods, his observances of ceremonies till at last an entire system was called *religious* or *religion.* There are others who derive *religion* from *religare,* to bind up, to fasten, to moor *i. e.* what binds or holds us back. But it is quite clear that if *religio* or religion originally meant attention, regard, or reverence it did not continue to retain that simple meaning. The word has had such a vast and varied use that it is almost hopeless to invent such a comprehensive definition as to cover the meanings of all those who have used it, discussed it and lived by it. With some the word has been synonymous with all that is good and noble in this world, with others it had nothing to do with the affairs of the world. With some it was only another name for morality; with others it overlapped morality and expressed a sense of spiritual ecstasy. With some it expressed the relationship of the spirit of man with that Universal Spirit, God. With others it directed a number of ideas in which God had no place at all, while there were others whose conception of religion even directed the existence of what we call human soul or spirit. By way of illustration we will notice a few of these attempts at defining religion.

Kant, for instance, one of the greatest European savants, says, "religion is morality." According to him, looking upon all our moral duties as divine commands is religion. To the question whence originates the building force of those moral duties, Kant has no satisfactory reply. Having no faith in revelation, he cannot ascribe this authorship to God. What then does he mean by asking us to look upon moral duties as divine commands? He calls them divine because in his opinion we are directly conscious of them. In the words of Professor Max Muller, any outward divine authority is in the eyes of a Kantiah philosopher mere phenomenal or as we should say a mere confession of human weakness. Fichte, however, an equally great name in European philosophy, takes an exactly opposite view. He denies that religion is morality because he says religion is never practical and was never intended to influence life. In his opinion pure morality serves the latter purpose and religion is knowledge which gives man a clear insight into himself, answers the highest questions and thus imparts to us a complete harmony with ourselves and a thorough satisfaction to our mind. Apparently this seems to be very much like the *Gyan* of the Indian Vedanti of the school of Swami Shankaracharya.

Then there are the two definitions of Schleier Macher and Hegel expessing two opposite views. According to the former, "religion consists in our consciousness of absolute dependence on something which though it determines us we cannot determine in turn." The latter, however, declares that "the feeling of dependence is the very opposite of religion." According to Hegel, "religion is or ought to be perfect freedom," for it is, according to him, nothing more nor less than the Divine Spirit becoming conscious of himself through the finite spirit. This again sounds like Vedantism.

The next step from this was taken by Comte who has taught that man is "not only the subject but also the object of religion and religious worship. We are told that man cannot know any thing higher than man ; that man therefore is the only true object of religious knowledge and worship, only not man as an individual but man as a class." This last qualification is the keynote of Comte's philosophy and no doubt reads very solemn, even sublime. But it was reserved to Fenerbach to give the last of the brush and remove even " this last mystic hold " off the brow of religion. According to him " self love is a necessary, indestructible, universal law and principle and inseparable from every kind of love. Religion must and does confirm this on every page of its history. Wherever man tries to resist that human egoism, in the sense in which we explained it, whether in religion, philosophy or politics he sinks into pure nonsense and insanity, for the sense which forms the foundation of all human instincts, desires and actions is the satisfaction of the human being, the satisfaction of human egoism." Hegel's rough but curt criticism of this definition is so pertinent that we cannot resist the temptation of quoting it. He says that if the feeling of dependence were the sole test of religion then a dog would be the most religious of all creatures.

Thus if universal philanthropy or humanity is religion according to Comte, pure selfishness is religion according to Fenerbach. To the same school belongs the definition of Gruppe who says that " religious belief is a doctrine professing to be able to produce union with a being or the attainment of a state which, properly speaking, lies beyond the sphere of human striving and attainment." According to him, "religion is a pure invention of some body's imagination, the acceptance of which is due to the unconscious vanity of its founders, a belief in the happiness which it procures to its believers and the substantial advantages which society derives from it."

From the philosophers' definitions of religion we next proceed to the definitions of European theologians.

Martineau describes it as "A belief in an ever-living God, *i.e.* a Divine Mind and Will ruling the universe, and holding moral relations with mankind." Professor Flint defines it as 'man's' belief in a being or beings, mightier than himself, and accessible to his senses, but not indifferent to his sentiments and actions, with the feelings and practices which flow from such a belief. *Spinoza* says, "religion is the love of God founded on a knowledge of his divine perfections." *Reville* :—Religion is the determination of human life by the sentiment of a bond uniting the human mind to that mysterious mind whose dominations of the world and of itself it recognises and to whom it delights in feeling itself united. These definitions are objected to because they exclude certain systems of belief and practice which, although universally recognised as religious yet ignore the existence of God or gods (such as Budhism). Consequently an attempt has been made by Professor Max Muller and some other writers to invent definitions of religion which may be sufficiently wide and comprehensive to include all that has till now been known or styled as religion. He defines it to be "a mental faculty which independent, nay, in spite, of sense and reason, enables man to apprehend the Infinite, under different names, and under varying disguises." In anticipation of criticism he has taken pains to point out that by "Infinite" he does not mean God but "Indefinite," thereby including Budhism as well. With great deference to these great names we cannot help remarking that we have quite failed to realize the necessity of finding such a definition of religion as may cover all those forms of belief or faith that have to this day been, whether rightly or wrongly, described or styled as religions. This, in our humble opinion, is not the correct way of teaching "what is religion." It may be a suitable definition for historical purposes but certainly not for theological or ethical or moral.

LAJPAT RAI.

---o---

OUR STRUGGLE FOR FREEDOM: HOW TO CARRY IT ON.

No patriotic Indian can return to his country after a trip to England, including a visit, however short, to other countries in Europe, without being forcibly struck by the intense desire for political liberty and freedom that fills the European atmosphere and that distinguishes the West from the East. He finds that in Europe people are always agitated about their political rights and are extremely jealous of interference with or suppression of popular rights and privileges. Life in England or in Europe is a great struggle—constant, unending struggle for light and liberty. Freedom from limitations and restrictions, removal of disqualifications and trammels, be they of any nature, perfect freedom from bondage of everykind, is the ever increasing and ever recurring cry of modern Europe. Democratic spirit is the key-note of Western Civilization in all its branches and departments, but in politics it rules almost supreme. The Government of the people, by the people and for the people is the ideal all over whether in Domocratic England, Monarchical Germany, Autocratic Russia or Republican France. The Press, the pulpit and the platform are all ringing with the cries of "away with the tyrants and autocrats who stand in the way of the democracy and who desire to check or stop the wheel of progress onwards or who have the audacity of trifling with the wishes of the people." One should be here in Europe to realize the truth of the above remarks on occasions when anything is done or attempted to be done by the various Governments in power, which is opposed to the democratic spirit of the times or by which a popular demand is thrown out or anything else is done which is opposed to the wishes of the people or which does not tend to further their interests. In July last the rejection of the London Tramways Bill by the House of Lords afforded such an occasion. The City of London, as our readers know, is situated on the banks of the Thames. The river divides the city into two main divisions one on each side of the river, the tramways end on each side and are not allowed to run across the bridges. This results in great inconvenience to the people as they have to leave the tramway at one end of the river, cross the bridge on foot and then take another tramway at the other end. For busy London people, men and women, boys and girls who come to the city every day from miles for business and then return to their homes after business hours, this means a great waste of time and money. The London County Council, therefore, proposed to take their tramways across the bridges and thus add to the comfort and the convenience of that great mass of people who cannot afford to engage cabs and hansoms. The Bill passed the House of Commons and was rejected in the House of Lords on the ground that its acceptance involved the destruction of the spectacular effect of the bridges and would make them look ugly. The days and nights that followed the rejection of this bill presented a spectacle in London which required to be seen in order to be fully realized and which is past all description. People were mad with rage and frenzy and on all sides and from all quarters you heard the cry " down with the Lords," " down with these heriditary robbers and thieves." In clubs, in theatres, in political meetings, on the tramcars, on the ' buses, ' in trains, everywhere in fact, the audacity of the House of Lords was the one absorbing topic of discussion and comment, and the proposal for abolishing the House of Lords was being freely and seriously discussed. It found loud expression in the columns of the democratic press, was re-echoed in society papers and was exhibited on the stage. Angry resolutions were passed at the meetings of the London County Council and at other public meetings whether convened for that special purpose or not. For a few days the atmosphere was surcharged with revolutionary ideas. The semi-official liberal and radical press joined in the cry and demanded the abolition of the House of Lords as the only remedy. The

Tory press could not but disapprove of the action of the Lords and was either discreetly silent or printed indifferent paragraphs. No serious attempt was made to defend the action of the Lords by anybody.

In short, the whole city seemed to be in a state of ferment and the public mind was intensely agitated. Even the *Daily News*, the organ of the Whigs, demanded an abolition of the House of Lords. The country resounded with the cries of " end it or mend it." Almost immediately following this, came the defeat of the Government on Irish supplies and the statement of the Premier that he intended neither to resign nor to dissolve the Parliament. On this question, of course, the country was divided and the Whigs and the Tories sided with their respective parties. But even the Tory papers acknowledged that a crisis had come and in a suppressed tone the *Times* also admitted that a great constitutional issue had been raised.

One of the Radical extremists wrote :—

" It is no less than Revolution! The King is dead. Mr. Balfour has established an autocracy to supplant the monarchy. As defiant of the nation as the Tsar and his bureaucracy, he laughs at public opinions and governs by paper constitutions. He has only to propose a measure prolonging the life of the Government indefinitely and the cowardly criminals at his back aided by the land thieves in the hereditary chamber will pass it. Defeated in the House of Commons, he ignores a hostile vote and continues the government of incompetence and corruption. This is Revolution."

Another paper after lamenting that the real government of the country was not in the hands of the electorate but in those of the rich wrote as follows :—" Let us rejoice, then, that we have been reminded before the election and not after it, of the Permanent Tory Opposition which will confront us after the battle is won. Now that we have the i·sue raised again, in sheer wantonness by the old and new nobility. Let us not suffer it to be dropped. We will come into power in 1906, not only with a mandate upon the fiscal question and education and the publicans and Chinese slavery and labour legislation, but upon that monstrous survival of the bad old times which we call the House of Lords."

At about the same time occurred another incident which showed the ascendancy of the democratic spirit in this country. The Government announced what was practically a dropping of the Unemployed Bill and said there was no chance of the Bill being passed into law this session. This announcement met with a chorus of disapproval from the public, and at once a number of monster demonstrations of the unemployed were organised.

Thousands of the unemployed assembled in different places and protested. In some cases thousands marched to London to prove to the Government the intensity of feeling on the subject.

At a meeting of the unemployed at Manchester a regular march to London was proposed. In discussing the proposed measure one of the speakers said: "They had no hesitation in declaring that such a march would be a menace to the towns they passed through, but if the Government wanted to prevent it, they must give the legislation asked for." Another speaker said that if in the opinion of the authorities, "Human life was not worth any consideration, they, the unemployed, would say that they were not prepared to consider property (Hear, Hear). They would take immediate steps to see to it that they had that which was necessary for their sustenance and they would not be particular where they got it." The demonstrations of the unemployed men were supplemented by similar demonstrations of the unemployed women, and the wives of the unemployed in London who eventually sent a deputation to the House of Commons to meet the Premier. The result was that all parties had to give in and the "Unemployed Bill" was taken up and passed into law.

Then there is another question that has been agitating a section of the British public for several years past, *viz.*, the Education Act. This Act forces Non-Conformists to pay rates which they consider iniquitous. The Bill was passed in the teeth of a great and vigorous opposition and the Non-Conformists have not yet been reconciled to it. A great number of them every year refuse to pay taxes voluntarily and the same is realized by the seizure and distress of their property. This has been going on for the last three years and still continues. The methods of agitation followed by the Irish nationalists are too significant and well known to need special mention. In the House of Commons they obstinately obstruct business and at times make the transaction of it almost impossible. Their policy in this respect is open and avowed. In the country itself they throw as many difficulties in the way of the Government as they can.

Their success in these methods is well known and, as a result thereof, they have extorted many valuable concessions from unwilling and hostile Parliaments. In other parts of Europe they go a step further and in the demand for political liberty have recourse to Anarchist methods, which at times culminate in murders, assassinations and crime. This is wicked no doubt, but it shows how intense is the desire for political liberty and at what risk and under what conditions people are striving to get it, in their own way and according to their own means. Now, on seeing and studying all this, one cannot help contrasting the same with political conditions that prevail in India. Not that he necessarily wishes that all of these methods may be adopted by his countrymen but because he keenly feels by contrast the apathy, the indifference, the want of earnestness, the absence of a spirit of sacrifice for the cause and for the principle, the collossal timidity and the consequent failure of those who carry on political agitation in India. There are neither leaders nor followers who fully realize what political freedom is and what stupendous efforts and sacrifices are required of them in order to get to even the fringe of the same. One is apt to feel that a set of wordly-wise (or perhaps unwise), greedy and cowardly people as we are, we do not deserve a better treatment at the hands of our rulers than what they accord to us. Why ? What sacrifices do we undergo to deserve what we want ? Anything more than the trouble of attending the annual session of the Congress and enjoying a holiday ? Yes, a few do more than that. They write articles and deliver speeches. A few do even more than that, they subscribe *small* sums of money for the political propaganda. But what proportion does that bear to their incomes or to their expenditure on luxuries and holidays, &c., you should not ask. Because in answer to that question even the greatest and the loudest of *Indian Patriots* will have to hide his head in shame. But why be so hard on them? Have they not big families, sons, grandsons, daughters, wives, mothers, and last but not the least, their great selves to provide for? Why, have they not to leave estates, build palaces and otherwise provide for the dim uncertain future? Yes, they have to do all that, and we have no quarrel with them for doing so. Only we object to their assuming that they are patriots. In our humble opinion no one is entitled to call himself a PATRIOT who holds anything (excepting his religion, of course,) dearer than his country. But this is a very high and almost unapproachable ideal, you will say. Very well, let us in any case try to do something better and more tangible than we have been doing heretofore. Let us, at the close of each year, feel certain of some progress. Let us take stock and say if we are, to be sure, making substaintial progress. Looked at from this point of view even, I am afraid we cannot hold out a cheerful and promising record. Our past record shows that in truth, the struggle for freedom has not even yet commenced, we have done absolutely nothing to inaugurate it. The country is as yet wanting in those conditions which must precede the dawn of an era of real, earnest struggle.

Where are the political thinkers of the country, whose sole thought by day or by night, sleeping or waking, should be, how to initiate and carry on the struggle for freedom? Where are the political Sanyasis whose sole work in life should be the preaching of the gospel of freedom, who should, even at the point of the bayonet, say with Galelio, "there they are, I see them moving"? Where are the *Vaishyas* of the movement who will only earn and make money for the struggle and who will finance it; who will live poorly and modestly and save every pie for the sacred cause in order not to let it suffer for want of the sinews of war? And last but not least where are the people who will quietly, ungrudgingly, without complaint or murmur, suffer for the cause and in their persons prove the truth of the saying that "the blood of the martyrs is the seed of the church"? In short, where are the people who will raise agitation for political rights and liberty to the dignity of a church and live and die for the same?

Let us look round and find out if there are men in the country who are fit to properly initiate and inaugurate the struggle for freedom. Bengal is renowned for its' writers and speakers. Let some of its best sons consecrate their lives to the cause. Their *only* business in life should be to write books, tracts, pamphlets, articles and notes, also to give speeches all over the country expounding what liberty is, how it was won by other people and how it can be won by us. Let them seek no payment for their labours but what is sufficient for their sustenance. Let them build no houses, create no estates and live simple frugal lives. If possible, let them be *celibates*. Maharashtra has justly earned a name for statesmanship and powers of organisation. Let some of its best sons consecrate their lives to the work of organising political movements in India. Our revered friend, Mr. Bal Gangadhar Tilak, is one of the fittest persons to undertake the work, if the Government which has been persecuting him so long, is inclined to let him alone, which is not likely, he having roused its worst suspicions. Well, in that case, the best thing for him is to bid good-bye to his motherland, be a voluntary exile and take his residence somewhere abroad. He should devote himself to the task of influencing English and foreign public opinion in favour of political reforms in India. The other leader who is fitted to do this work is Mr. Gokhale. I may be pardoned for hazarding an opinion to the effect that the Supreme or any other Legislative Council Chamber is not the place for him. He has shown the way to others, he has proved to the world sufficiently that even poor Indians can hold their own against clever autocratic bureaucrats of the class of Lord Curzon, and that is enough. Let the non-official members of the Bombay Legislative Council find another representative champion for the Supreme Council and leave Mr. Gokhale alone, to be the whole-time Secretary of the Congress, to organise a central office, to go about, and guide the Provincial Congress Committees. The other provinces, also, should, if possible, prevail upon one or two capable persons in each centre to renounce their professions and take to the work of carrying on political agitation and spreading political propaganda.

If there are any provinces which cannot fix upon their own leaders, let them follow the lead of the better situated and more lucky ones and assist in bringing about one compact political organisation determined to carry on the struggle for political right.

As to actual work, we think, the time has come for more vigorous measures and for a substantial change in the methods of our agitation.

Bengal has just shown the way in agitating against the Partition of Bengal. What Bengal has done should be done by every province in ventilating its grievances. Besides occasional provincial demonstrations like those recently held in Bengal, we ought to improve upon the general annual demonstration at the Congress session by arranging to bring about a greater and a bigger meeting every year attended by no less than a hundred thousand persons from all parts of India. The educational and the political value of such gatherings cannot be over-estimated. Let the next session of the Congress at Benares set the example. Actual deliberative work should be done by a smaller conference attended by not more than a hundred of the best men of the country. Two whole days may be reserved for this work and *one day*, the opening day, for popular demonstration, at which speeches may be delivered to the assembled masses from different platforms by different men in their own vernaculars. The executive and administrative work of guiding the movement all round the year should be done by a still smaller standing Committee of 20 to 30 men. This committee ought to meet at least twice or three times a year, and if Sir Pherozeshah Mehta cannot spare time to attend its sittings at some central place, let us unanimously agree to fix Bombay as the headquarters and meet only there. Or if that be not acceptable to our Bengal friends who are equally indispensable, let Bombay and Calcutta have the honour of being the meeting place every alternate year. For the sake of unanimity and for the sake of our motherland let us all agree to this even though it may be inconvenient and expensive to Madrassees and Punjabis to do so.

Then the next thing which the whole country ought to do simultaneously with the above is the adopting of and giving effect to the Bengal resolutions *re* the boycotting of English goods. This in my opinion is the most effective way of bringing the Government to its senses and will be most telling on England. Even if we cannot do without foreign goods let us import them from Japan and China first and from Germany, France or the United States next. Let us try to gain the sympathy and good-will of the Indian retail-sellers, and there cannot be the least doubt that we can carry on an effective political propaganda. There is another thing which I would do, *viz.*, to spread a knowledge of English laws and Regulations broad-cast. Let the people realize the full significance of the laws under which they live and demand the full pound of flesh given to them by the same. If all these measures carried out for a number of years fail to make an impression upon the Government, though I am sure they will, then there will be time to think of more effective methods of constitutional agitation to bring about the desired reforms in the government of the country.

I have my own ideas about carrying on the Indian political campaign in England which I reserve for another occasion.

LAJPAT RAI.

INDIA AND ENGLISH PARTY POLITICS.

I am of opinion that those who talk of identifying the Congress with the Liberal Party in England, presume too much. Firstly, they assume without justification and perhaps against all experience that the Liberal Party, as a party, are prepared to open their arms to them. My experience tells me just the otherwise It is true that the response to the circular letter of the Chairman of the British Committee of the Indian National Congress, asking for platforms for the Indian Delegates came mostly from the Liberal and Radical Associations of England, including Trade Unions, Labour and Socialist circles. It is equally true that what little hearing we received in England was given to us by the Liberals, but then we cannot shut our eyes to the fact that the Liberal leaders and the Liberal executives kept themselves as much aloof as the Conservatives. These latter are in substantial agreement with the Conservatives in keeping Indian affairs out of party politics. At the discussion of the last Budget in June there was only one influential Liberal (Sir Charles Dilke) who spoke in favour of Mr. Herbert Robert's motion for a Parliamentary enquiry. The other leading Liberals went in a body against it. You have only to be a few days in England to come to the conclusion that the Liberal executive is as indifferent to the Indian affairs as the Conservatives and that as a party the Liberals are not prepared to receive your advances. For the time being some of them may utilise you for party purposes in those matters in which they differ from their rivals, the Tories, but beyond that they will not go. As such, it is futile to discuss the wisdom or the non-wisdom of identifying the Congress with the Liberals as a party. The question is, at present, outside the range of practical politics. Though it were possible to do so, I would rather have the Indian affairs fought and discussed on party lines. So far I am quite in agreement with Sir Pherozeshah Mehta. Any one even slightly acquainted with political life in England will tell you that, as a rule, English politicians are not prepared to devote any time and attention to any matter which does not further party interests. Matters outside party politics receive hardly any consideration. Nobody cares for the same. People do not feel sufficiently interested to spare any time or attention for matters which do not seem to concern them in any way. The Press cannot afford to spare space for them or it does not pay them. The man in the street is absorbed in his own affairs. The ordinary citizen or voter argues that a matter upon which both parties agree and hold the same views must be well looked after and needed no care on his part. To be just and fair to English Liberals, I must say that those who could be approached were found to be very sympathetic and for the time being at least appeared to have been touched by the tale of woe narrated before them. Some of them passed resolutions of sympathy and so on, but beyond that I don't believe they will take any further trouble of pressing it either on their representatives in the House of Commons or on their party leaders as such. So far the greatest sympathy has been expressed by the Labour and Democratic and Socialist circles. The working men in England are now awake and they are as much disgusted with the present system of class Government as we are. They are pushing forward their own candidates and they hope to return a solid body of Labour members in the next General Election. The Democratic and Socialist sections are in favour of Home Rule for India and so, of course, are the Irish. These are the people upon whose active sympathy Indians can safely rely and who might help Indians if they are sufficiently strong to make themselves heard. But they are poor; and poverty in England is, perhaps, a greater curse and calamity than anywhere else in the world. They generally denounce the Liberals as well as the Conservatives, though their members in Parliament seem to have a certain sort of alliance with the Liberals. They are perfecting their organisations and are advancing steadily. The Socialists and the Democrats are allied with them. I was much impressed with their sincerity of purpose and genuineness of sympathy, and I am of opinion that it is this class only with which at present an alliance is possible, if any. It is no doubt true, that in high Whig circles this class is not looked upon with favour and very reasonably too. They aim at their overthrow and claim a share of the power of which the former have been enjoying an exclusive monopoly so far. The fact that of all countries in the European world, England is the most Conservative and very slow to adopt new ideas makes it probable that the Labour and Democratic influence will take a long time to develop and to attain the power which they aim at. But all the same it is hopeless to expect anything at the hands of the Liberals for India. When in power they might send a sympathetic Viceroy but that they cannot and will not follow a systematic, persistent policy of advance in applying Democratic principles of Government to India, is as certain as that Sun will set this evening and rise to-morrow morning.

There are some good Liberals who sincerely desire to rule India on sound Liberal principles, but at present they are in a hopeless minority, their voices do not count for much and there is little chance of their gaining any prominence or coming to the front Benches, in the near future.

Under the circumstances, the only advice I can offer my countrymen is as follows :—

(1) That they should mainly look to themselves and their own exertions for political progress. The English voter, whether Liberal or Conservative, is a sympathetic creature no doubt, but then he is absorbed in his own troubles and affairs and to care for us has neither the time nor the inclination to attend to anything which does not directly concern him or which is likely to affect his pocket injuriously.

(2) That if there is any class in England which deserves our confidence and upon whose votes we can place any reliance at all it is the Labour party, including the democrats and the Socialists and the Irish of course

REPRESSIVE MEASURES IN BENGAL.

RESOLUTION XIII, OF THE 21ST INDIAN NATIONAL CONGRESS HELD AT BENARES 1905.

Mr. President, brother-delegates, ladies and gentle-men:—I am afraid I cannot deliver a speech in the strain which we have been hearing on the resolution of the "Partition of Bengal" and the present resolution before you. I give it my heartiest support on two grounds. You have been hearing of the misfortunes of our brethren of Bengal. I am rather inclined to congratulate them on the splendid opportunity (cheers) to which an all-wise Providence, in His dispensation, has afforded to them by heralding the dawn of a new political era for this country (cheers). I think the honour was reserved for Bengal, as Bengal was the first to benefit by the fruits of English education. Bengal up to this time—excuse me for saying that—the Bengal lion, by some cause, had degenerated into a jackal, and I think Lord Curzon has done us a great service by provoking the lion in his own den (cheers) and rousing him to a sense of conscientiousness of his being a lion. I think no greater service could have been done to India, to the cause of India or to Bengal, by any other statesman. There are times, gentlemen, when I am inclined to pray that from time to time God might be pleased to send. Viceroys like Lord Curzon to this country, in order to awaken the people of this country to a sense of their responsibility in this matter. Gentlemen, I believe, and I believe earnestly, that the political struggle has only commenced, it was only in the fitness of things that, when Congress attained its majority, the attaining of that majority should have been preceded by a manly and vigorous protest on the part of the people of this country. It is only in the fitness of things that the movement's coming to age of majority should have been preceded by a vigorous and manly declaration of its approaching manhood. I think in the circumstances like ours, in conditions like ours, we are perfectly justified in taking the attitude that our brethren of Bengal have taken. What else was left for you? It has been explained that all possible things that could be done in the name of constitutional agitation have been exhausted. What was the example given to you by your fellow-subjects in the other parts of the Empire? Englishmen have been our teachers in all branches of human knowledge. Englishmen have given us constitutional rights. Was it not perfectly right to take a page from the book of the Englishmen on the methods of constitutional agitation and adopt those methods which will be appreciated by themselves? Now let us see what Englishmen in England do. I do not say that our conditions allow of our exactly copying or imitating them, but surely we have a right to adopt that spirit, understand that spirit and follow it. Let me tell you what are the methods adopted by Englishmen in England when they have a grievance to be listened to by Government. The method which is perfectly legitimate, perfectly constitutional and perfectly justifiiable, is the method of passive resistance (cheers). Although I am not at the present moment quoting any social democrat or làbourman, I must admire them ; I have great respect for them. I must tell you that the message which the people of England wanted to send to you through me was the message that in our utterance, in our agitations and in our fight and struggle for liberty, we ought to be more manly than we have been heretofore (cheers). An Englishman hates or dislikes nothing like beggary. I think a begger deserves to be hated. Therefore, it is our duty to show Englishman that we have risen to the sense of consciousness, that we are no longer beggars and that we are subjects of an Empire when people are struggling to achieve that position which is their right by right of natural law (cheers). Gentlemen, in every stage people were arbiters of their destiny, but we are not so at the present moment. We are perfectly justified in trying to become arbiters of our own destiny and in trying to obtain freedom. I think the people of Bengal ought to be congratulated on being leaders of that march in the van of progress (cheers). I rather envy them. I am rather jealous of them; at the same time I am proud of them. They have begun the battle, they have begun the fight and they have begun it in right manly style. They have effaced all those taunts, they have effaced all those insinuations against them of being timid and cowardly; they have exhibited a manliness, they have exhibited a spirit in this battle which has to be commended to other Provinces of India. If the other Provinces of India will just follow their example, I say the day is not far from distant sights. But if you simply go there as a beggar without the consciousness of your power, of your right to demand your rights, you go there simply to be rejected (cheers). If, therefore, you want to be heard, and you want to be heard with respect, you must approach with determination, with evidences of determination, with signs that you are determined to achieve your rights at any cost. Unless you do that, the goddess of liberty is very jealous. She shall never allow you to approach her and she shall never allow you to enter her portals. You must remain outside because you are profane : you cannot enter because you are not sufficiently pure ; you must purify yourselves through the ordeals of fire of self-sacrifice. The goddess of liberty is the most sacred goddess in the world, and before you can approach her, you should show by your life, life of self-denial, that you are fit to enter her temple (cheers). What have we been doing to be fit to approach that temple? I am afraid that our record is extremely poor and extremely humiliating: it is extremely bad to look at. But there are signs of the rising sun. And if the people of India will just learn that lesson from the people of Bengal, I think the struggle is not hopeless. We are just awakening to a sense of our duty and a sense of responsibility to the motherland. It may be that with the consciousness of that strength we may tread the right way, the right path in the struggle for freedom. I have only to say one word about that part of the resolution which deals with repressive measures. I think the repressive policy of this Government is very encouraging. A Government commanding 260,000 or 500,000 soldiers stooping to strike us by striking at our boys (cries of shame) ! I say what have these wise statesmen of Government come to ? Are they not displaying disgraceful weakness, a weakness of which the people are conscious? It would be difficult for them to remain where they are. What would people conclude that this mighty Covernment, with so many guns and canons, with so many armies and with such array of statesmen, have begun to fight with boys (cries of shame)? I say that, as friends of order, as friends of peaceful progress, as friends of the present government, because we are not ungrateful, we advise them to eschew these weak methods, disgraceful methods, and re-assert their manliness by pursuing paths of righteousness. If we were to adopt the methods of revolutionists, if we were to adopt to some secret methods which the Government of Lord Curzon has adopted in pushing forth the Partition Scheme, if we were to adopt the same methods that the Government of India and beauracratic rulers are adopting in dividing people against people, in setting the Hindu against the Mahomedan (shame), the Hindu against the Sikhs, it will be a dangerous game. I say that the Government is giving weapons which are sharp but which are disgraceful and which show signs of weakness. I, therefore, say that it is a dangerous game which the Government is playing. It might injure them at any moment. Therefore, as friends of Government, as friends of order, we warn Government against treading this path of danger and difficulty. Let Government remember, and let you, gentlemen, also remember, that people once awakened and awakened rightly, cannot be put down (cheers). It is impossible for the Government of India, after a century of British rule, after a century of liberal education, after having put the books of Burke, Bain and Mason in our hands, to put us down like dogs and slaves. That is impossible. The Bengalis have just now shown. They are only now showing that the task is impossible even for a mighty government like the British Government. Therefore, wisdom requires, statesmanship requires, that people should be governed on right lines, on liberal principles, on those democratic principles which are just now stirring the whole world.

The wave of democracy is out. I defy any Government in the world where there is any just civilization to keep the people out of their rights for any length of time. The history of Europe is before you. What is the fate of the autocratic methods? We pray our Government not to adopt those methods. As my friend the Chairman has been telling English audience, the British Government is foolish in following Russian methods. We are great admirers of British rule. As people who are benefited by that rule, we call upon Government not to trample under foot the best traditions of British rule, but to re-trace those steps and not leave the people of this country under the impression that their Government is going to adopt nothing better than Russian methods. If these methods continue, gentlemen, what will be the difference between the Russian Government and the British Government? There will be nothing left for the people of this country to be loyal to the British Government if these things are taken away—if the rights of meetings, if the rights of petitions and if the rights of constitutional agitation are taken away from us. Let my Governors tell me what shall be left to us to be loyal to them? Why shall we be loyal to them? I, therefore, say that it is in their own interests that they ought to retrace their steps and follow the noble example which has been set by some of their noblest statesmen, and remedy the state of things that exist. One word more and I have done. I see the time is going fast (cries of "go on"). No, I am not going to break the rule. I think I have already exceeded the limits. There is only one word I should like to say. If you have adopted this manly and vigorous policy, be prepared for the logical consequence (cheers). Don't conceal your heads. Don't behave like cowards. Once having adopted that manly policy, stick to it till the last. Glorify yourselves as I have told you. Is it not a matter of shame for us that this National Congress in the last twenty-one years should not have produced at least a number of political Sanyasis that could sacrifice their lives for the political regeneration of the country? Now that the Congress has come to a stage when it could become a father, a parent, I earnestly appeal to you to let it have its legitimate offsprings, a band of earnest missionaries to work out the political regeneration of the country (cheers). There is no use of our talking aloud, there is not much use of our showing signs of discontent and disaffection, unless we are true to ourselves, true to our noble country, true to the mother-land, true to the cause of political regeneration and political agitation. If you show, in a few years, to our rulers that we are steadfast in our determination, that we are steadfast in our devotion to our cause, I assure you that there is no power in the world that can prevent us from going forward (loud and continued cheers).

EDUCATION IN INDIA.*

It has now more than abundantly been established that the efficiency of a nation depends upon the amount and nature of brain power which it can put forth in

* The conclusions and comments noted above are based on the figures of 1901-1902. We know that since then someting more has been done by the Government of India towards extending the scope and

the affairs of life. In an address delivered some two years back, Sir Jhon Lockyer, the illustrious President of the British Association, traced conclusively and convincingly the intimate relation that exists between the provision made by a nation for the higher education of its people and the position taken by that nation in the ceaseless competition between the great countries of the world. Relying upon facts and figures, he compared the educational facilities and the intellectual out-put of Great Britain and Ireland with those of its rivals, Germany and United States, and came to the conclusion that the latter were much in advance of the former. Nay, he went a step further and held out young Japan as an example to be followed with profit in the matter of intellectual efforts. Those who are in touch with the current literature of the West, must have been struck by the extreme importance which all the civilized nations of the world have, by experience, begun to attach to education as the foundation of all national greatness both in point of wealth as well as of intellect. If, then, in the struggle for life, education and educational efforts are matters of supreme importance to advanced, independent and self-governing nations like the English, the German and the American, it only stands to reason that they are of still greater importance to a country like India where igno-

---

sphere of education in this country. An examination of what has been done in these years and whether that justifies the Policy and attitude of the Government towards private enterprise in education may better form the subject of a separate article wherein we may compare the results achieved by the Government of American and European states in the matter of Education.

rance and superstition reign supreme, where penury and poverty are the order of the day, where want and starvation are generally prominent, where independence of thought and action is almost unknown, and where the destinies of the nation are completely in the hands, and at the mercy, of a handful of foreigners who, in spite of all the generosity and benevolence of intentions that they can put forth in the Government of this country, are loth to admit the sons of the soil to any decent share in the management of the affairs of their own land. In a country where the economic circumstances brought about by an alien rule force the people to look to other countries for even the necessaries of life, where the unlimited resources provided by a bountiful Providence are closed to the sons of the soil and are only accessible to clever, energetic, and enterprising foreigners, where the wealth of the country is being daily drained out of the country, and where a fairly intelligent population are, for want of education and opportunities, being reduced to the position of drawers of water and hewers of wood, education, I say, is a question of life and death. Our future principally depends upon the amount and the sort of education we shall receive.

Having once put the educational machinary into motion, our rulers have of late been showing signs of great dissatisfaction with the results. The history of English education in this country shows that originally the framers of Government Educational policy were actuated partly by selfish and partly by philanthropic and high motives. To quote the words of the Government of

India resolution of 1904:

They regarded it as a sacred duty to confer upon the natives of India those vast moral and material blessings which flow from the general diffusion of useful knowledge. They hoped by means of education to extend the influence which the Government was exerting for the suppression of demoralizing practices, by enlisting in its favour the general sympathy of the native mind. *They also sought to create supply of public servants to whose probity, offices of trust might with increased confidence be committed,* and to promote the material interests of the country by stimulating its inhabitants to develop its vast resources.

The italics are mine. This policy appears to have been faithfully carried up to 1882, by which time the out-turn of the educational activity in the land had come to be immensely in excess of the requirements of the administration merely. To quote the resolution again:

The growth of schools and colleges proceeded most rapidly between 1871 and 1882, and was furthur augmented by the development of the Municipal system, and by the Acts which were passed from 1865 onwards providing for the imposition of local cesses which might be applied to the establishment of schools. By the year 1882, there were more than two million and a quarter of pupils under instruction in public institutions. The Commission of 1882-83 furnished a most copious and valuable report upon the state of education as then existing, made a careful enquiry into the measures which had been taken in pursuance of the Despatch of 1854, and submitted furthur detailed proposals for carrying out the principles of that Despatch. *They advised increased reliance upon, and systematic encouragement of private effort* and their recommendations were approved by the Government of India.

The italics are again mine. This was the first step towards reaction. The Anglo-Indian bureaucracy raised a cry against high education and bitterly complained that the Government was entirely wrong in spending large sums out of their resources on high education. It was thus laid down as a principle of policy to gradually withdraw from the work of secondary and high education and confine the energies of the State to the task of extending Primary Education. In pursuance of this policy some Government Colleges were abolished, a few transferred to private management, and the fees in all Government and aided colleges were greatly raised. To the great misfortune of those provinces which had only recently come under the British rule and where education had only very recently been introduced, as the Punjab, the policy formulated by the Government of India in 1882 affected them most injuriously and was very effectual in retarding high education therein.

As a natural result of this policy, however, the people of the country began to look up for themselves, and systematic efforts were made by them to provide against the loss likely to follow from the partial withdrawal of Government from the field. This withdrawal of Government, or the contraction of Government expenditure on high education, and the raising of fees, have had different effects in different provinces, but so far it has had only a most disastrous effect in the Punjab.

The truth of this remark will appear from a glance

at the following table in which the 5 large provinces range themselves according to fee incidence ;—

Punjab	5·4
Bengal	3·9
Madras	3·5
Bombay	3·0
United Provinces...	3·0

The following figures show that of all the 5 important provinces into which British India proper is divided, the Punjab is only next to the most backward of them in the matter of University education.

The following table gives the number of boys of school-going age of which one is an Arts College, in the 5 University provinces of India :—

Bengal	711
Madras...	755
Bombay	1,029
Punjab...	1,319
U- P.	2,502

The following table shows the increase in all British India in the total number of collegiate students in the 3 quinquenniums that have elapsed since 1882 :--

1887-88 to 1891-92	4,364
1891-92 to 1896-97	1,509
1896 97 to 1901-02	3,215

Thus it took full 10 years for the private colleges to develop in order to reduce the decrease that was so marked and startling in the second quinquennium of this reactionary period.

During the last quinquennium while Bengal gained 1,766 pupils (collegiates)

Bombay	877
Madras	239

Punjab with the N. W. F. P. only gained 160 while the U. P. fared still worse and only gained 44. In 1896-97 the number of scholars receving education in Arts Colleges in the Punjab was 1,101. In 1899-00 it rose to 1,180 and in 1900-01 it was only 1,152.

The following figures show that but for the private colleges, the collegiate education in India would have fared disastrously, as in 1901-02 there were only 4,000 students in Government Colleges and 12,000 in privately managed colleges, 54 per cent. of the latter only being in aided institutions—the unaided colleges of Bengal alone educating no less than 4,541 of them. The figures of increase in the number of students in different classes of institutions show to what extent, during the last quinquennium alone, private enterprise in education has come to the rescue of high education in this country. This increase is divided as follows :—

Government Colleges	448
Aided Colleges	998
Unaided Colleges	1,695

With the exception of Bengal, where the average annual cost of educating a college student is the lowest because of the very large numbers receiving education in cheap private colleges, the cost is the lowest in the Punjab, as shown by the following table :—

U. P.	278
Madras	195
Bombay	188
Punjab	136

Bengal 97

while the total expenditure on collegiate education stands thus :--

Bengal ...	... ...	$8\frac{1}{4}$ lacs.
Madras ...	... ...	$6\frac{1}{3}$ lacs.
U. P. ...	... ...	$4\frac{1}{4}$ lacs.
Bombay	... ...	$3\frac{1}{2}$ lacs.
Punjab ...	... ...	$1\frac{3}{4}$ lacs.

Of these $25\frac{2}{3}$ lacs, only 8,96,000 are furnished by Provincial Revenues while fees contribute $9\frac{3}{4}$ lacs, *i. e.*, 80,000 *over and above the contribution of Government.*

During the last quinquennium the expenditure from public Revenues has actually diminished by Rs. 67,000 while that from fees has increased by Rs. 231,000.

Compare with the above the amount of money contributed by the Government of Great Britain and Ireland on University education alone, viz. £ 1,55,600.

The University of London alone gets a grant of £8,000 (see Contemporary Review of December 1903, P. 838) ;the University of Berlin gets a grant of £1,68,780 from its Government and the University of Tokio (in 1895) £ 1,30,000.

SECONDARY EDUCATION.

Descending a step lower and looking at secondary education we shall find that altogether a sum of Rs. 126,84,000 is spent on secondary schools, of which only Rs. 32,76,000 are contributed by public funds (Imperial and Provincial Revenues, Local and Municipal Funds all together) and Rs. 60,76,640 by fees only, the balance being made up from private sources.

In the Punjab the fee-ratio of expenditure is shown

in the following quotation from the Review of H. H. the Lieutenant-Governor on the Education report for 1900 01.

It is interesting to notice that on the average native parents are called upon to pay Rs. 1-3-0 per annum for the education of a son in a Primary School; Rs. 11-8-6 in a Secondary School; and over Rs. 80 in an Arts College. These figures, hower, do not take into account assistance given in the form of scholarships.

In the *Nineteenth Century* for Oct. 1903 appeared an article on "London Education" from the pen of the Hon'ble Mr. Sydney L. C. C., in which the writer has noticed the work of the London county council in providing improved educational facilities for London boys and suggested desirable reforms and changes. Commenting upon the facilities which exist in London for secondary education the writer remarks that:

Every year about *eight hundred* of the ablest boys and girls in the public elementary or lower secondary schools, between eleven and thirteen years of age, are picked by competitive examination for two to five years of higher education. *These two thousand scholarships provide for the cleverest children of the London wageearners a more genuinely accessible ladder than is open to the corresponding class in any American, French, or German city.* In addition to these maintenance scholarships there are *free places at most of the London secondary schools,* from St. Paul's downwards, which are utilised, as is found to be the case with all provision of merely gratutious secondary education, by the lower middle and professional classes. *Above these opportunities stand the intermediate and senior county scholarships, and others provided by various trust funds, probably altogether about two hundred in each year*, for candidates between fifteen and nineteen years of age. These serve partly to carry on the best of the junior scholars; partly to admit to the highest secondary schools the ablest children of parents ineligible for the lowest rung of the ladder; and partly to take the very pick of London's young people to the technical college and the university.

This scholarship scheme has now necessarily to be revised, to bring it into accord with the changes lately made in the school-leaving age and the pupil-teacher system. Practically all children now stay at school until fourteen, and it is no longer necessary for any substantial payment towards the maintenance of the scholarship to begin before that age. On the other hand there is a consensus of opinion that, when a child passes from an elementary to a secondary school, it should do so before the age of twelve, and should remain for not less than four years. It looks as if the limit of age for the normal junior scholarship should be reduced from thirteen to twelve, and its duration extended from two to four years, whilst the annual maintenance allowance up to the age of fourteen might be reduced to 5l, rising to 10*l*, and 15*l*, in the last two years. And if the need for pupil-teachers causes the number of scholarships to rise to 2,000 a year, it would perhaps be possible to effect the further desirable reform of beginning the selecting process by a preliminary examination, conducted, by the head-teachers themselves, in their own schools, of all the children who had attained the fifth standard before the age of twelve; and of undertaking to award the scholarships, not to any fixed number of winners but to all who, in the subsequent centralised competitive examination, reached a certain percentage of marks Such a reform would organically connect the scholarship system with all the public elementary schools, instead of, as at present, only about a third of them; and would bring London's 'capacity-catching machine' to bear on every promising child.

There must, however, be an adequate supply of efficient secondary schools for these picked scholars to attend, not to mention the needs of those who can afford to keep their boys and girls at school until seventeen or nineteen. There is a common impression that the public secondary schools of London are few and inefficient. Yet, including only Foundations, of which the management is essentially public in character, *London has to-day certainly not less than 25,000 boys and girls, between seven and nineteen in its secondary schools, actually a larger number than either Paris or Berlin. In the background, and not included in this calculation, stands the hord of private adventure 'commercial academies' and 'colleges for young ladies' of the genteel suburbs.* These we may leave gently on one side. The publicly managed schools number about ninety, well dispersed over the whole country, ranging from those like Parmiter's School (Bethnal Green) and Addey's School (Deptford), where the leaving age is sixteen or seventeen, through the dozen admirable institutions of the essentially public Girls, Public Day School Company, up to such thoroughly efficient 'first-grade' schools as the North London Collegiate, for girls (St. Pancras) and Dulwhich College (Camberwell) and St. Paul's (Hammersmith) for boys. Yet so dense is

London that, with one or two exceptions, the very existence of these schools is forgotten by the ordinary citizen and is often ignored by the legislator or administrator. Many a middle class family which could well afford to send its boys and girls to secondary schools is unfamiliar with those which exist within a mile of its home. Even to the best informed educational administrators the real state and quality of the London secondary schools taken as a whole, are far less accurately known than those of the elementary. All the information points to the conclusion that the efficiency varies immensely from school to school; that nearly all of them have good buildings, mostly well provided with science laboratories and suitable equipment; and that, where any school falls below the mark, the weak point is the staffing. *In at least a third of the London secondary schools the income from fees and endowment is insufficient to provide more than one good salary which goes to the head teacher whilst the assistants, who are to be university graduates, are paid, for the most part, less than is earned by an ordinary certificated teacher in a board school.* Yet even recognising all the shortcomings of these schools, the department of secondary education is not one which will give the London County Council any serious trouble. About forty of the publicly managed schools are sufficiently well off to be independent of its aid, and these, nearly always charging high fees, and providing an education of high grade may be left to themselves. The other fifty, including practically all those in need of help, have already shown by their cordial co-operation with the Technical Education Board their willingness to fall into line. It would, of course, be necessary to disturb the present governing bodies, on which the local authorities are already well represented, *and it would be unwise for the Council to interfere in the details of administration. In no department is it so important to maintain variety and independent experiment as in the secondary schools.*

But construct what scholarship ladder we will, the secondary schools can be used only by a small fraction of the population. For the secondary education of the masses there has been organised, by the School Board on the one hand, and the Technical Education Board on the other, an extensive assortment of evening classes; providing instruction in every imaginable subject of literature, science, art, and technology. The classes of the School Board, which enrol over 1,20,000 students for the winter session and have an average attendance of half that number, are conducted in 410 of its day-school buildings, mainly by the younger and more energetic of its staff of day teachers. The work of the Technical Education Board, dealing usually with a more advanced stage and older scholars, is concentrated in the forty polytechnics, art schools, and technical institutes under its management or control which have in the aggregate about 50,000 students. Here the lecturers and teachers are specialists in their respective subjects, teaching in institutions specially equipped for their work. At six of the polytechnics, the highest classes have been included in the faculties of the reorganised London University. These two schemes of evening instruction have now to be co-ordinated, differentiated, and developed. There can be no question of stopping either the one or the other ; on the contrary, both sides of the work will have to be increased. It *ought not to be too much to ask that every boy or girl who leaves school at fourteen or fifteen should, up to twenty one, be at any rate enrolled at some evening-class institution even if attendance is confined to an hour per week.* Yet there are in London over 6,00,000 young people between fourteen and twenty-one and not a third of these are at present members of any sort of institution, recreational or educational. Out of 84,000 boys and girls between fifteen and sixteen, only 21,000 are on the rolls. What is happening to the others ? We cannot, as yet, compel them to come in, as the Bishop of Hereford proposes, though this is done in various parts [of Germany and Switzerland. But we might try the experiment of using the school attendance officers to look after those who have not joined an evening school, using the method of persuasion, just as they look after the younger defaulters from the day school. Meanwhile we could bring the whole of the evening instruction in each borough into a single hormonious organisation ; we could allocate the work in such a way as to provide appropriately for each age and each grade, and avoid overlapping ; we could take care that each subject is taught under the most effective conditions, and properly co-ordinated with more advanced instruction elsewhere ; and we could arrange for the progression of the students from stage to stage, until they reach the highest classes of the nearest polytechnic, or the technical college itself.

The italics are everywhere mine and adopted to enable the reader to compare the existing state of things in India with the existing state of things in London or with what in the opinion of the writer in the Nineteenth Century should be the state of things there.

It will thus appear that while the London authorities are anxious to see that every *boy and girl*, whether rich or poor, is in receipt of *some sort of secondary education* up to the age of 21, the authorities in India have ruled that the classes in the rural schools be so formed as to exclude the possibilities of scholars reading in them joining the ordinary secondary schools in towns.

The statement that in at least a third of the London secondary schools *the income from fees and endowment* taken together is insufficient to provide more than one good salary which goes to the head-teacher whilst the assistants who ought to be university graduates are paid for the most part less than is earned by an ordinary certificated teacher in a Board school, is significant and may with profit be pondered over by the educational authorities in the Punjab who are so strict towards the private schools and are at times inclined to exact higher standards of efficiency than even those observed by some of the Board and Mission Schools in the province. If even London tolerates the existence of inefficient secondary schools wherein the income from the fees and endowment together is so meagre, surely there can hardly be a case against similar schools in India which is educationally so backward.

PRIMARY EDUCATION.

Coming down to the Primary School we find the state of things still gloomier. The total expenditure on Primary Education is Rs. 1,05,45,000 to which the Public funds (Revenues, Local and Municipal) all contribute only Rs. 60,50,000 while from fees are realised Rs. 31,15,211. The Provincial and Imperial Revenues contributed only 13⅓ lacs (see page 178 of report.) As compared with the magnificent figure of 13⅓ lacs of Rupees spent by British Government on Primary Education in India, the Parliament of Great Britain and Ireland voted £ 1,24,17,368 for elementary education in those islands in 1901 alone. The extent and enormity of the evil have been recognised by the Government of India in their resolution of 1904, Paras 14, 15, and 16.

How, then, do matters stand in respect of the extension among the masses of primary education? The population of British India is over two hundred and forty millions. It is commonly reckoned that fifteen per cent of the population are of school-going age According to this standard there are more than 18 millions of boys who ought now to be at school, but of these only a little more than ⅙ are actually receiving primary education. If the statistics are arranged by Provinces, that out of a hundred boys of an age to go to school, the number attending primary schools of some kind, ranges from between eight and nine in the Punjab and the United Provinces, to twenty-two and twenty-three in Bombay and Bengal. In the census of 1901 it was found that only one in ten of the male population, and only seven in a thousand of the female population were literate. These figures exhibit the vast dimensions of the problem, and show how much remains to do done before the proportion of the population receiving elementary instruction can approach the standard recognised as indispensable in more advanced countries. While the need for education grows with the growth of population the progress towords supplying it is not so rapid as it was in former years. In 1870-71 there were 16,473 schools with 607,320 scholars; in 1881-82 there were 82,916 with 2,061,541 scholars. But in 1891-92 these had only increased to 97,109 schools with 2,837,607 scholars, and the figures of 1901-02 (98,538 schools with 3,268,726 scholars), suggest that the initial force of expansion is somewhat on the decline, indeed the last year of the century showed a slight decrease as compared with the previous year.

On a general view of the question the Government of India cannot avoid the conclusion that the primary education has hitherto had insufficient attention and an inadequate share of the public funds. They consider that it possesses a strong claim upon the sympathy both of the supreme Government and of the Local Governments, and should be made a leading charge upon provincial revenues; and that in those Provinces where it is in a backward condition, its encouragement should be a primary obligation.

It may be remarked that these obligations were also admitted in 1882-83, but little was done to fulfill them, as will be clear from a perusal of the following facts and figures which we cull from vol. II of the Government of India's reports on the progress of Education between 97-98 to 1901-02.

NO. OF PRIMARY SCHOOLS FOR BOYS.

1886.	91-92.	96-97.	1901-02.
84,673	91,881	97,881	92,226

which means an actual decrease of 5,655 in the last 5 years. The Punjab showed this decrease to the extent of 42, *i.e.* in 1901-02 there were 42 Primary Schools less in the Punjab and N. W. Frontier Provinces combined. In 96-97 there was one school for a group of 5·8 towns and villages. In 1901-02 there was one for a group of 6·2. In the Central Provinces there is one Primary school for 23·4 towns and villages, in the United Provinces of Agra and Oudh one for 15·6 and in the Punjab one for 14·5. In the Central Provinces the mean average distance in miles between each boy's Primary school is 8·2 miles and in the Punjab 7·1. This does not mean that schools are equally distributed over the whole area. The fact is that in some districts there is no school for many tens of miles.

During the last 5 years, while the number of Schools fell by 5,655, the average strength per school rose only by 2 (*i. e.* from 31 to 33 per school). The following figures will show the progress made by primary education in the number of scholars receiving education. In 96-97, 30 lacs and 28 thousand boys received instruction in Primary Schools for boys but in 1901-02 the number fell to 30 lacs and 9 thousand (a fallof 17,000). In the Primary Schools attached to secondary schools the numbers in 96-97 were 31 lacs and 83 thousand and in 1901-02 the numbers were 31 lacks and 84 thousand *i.e.*, an increase of 1,000. Total loss 16,000. In the Punjab and N. W. F Province (combined) the numbers in the former schools were 10 lacs and 8 thousand in 96-97 and the same in 1901 and 1902, but in the latter class of schools it rose slightly, *i.e.*, by 4,000.

In the Census Returns of 1901-02 only 13 million males in British India have been entered as able to read and write out of a total male population of 117½ millions which means that 104½ millions cannot read and write at all. In 1901-02 only 174 out of a 1,000 boys of school-going age were receiving instruction, *i.e.*. 826 went without any education at all. But in the Punjab 914 out of a 1,000 went without any instruction at all. Thus in the matter of Primary education, the Punjab—that nursery of the Indian soldier—the land of the brave and the loyal Sikh—is the most backward of all the Provinces, even Assam, Burma and Central Provinces showing much better figures (*i.e.*, 197, 167, 137 per thousand respectively) against 86 of the Punjab.

Now to judge of the quality of education imparted in these schools we have only to examine the figures relating to the average cost of a school and the average annual cost per pupil, the former being less than 10 Rs. a month and the latter being 3·7 (per year). The following figures show that there has been practically no improvement in this direction within the last 10 years.

Average annual cost of a boy's Primary School :—

91-92	96-97	1901-02.
94	101	114

or say the improvement can be valued at less than one Rupee per month.

Coming nearer home we find that in the Punjab the progress has been in the other direction. In 91-92 the annual cost of a boy's Primary School in the Punjab was Rs. 222, in 96-97 it fell to Rs. 195 and in 1901-02 it could only slightly rise to Rs. 202. The net result is that as compared with 91-92 there is a falling off of 20 per year. The increase in the average cost of educating a boy may be judged from the following figures.

	91-92.	96-97.	1901-02.
General average cost ...	3·2	3·2	3·7
Punjab	4·4	4·4	4·9

Now let us examine the so-called "unparalleled liberality" of the British Government in paying the teachers employed in the schools.

The following table shows the average of monthly pay of primary school teachers:—

		Government School	Board School
Madras ...	Head Master	Rs. 8 to Rs. 20	Rs. 8 to Rs. 15
	Assistant Master	,, 5 to ,, 10	,, 5 to ,, 12
Bengal ...	Teacher ...	,, 3 to ,, 8 approximately.	
Punjab ...	do ...	,, 8 to ,, 55	Rs. 4 to Rs. 40
Central provinces...	do ...	,, 6 to ,, 20 in general.	
Bombay ...	do ...	,, 7 to ,, 60	Rs. 7 to Rs. 60 Rs. 7 to Rs. 65
U. P. of Agra and Oudh ...	do ...	,, 2 to ,, 17	aided 2 to 2 unaided 2 to 2

I do not know how to characterise the conduct of a Government who expect teachers who get the royal salary of Rs. 2 to 5 a month to spread and strengthen the sentiment of loyalty amongst their pupils. In these days even an ordinary illiterate day-labourer gets 6 annas per diem. The prosperity of this country under British rule may better be judged by these scales of pay which we have given above. Any furthur comments are not needed-

Compare with this the following figures giving the annual cost per child in the Primary Stage in Great Britain and Ireland.

	Board School.	Private School.
England and Wales.	£3-0-9d. *i. e.*, Rs. 45-9.	£2.6s.4d., *i. e.* R. 34-12
Scotland.	£2-17-4 *i.e.* Rs. 43.	£2-15s-6d-*i.e.* Rs. 37
Ireland.	£2-10-11 *i.e.* Rs. 38..	

The average pay of a teacher of Primary School in Great Britain and Ireland is £129 sterling per annum, *i. e.* RS. 1,935 or say more than Rs. 150 per month.

So long as the cost of General Administration remains what it is, and no reduction is effected by the larger employment of native agency for the high-paid and costly European agency, and so long as the military is maintained on that ruinous scale as at present, there is little prospect of increased expenditure being incurred on education from Provincial and Imperial Revenues. Every sensible man will agree with the Government that the wider extension of education in India is chiefly a matter of increased expenditure; and any material improvement of its quality is largely dependent upon the same condition. A Government which could heretofore afford to spend only a crore and 4 lacs upon the education of more than 24 crores of its people in its charge is not in a position to assume that supreme position in matters educational which it has, by its recent policy, decreed to itself. While the Government in India cannot afford to give more than 1 crore and 4 lacs for the education of more than 24 crores of its people, compared with about 19 crores spent by the Parliament of Great Britain for the same object, the former aims at officialising, supervising and controlling every educational agency in the land. In the name of sound education they decry those institutions which, if not up to date in the supply of appliances and apparatus, if not quite up to the mark in the efficiency and competency of their teachers, if not located in beautiful buildings, if not possessed of grand and inspiring surroundings, are at least helping the cause of education and literacy in the land. A Government which pays teachers at the munificent rate of from 5 to 10 or 20 Rupees a month in Government and District and Municipal Board Primary Schools, and at the lowest rate of 4 and 5 Rupees a month * to teachers in the Secondary Schools is surely not in a position to vote the Private Schools out of existence even if the managers of the latter cannot treat their teachers better than or so well as the Government does. In a country where the number of male literates per 1,000 of the male population ranges from 54 to 378 with an average of 102 for the whole of India; where the number of boys in the Primary stage per 1,000 of male population of school-

* See page 71 Vol. II. of the report for 97-98 to 1901-1902.

going age ranges from 63 in the N. W. F. P. and 68 in the Punjab to 232 in Bengal with an average of 174 for the whole of British India; where the Government can only spare 13½ lacs of Rupees upon elementary education for a population of more than 24 crores; in a country where in some parts of it, only one out of 278 is in the secondary stage of an English School and one in 1,032 in the same stage of a vernacular school; in a country where on the average only one out of 1,079 of a population of school-going age is in an Arts College, the Government can hardly be justified in assuming that aggressive and dictatorial attitude towards private enterprise in education which it has lately done.

Even in advanced countries where a very large part of Government Revenues is spent upon education; where education is considered as a national asset; wherethe number of literates in the population is over 90 per cent; where education is compulsory; even in such countries the Government is not so hard or does not require high and rigid and almost impossible standard of efficiency from private Schools and Colleges as the Government has lately been laying down for the same class of institutions here in India. We wonder why the Government of Lord Curzon should have forgotten that the systems of education now prevalent in England, United States and Germany, which he has taken as his models, are the growths of more than a century at least if not of centuries; that all those countries are self-governing countries, where the interest of the rulers and the ruled are identical and where the former only exist for the benefit and the protection of the latter. To apply the systems, standards and principles in force in these countries to India is more absurd than even the putting of the cart before the horse. But even in England the voluntary and denominational schools were the pioneers of education and till lately enjoyed—nay, to a great extent even now enjoy—the freedom which the Government of India by their recent policy refuse to the private Schools and Colleges of this country.

It is not strange, then, that the people of India should be suspicious of the intentions and the motives of the Government, and that the recent policy of the Government in matters of education should have raised a storm of indignation in the land. We say, why should the Government prescribe a tuition fee for the private school and the private college in this land where dense ignorance prevails, where more than 90 per cent. of the population is illiterate, and where the Government of the country cannot spend more than 1½ annas per head on education? Again, we ask why should the Government, if it is honest and actuated by the best and the highest motives, in a country like this, throw obstacles in the way of private enterprise in education; why should it try to prevent the same from competing with the Government institutions; why should it frame such rules and regulations as to take away all liberty of action and freedom of initiative from them and compel them to submit to dictation and supervision from Government and its officers? If under the circumstances the Government is misunderstood and its motives and intentions misconstrued, it has only to thank itself for these misunderstandings and misinterpretations.

Under the new regulations the Government has almost made it impossible for a new private educational institution to come into existence and to thrive. No private school or college can, under the present rules, dare to make an humble beginning. Large funds, high-class buildings, official good will and a very high state of efficiency in all respects, are the conditions precedent even for a start. Under the present rules, institutions like the great Metropolitan one of Calcutta, the Fergusson College of Poona, the D. A. V. College at Lahore, would not have come into existence. Similar attempts are, as a matter of fact, impossible under the new policy. The conclusion, which the people then are irresistably led to, under the above circumstances, is that the Government of this country is neither willing to spend its own Revenues on education, nor will it tolerate the doing of it by people for themselves unless the latter are prepared to place their funds and efforts under the control of the former.

THE SWADESHI MOVEMENT.

It is commonly supposed that there are two sides to the Swadeshi movement, one the political and the other the economic. Pure Swadeshi, as some of the Anglo-Indians choose to call it, is an economic movement and they profess to have a great sympathy for the same. Boycott of foreign made goods is held to be a political weapon upon the uses and ethics of which there is a great divergence of opinion. The Anglo-Indian can see nothing but mischief in it. In their opinion it is morally wrong, politically pernicious and economically unsound and impracticable. But there are a number of Europeans and Americans who see nothing pernicious in it and consider it to be not only a perfectly legitimate weapon but a very powerful and effective one to bring pressure upon any imperial race having commerce as its principal business. Amongst the Indians themselves different classes of people look at it from different points of view. Firstly, there is that class who can never see differently from their Anglo-Indian patrons. The opinions of this class do not count for much and need not be considered at all. Secondly, there are those, who both by nature and habit are in favour of *peace at any cost.* They cannot approve of any methods which are calculated to cause the least disturbance in the relations of the different persons and communities, whether Indians or aliens, who are in some way or other interested in India. These good people have great faith in moral persuasion and prayers—prayers addressed to the Great Ruler of the Universe as well as to our rulers in affairs mundane They believe that a combined force of these two is sure to bring about a quiet, bloodless, moral revolution in India which will set matters right and remove all the political disqualifications and disabilities from which the Indians at present suffer and which result in so much hardship, oppression and wrong to the people of this country.

Personally I am a believer in the efficacy of prayer as an instrument of religious discipline but it will require a great stretch of imagination and an inconceivable amount of credulity on my part to accept that prayer to the Almighty coupled with prayers to the ruling nation are likely to lead to any practicable results, in matters political and international. Prayers to the Almighty may be useful in intensifying your desire for political liberty and political privileges. Prayers to the ruling nation may be useful to you in proving the *uselessness* of appealing to the higher sense of man in matters political, where the interests of one nation clash with those of another and in driving you to the conclusion that human nature, constituted as it is, is extremely selfish and is not likely to change or bend unless the force of circumstances compels it to do so in spite of itself. But beyond this I cannot pin my faith on prayers. The third class of Indians consists of those estimable gentlemen who believe in the righteousness of the British nation as represented by the electors of Great Britain and Ireland and who are afraid of offending them by the boycott of English made goods. If there are any two classes into which the British nation can roughly be divided they are either manufacturers or the working men. Both of them are interested in keeping the Indian market open for the sale and consumption of their manufactures. Any movement aiming at the closing or contracting of this market is sure to offend them. They are said to be our only friends to whom we can appeal against the injustice of the Anglo-Indian bureaucracy. Offend them, say these friends, and you are undone. You lose the good will of the only class who can help you and who are prepared to listen to your grievances. But these good friends forget that, boycott or no boycott, any movement calculated to increase the manufacturing power of

India is likely to incur the displeasure of the British Elector. The latter is a very well educated animal, a keen man of business who can at once see through things that are likely to affect his pocket however cleverly they might be put or arranged by those who hold an interest which is really adverse to his. He is not likely to be hood-winked by the cry of Swadeshi *minus* the boycott because really speaking and effectively worked and organised both are one and the same.

The Swadeshi aims at the production of those articles at home which are at present imported from abroad. The boycott means the discontinuance of the consumption of those articles not made in this country. So far, then, it is not likely to be of much use to drop the boycott in order to secure for us the continuation of the friendly attitude of the British Elector. But then we may go a step further and maintain that up till now the alleged friendliness of the British Elector has been of no good to us. Past experience shows that they have more than once stood between the people of India and some of its more nobleminded Anglo-Indian rulers whenever the latter tried to obtain economic justice for the former. The latter from their knowledge of the growing seriousness of the economic situation in India have now and then made a bold stand for Justice to India against the demands of the British manufacturer, but they have almost always had to give in because the latter proved too strong for them. Here then we are on the horns of a dilemma. To our wrongs the British Elector is indifferent, to our rights, even if supported by good Englishmen in India, they have been opposed. The British Elector has no doubt a sympathetic ear to the tales of wrong and oppression that you may carry to England but unfortunately he is too busy and too absorbed in his own affairs to spare any time, to listen to your tales or to take a serious view of them. The burden of the empire is too heavy to be conveniently shifted from the shoulders of a few—magnificently paid for the work—to those of the English people. The struggle for wealth, for luxury is too keen and too intense to leave the latter any leisure or inclination for the study of the ethics of Imperialism. Under the circumstances the sympathy of the British Elector is for the present at least a negligible quantity. The question directly put comes to this;—are the British prepared to give us full political privileges in exchange for open markets for their goods? Any attempt to answer this in the affirmative must be put down as chimerical. But even granting that the argument has some force, is it not worth our while to impress upon the Britons at home the enormity of the wrongs inflicted upon us by their representatives here in this country, by supplementing the Swadeshi by boycott? Admitting that Englishmen at home have the power to set matters right how are you to force their attention to the state of things in India except by directly threatening their pockets? The logic of losing business is more likely to impress this nation of shopkeepers than any arguments based on the ethics of justice and fair-play. The British people are not a spiritual people. They are either a fighting race or a commercial nation. It will be like throwing pearls before swine to appeal to them in the name of higher morality or justice or on ethical grounds. They are a self-reliant, haughty people, who can appreciate self-respect and self-reliance even in their opponents. It is then for the Indians to decide whether they mean to continue to appeal to them in the name of political justice, fair-play or whether they intend to attract their attention to the existing intolerable condition of things in India by inflicting losses in business and by adopting an attitude of retaliatory self-reliance.

But then there is another class of Indians who tread on more solid ground than any of those spoken of above. This is the class who oppose the boycott on Economic grounds. Here we feel we are on more substantial ground. Theirs is no plea of expediency, nor does it arise out of fear of the authorities in India or of the British Elector at home. Their warning note has a scientific basis and deserves the most careful and attentive consideration of all patriotic Indians. Whether Free Trader or Protectionist, you cannot dismiss them offhand nor treat their reasoning with contempt. They may be fadists (a term which in their turn they apply to Swadeshists) but they are neither cowards nor traitors. Speaking for myself I am an out and out Swadeshist and have been so for the last 25 years, in fact ever since I learnt for the first time the true meaning of the word patriotism. For me the words Swadeshi and patriotism are synonymous though I do not maintain or insinuate that those who are freetraders are not patriots. I advisedly do not say "not Swadeshists," because I am not prepared to say that those Indians who are free-traders are not necessarily Swadeshists. Be it as it may, I am personally inclined to attach the greatest importance possible to the Swadeshi Movement. I look upon it as *the* remedy upon the right and continued use of which depends the alleviation of the sufferings of our country. I regard it *as the salvation of my country. The Swadeshi* ought to make us self-respecting, self reliant, self supporting, self-sacrificing, and last, but not least, *manly*. The Swadeshi ought to teach us how to organise our capital, our resources, our labour, our energies and our talents to the greatest good of all Indians, irrespective of creed, colour or caste. It ought to unite us—our religious and denominational differences notwithstanding. It ought to furnish us with an altar before which we can all stand in the fullest sincerity of our hearts and in the deepest strength of faith to pray for the good of our common mother-land, with a determination to stand together and work together. In my opinion *the Swadeshi* ought to be the common religion of *United India*. But all this notwithstanding, as a practical Swadeshist, I want a better understanding of the economic needs and requirements of the country and a practical programme of industrial development based on scientific calculations. As an indication of the lines upon which I shall like this programme to be framed, I cannot do better than quote from a very famed paper from the journal of the Royal Economic Society of London for the month of March 1906, under the heading of 'Protection of infant Industries.' Discussing the economic effects of a protective tariff the writer remarks:

"We see that when the import of goods is checked the exchanges are affected in a way which tends to raise prices at home; and that this rise continues until importation is again possible, unless such heavy duties are imposed that the country can be cut off both from importation and from exportation, and so become entirely self-contained. We find also in this process the explanation of the fact that the relief afforded by a protective tariff is frequently of a somewhat temporary character. For a few months the home producer has the field to himself: then his costs of production gradually rise: at last he finds foreign competition pressing on him once more; and finally he falls back upon the fatal demand for more Protection.

But this—the common course of protection in both the new and the old countries—is not the only possible course in theory. It is caused, so far as I can see, principally by the attempt to do too much at once. Your new country is inclined to be generous to its home manufacturers, and to start manufacturing in all lines at once: by so doing it fritters away energy, and spreads expenditure over a wide field which if concentrated might produce imposing results.

For, supposing that a new country would consent to do one or two things at a time, its difficulties would probably be far less. If it started, for instance, by attempting to found one textile or one branch of metallurgical industry, it could afford to give to its infant for a few years a genuine and important assistance. Gold prices would, of course, still be to some extent affected, but in an infinitely smaller degree than when a dead set is made against all manufactured goods at once. And by concentrating the money which is available on one end instead of dividing it among several hundreds, more real progress would indubitably be made. After all, under modern conditions, no industry ought to remain an infant for more than five years: during those years it probably needs more assistance than can easily be given it under a general Protective System; later on, the less help it has, the better.

Other important gains could be made—both political and economic—by this system of concentration. In the first place, the opportunities for log-rolling would certainly be diminished. If the system were once established, a most salutary division of the Protectionist forces would assuredly take place: as it is, the tendency in many countries is for everybody to favour protection on the off-chance that he may make more by it than he loses: on the system proposed everybody would know that only one or two industries were to be protected at a time, and those only for a few years. Again the present certainty that a protective system will last much longer than there is any need for it would be removed. For as only one or two industries would receive help at any one time, all the other industries would combine to reduce that time to a minimum in the hope that their turn would come next."

In my opinion, the leaders of the Swadeshi movement including men actually engaged in business ought to put their heads together and promulgate an industrial pronouncement for the next five years, prepared on the lines indicated in the above extract.

INDIAN PATRIOTISM TOWARDS THE EMPIRE.

In May last (1906) the Director of Public Instruction of the Panjab issued a circular order to all the headmasters and managers of Government, aided and unaided, schools, in the province, requiring them to celebrate the empire-day in a certain way. One of the items of the programme laid down by him for observance was "the recitation of Urdu poems, on loyalty to the Crown of England and patriotism towards the empire." We do not know if the head of the Panjab Education Department was responsible for the wording of the above clause. The document seemed to bear on it abundant marks of that jingo statesmanship which has for a number of years, been in ascendancy in the councils of the British empire. One thing, however, is clear. The Government was sensible enough not to declare the empire-day as a public holiday. The compulsory celebration of the empire-day in 1906 was therefore confined to the schools, may be, to the schools of the Panjab only. We propose to examine in this paper if the step taken was educationally sound and in any way calculated to improve the moral tone of the schools where it was, by order, enforced.

Till lately the impression was that the British were, at least, frank by nature and valued frankness and sincerity on the part of others, however distasteful and unpleasant, at times, they may be to their imperial temper. The idea was that although conscious of the unnaturalness of their rule over alien races, they aimed at making it as pleasant and benevolent as they possibly could (if ever it is possible to make subjection pleasant and benevolent) consistently with the making of the largest profit out of it for themselves. Of course, nobody having sufficient experience of human nature ever took the Britisher at his word, when the latter professed to be moved by unselfish and altruistic motives in extending his rule over other nations and countries and governing them solely for the sake of humanity and civilisation. All the same, people believed that the British administration had not lost all sense of frankness and sincerity, until the new doctrine of the white man's burden was propounded by the banjo-bards, and the jingo poets had forced their muse to sing of the great sacrifices which the white man underwent in his civilising mission and his humane rule, undertaken for the sole benefit of the ruled. But even the jingoes, whether poets or statesmen, never thought of appealing to the subject races in the name of *Patriotism towards the Empire,* for the simple reason that in the mouths of the latter the expression was an absurdity, and a contradiction in terms. The subject races—the fact of whose subordination to Great Britain alone, confers upon the latter, the status and dignity of an Empire—may be loyal, whether, voluntarily or involuntarily, whether by free will, or by necessity, but to attempt to raise this sense of loyalty to the dignity of patriotism is sheer nonsense. No lexicographer, of any position whatsoever, will risk his reputation by speaking, even by inference of " Patriotism towards the Empire." The idea is monstrous and is for the first time being introduced into the English language by the presumptuous genius of the jingoes as an antidote towards the sacred sentiment of patriotism, in the development of which amongst the subject races, they see a dangerous enemy to their own despotic rule. The lexicographers, if they can be accepted as reliable guides, in explaining the meaning of English words to us, almost unanimously agree in expressing the general opinion, as to patriotism signifying "love of country." Johnson defines it as "zeal for one's country" and Webster as "the passion which aims to serve one's country." The *Encyclopædic Dictionary* says that patriotism is "devotion to the interest and welfare of one's country" and the *Century Dictionary*, as "the passion which moves a person to serve his country either in defending it from invasion or protecting its rights and maintaining its lands and institutions" and so on and so forth. But how can a subject race governed by another be patriotic towards its rulers passes one's comprehension, unless one accepts the theory that the latter rules solely for the benefit of the former? Even in this case it is love of his own country and certainly not patriotism towards the empire (signifying love for the empire) which evokes loyalty for the existing Government. Honestly speaking the two sentiments are antagonistic, *viz.*, loyalty to a foreign government and love for one's country, which is patriotism; unless the patriot is to reconcile his patriotism with loyalty by the idea that in loving the foreign ruler he loves his own country. It may be allowable to a patriot to soothe his conscience by identifying his loyalty with patriotism, but to carry it furthur and to extend it to the empire is coining a new expression with an entirely new meaning. When, therefore, in the name of the Empire, the British appeal to the patriotism of the Indians instead of to their loyalty, their object is to give a higher pedestal to the shame which every member of a subject race (having the least vestige of self-respect and honourable feeling in him) must feel at his political helplessness and at the political non-existence of his country. The object is to cover the shame of political bondage with the halo of glory that attaches to the word "patriotism" and thus to remove the sting that bites the consciences of those of the ruling race and puts to shame those among the ruled, as are still open to any sense of honour.

However commendable the motive and however praiseworthy the object may be, one does not require much common sense to see through the device. The fact is that human nature with all its inherent disposition towards selfishness is always apt to find excuses for its idiosyncracies and will not allow itself to be denied the pleasure of putting a gloss of high and pure motives on its basest and meanest acts, whereby it deprives others of the simplest rights of humanity and the priceless treasure of liberty. No wrong-doer, however educated and cultured he may be, can at times help feeling mortification at the wrongs which in the pursuit of self-interest he has inflicted or does inflict upon others, and it is then that his guilty conscience runs riot in search of pleas and justifications for his wrongful conduct. Makers and rulers of empires are no exception to this general rule, which governs human nature everywhere and in every phase of life. Now empires are neither made nor maintained by right. They are made by might, both physical and intellectual, including that diplomacy and cunning without which no supremacy can ever be gained over other peoples and nations. "Only by force can empire, as a rule, be created; only by force can empire, as a rule, be maintained," rightly remarks Mr. Goddard in his excellent book on *Racial Supremacy*, although instances are not wanting in which wise and sagacious empire-makers and their equally clever successors have maintained empires for a longer period than they otherwise could, by doses of benevolence and justice in the management of its affairs. But racial supremacy is one of those necessary evils of which the world can never be purged. Its roots are deep. No amount of philosophizing and high thinking will see its complete overthrow from the world, and as long as this necessary evil exists, which is tantamount to saying that it must always exist, you cannot do away with empires and empire-makers. Still that is no reason why those who are the victims of empires and empire-makers should feel grateful to their masters for having extended their empire over them and for having included them in the category of their subjects. As to the ethics of empire-making and as to the claims of the British to the gratitude of those included in their empire, we will prefer to quote some English authorities on the subject rather than give expression to our own views.

First, as to what does "empire" signify? In the language of Mr. J. G. Goddard, a member of the new House of Commons, it "simply means rule, dominion, sway." According to Lord Rosebery, empire is "the predominance of rule." According to Herbert Spencer "not the derivation of the word only but all its uses and associations imply the thought of predominance— imply a correlative subordination. Actual or potential coercion of other individuals or communities is necessarily involved in the conception." In the words of Mr. Goddard then "imperialism is the spirit of rule, ascendancy or predominance; the rule of one race of people by another race of people involving—of course, the subjection of the former to the latter."

Mr. J. M Robertson, another member of the House of Commons, also defines empire as "rule over other communities than his own." Mr. Joseph Chamberlain, the jingo imperialist of modern England, has, however, assured us that "the new conception of empire is of a voluntary organisation, based on community of interests and community of sacrifices, to which all should bring their contribution to the common good."

How far this is in accordance with existing facts has been made clear by Mr. Goddard in examining the above statement, in his book referred to above. In the opinion of this writer imperialism tends to demoralise the dominant race, while it is simply the bane of the subject races. Taking the case of India as the most prominent and pertinent instance of the government of one people by another people, he concludes by saying that India is ruled in the interest of the dominant race rather than in hers and endorses the well-known remark of John Ruskin that "every mutiny, every danger, every crime occurring under our Indian legislation arose directly out of our native desire to live on the loot of India." The writer further condemns imperialism on the ground that it is destructive of liberty and applying it to the case of India he pronounces an indictment on imperialism in this country in the following terms :—

Here we have countless millions denied the rights accorded to the English agricultural labourer, taxed to pay for a Government in which they have no voice, condemned to support an army they cannot control, rack-rented for land they cultivate mainly for the benefit of others, compelled to yield interest on an expenditure they did not make, and generally reduced to the condition of hewers of wood and drawers of water, with sufferance as the badge of all their tribe.

Discussing the ethics of empire the same writer examines the claims of the dominant races in placing themselves in *quasi loco parentis* over subject races, as follows :—

The bond which unites father or mother with son and daughter is one of mutual affection and so far from self-sacrifice on the part of the dominant race being present, the opposite characteristic is manifested, and there is certainly no constant endeavour to promote the welfare of the putative child. The most serious flaw in the analogy, however, has reference to the main purpose of control. For the primary object of the parental rule of children, is to develop their faculties, and that for their own benefit. *It is a temporary and not a permanent rule, devoted to the purpose of rendering the child a self-governing person, capable as manhood is reached of exercising similar rule.* The primary object of racial rule is not *to develop the faculties of the governed* ; even if some development takes place, it is not for their own benefit ; the rule is regarded not as temporary, but rather as permanent and it is not devoted to the purpose of rendering them capable of exercising similar rule. No doubt, in point of time, the infancy of man is incomparable to the infancy of a race, and a far larger period is requisite for development. But a dominant nation does not work for or contemplate the abrogation of its power, even in the distant future ; its rooted idea is that of its own supremacy ; its constant aim is to secure the maintenance and generally the extension of that supremacy ; its fundamental conception of the relations which exist is subjective and not objective. Hence, on almost all points the analogy is absolutely false and misleading. One, and one only, of the many parental functions is selected, and the rest are implicitly or explicitly ignored. The maturity of the parent and the immaturity of the child are at the outset assumed to respectively distinguish the two races ; and then from a distorted simile an attempt is made to convert the temporary and qualified and specialised control which a parent exercises into a justification for the permanent and unqualified and general control which a nation claims.

Passing to the consideration of the second hypothesis of the imperialist, viz., that benevolence characterizes despotism, Mr. Goddard points out that in order to make despotism benevolent the one condition essential—that the power should be vested in one individual—is wanting in the case. Thinking on the same line I have often wished that we had been ruled by Queen Victoria or by

King Edward, or by any other single individual exercising the power of a despotic monarch rather than by the Parliament of Great Britain and Ireland representing the British nation, for you can, at times, successfully appeal to the humanity and benevolence of individuals but to hope for justice and benevolence from a nation is hoping against hope. The rule of a foreign democracy, is, in this respect, the most dangerous. The democracy is swayed by so many diverse interests and motives that it is simply impossible to expect anything like unanimity or even a preponderance of opinion in dealing justly with a subject race, because justice to a subject race often clashes or is inconsistent with the interest of some class of the ruling democracy. Whenever an attempt is therefore made to do justice to the former, the latter rise up, raise a storm and prevent the Government from doing the right thing. Looking to the history of the cotton duties in India, every one will see the truth of my remarks. How many times have the Government of India been overruled in the matter, simply because the Home Government can not afford to risk the opposition of Lancashire and incur its displeasure ?

As a matter of fact, we are at present ruled by a democracy which represents the British nation and in the appointing and controlling of which the Sovereign has really no hand. In my opinion the benevolence of an individual has greater chances of being effective than that of a whole nation. To me the benevolence of a whole nation seems to be nothing more than a myth and a fiction, as there can never be an absolute unanimity both as to what constitutes benevolence in given circumstances, as well as to how it is to be reduced into practice. Applying the benevolence plea to the case of India and other subject races of Britain, Mr. Goddard concludes (a conclusion in which other eminent authorities agree) that the plea is simply untenable. Examining the plea of benevolence in imperial relations in the light of historical facts Mr. Goddard says: "The truth is that whilst it does not necessarily give rise to exalting acts of cruelty, so far from its ever being largely tempered by benevolence, it has invariably one prominent characteristic, namely, the exploitation of its victims. The primary object and result of alien government is not to confer benefits upon the subject races but to obtain benefits from them". He further says that:—

Perhaps......the most striking testimony to the virtues of benevolent despotism is seen in the employment of native races to fight our battles for us. Wild animals are sometimes lured to their doom by means of one of their kind trained to act as a decoy, and we occasionally hear setting of a thief to catch a thief. The process has been adopted with a magnificent effrontry and a grim sense of humour to the needs of aggressive imperialism, and having extended the empire by bringing the "inferior races" under our sway, by a master stroke of genius, we utilise them to still further extend and also to defend the empire and convert them into instruments for bestowing upon their brethren the boons which they themselves have obtained. It is very largely in this way that our Indian Empire has been built up.

Then let us see what another English author, Mr. J. A. Hobson, says about the sophistries of imperialism.

"The idea" he says "that we are civilising India in the sense of assisting them to industrial, political, and moral progress along the lines either of our own or their civilisation is a complete delusion, based upon a false estimate of the influence of superficial changes brought by Government and the activity of a minute group of aliens. The delusion is only sustained by the sophistry of imperialism which weaves these fallacies to cover its nakedness and the advantages which certain interests suck out of empire." Even the late Professor Seeley writes in the same strain where he says: "We are not disposed to be proud of the succession of the Grand Mogul. We doubt whether with all the merits of our administration the subjects of it are happy. We may even doubt whether our rule is preparing them for a happier condition, whether it may not be sinking them lower in misery." But what Professor Seeley states in rather halting language is expressed affirmatively by another great writer on India, Mr. W. S. Lily. "The test of a people's prosperity", says Mr. Lily, "is not the extension of exports, the multiplication of manufactures or other industries, the construction of cities. No. A prosperous country is one in which the great mass of the inhabitants are able to procure with moderate toil what is necessary for living human lives, lives of frugal and assured comfort. Judged by this standard can India be called prosperous?" His answer, of course, is a positive 'No.' He adds that "comfort is a relative term and that in a tropical country like India the standard is very low * * * * * * * * but millions of peasants in India are struggling to live on half an acre. Their existence is a constant struggle with starvation leading too often in defeat. Their difficulty is not to live *human* lives—lives up to the level of their poor standard of comfort—*but to live at all and not die.*"

Such then is the verdict of level-headed Englishmen on the result of imperial rule in India, which testimony is of hundred times greater value than the interested sayings of stock exchange brokers and speculators, whom the British System helps in hording up millions upon millions at the cost of the Indian peasant, the Indian labourer and the Indian handicraftsman. I could add the testimony of many more Englishmen as to the baneful effects of imperialism in India, but the fear of adding to the bulk of this paper prevents me from doing so, and I will conclude this part of the paper by adding one more quotation from the fascinating work of Mr. Goddard, wherein he shows how detrimental benevolent imperialism is to the interests of the subject races :—

The gravaman of the indictment of "benevolent despotism" is that it tends to perpetuate the despotism. Whilst in practice the benevolence, if manifested at all, is relatively small, and whilst even if it were exhibited to the fullest extent circumstances admit, it would be no adequate justification ; its supposed or actual existence obscures the facts, satisfies the conscience, and leads to acquiescence in the permanent withdrawal of liberty, instead of efforts towards its restoration.

It will be seen that in saying all this I have only discussed the general effects of imperial rule in India and have not even touched upon particular grievances. I have made no allusion to the brutal treatment we receive in South Africa, Australia and other parts of the empire, and I have made no mention of the disabilities from which we suffer in India. Is it then right to ask us to celebrate the empire-day? Is it then likely to improve habits of sincerity and truthfulness amongst our boys, by compelling them to glorify the empire? Is it then honest on the part of our teachers and professors and directors to flatter us by saying that we are either the sons of the empire or its citizens, while we are neither, but are treated as the subjects of the empire—the victims of the imperial spirit that rules? Britishers may or may not glory in their empire. Perhaps from the ordinary point of view they have every reason to be proud of it and to glory in it. It tickles their fancy to think of their possessions, their dependencies and their subjects, though the sober-minded amongst them have begun to talk loudly as to the evil effects of the imperialism on the morale of their own people. The once sturdy and vigorous, both in thought and in deed, the simple but the high-minded, the reserved but solid Britisher is perhaps exchanging his virtues for the comforts, ease and luxuries, which attend an unchecked sway of empire and the bumptiousness and the vulgar pride of unbounded intoxication of uncontrolled power. Be however as it may, we do not and we cannot object to the Britisher at home or in India celebrating his empire-day, but it is nothing short of adding insult to injury to ask us and our boys to do so. Devoted patriots, as the British are, is it fair on their part to ask us to celebrate the empire-day in the name of "Patriotism towards the empire"—

a patriotism which we do not feel, which does not inspire us with noble thoughts and which evokes neither love nor homage in our bosoms? As helpless victims of the aggressive imperialism, as servants of the Crown and as students of schools and colleges, we might silently put up with the humiliation, but I dare say I am not wrong in reading the hearts of the bulk of my educated countrymen when I say, that the idea is simply revolting and extremely provoking to their sense of honour and shame. Those Britishers and Indians who thus trade in hypocrisy, and who thus would inoculate the minds of the innocent boys and girls with the serum of hypocrisy, are doing a positive injury to human nature, and to the principles of sound education without doing any good to British rule in India. In the name of loyalty we are prepared to submit to any order which the authorities issue, but we earnestly beg of them not to drag our patriotism into the mire and not to force us to compromise the same. The demands of patriotism are sacred and ennobling, which require no hypocrisy, and which evoke the deepest feelings of love for our country and for our people.

——o——

THE NATIONAL OUTLOOK: THE GREAT NEED OF THE SITUATION.

Problems of the gravest import await our solution —"problems which need all our nerve, all our determination, all our courage, all our hope and which affect the life and death of us all," were the words uttered by one of the most popular divines of England, portraying "national perils" for the consideration of his countrymen. Well did he say that the conditions of things then or at any time may be looked at in two different ways. There is one set of facts, which when considered exclusively, would make us hopeless pessimists. There is another set of facts which when taken by themselves may furnish good ground for the most sanguine optimism.

The truth, however, generally lies between the two. While pessimism is positively harmful as dispiriting and discouraging, optimism may be misleading as tending to produce a frame of mind which is always sanguine, prone to ignore difficulties and to neglect very necessary precautions. The best and the safest course, therefore, will be to steer clear of extreme views, to weigh the situation as accurately as may be possible in the light of our own history, that of the ruling race, and that of other countries and people similarly situated. Practical wisdom lies in eschewing, over-estimating as well as under-estimating. While it is no good under-estimating our difficulties and overestimating our capacities, it is perhaps more harmful to have a very low opinion of ourselves and our people. Both are equally bad; though if compelled to make a choice between the two, I would rather choose the former than the latter. Keeping the past history of the Hindus in mind I would rather see them indulge in optimism than in pessimism.

We have so long been in doubt about ourselves, about the world and about the good in the world that it is time to exchange this latter attitude of mind for confidence in self, confidence in our people, and hope for a better future, which may give us better opportunities to use and enjoy the good and the beautiful in the world. We have known enough of misery and it is time we made up our minds to discard it at any cost, even at the risk of having to suffer and undergo greater misery in the attempt to achieve the desired end.

But while recommending this attitude of mind to the nation at large, I cannot help asking those engaged in the work of awakening the people to a sense of their rights, to make no attempts to under-estimate the difficulties or to ignore them. I know there are a number of people, ill-disposed towards us, who exaggerate our difficulties so that we may sink under their weight and give up all efforts to rise. These honourable gentlemen, past masters in the art of diplomacy as they are, leave no stone unturned to make us and our people believe that there is no hope for us; that it is perfectly futile for us to make any attempt to gain our liberty; that, in fact, we are happier now than we can possibly be in a state of Self-Government. While they do not scruple to threaten us with fire and sword now and then, at other times they are disposed to use the milder weapon of persuasion, trying each in turn and hopeful of favourble results. While constantly dinning into our ears the vastness of the resources of their empire, more than sufficient in their opinion to bring down the whole of Asia to their feet, they never forget to remind us of our shortcomings and failings and weaknesses—our state of disunion and our helplessness in their grip. While some of us they threaten, others they cajole and flatter, going even so far as to bribe some, who are susceptible of being won over in that way. Our wisdom, moderation, prudence, and humanity are all, in turns appealed to, nay, our patriotism also is requisitioned at times on their side. All our weak points are assailed and a superhuman effort is being made to persuade us to give up all efforts to win Self-Government, the latter being at times painted as very pernicious, injurious and harmful, in the case of Asiatic peoples. Oh, how shocking must it be to those who believe in the innate sense of goodness and justice of human nature and in the native integrity of human conscience! But self-interest blinds a man and it is no wonder, that blinded by self-interest, carried away by the lust of gain and power, these imperial wolves in the shape of men, should belie their innate good natures and in the degradation of their own souls try to bring down even truth and uprightness. One is at times disposed to lose all faith in the goodness of human nature when one sees these *professed friends* of ours preaching sermons of unswerving loyalty, and forbearance and moderation to us, in their efforts to make us believe that our state of complete subservience is nothing but perfect bliss for us, and that an attempt to throw it off is sinful and likely to land us in greater disasters. I will advise my people to decline to listen to these friends of ours, if they desire to go forward and to attach no weight whatsoever either to their threats or their promises or their reasoning but all the same, to try to study the situation well, find out the truth and do what is right and just, be the consequences what they may. At the 22nd session of the Indian National Congress our worthy president, the grand old man of India, has laid down our political goal. The aim of all our efforts and the object of all our agitation, has been placed before us in clear, unambiguous and unmistakable terms. In a happy and inspired moment Mr. Naoroji struck upon that noble word—"Swaraj," which sums up all our political aspirations. Henceforth, "Swaraj" is our war-cry, our all-inspiring and all-absorbing aim in life. Henceforth, the duty of our earthly existence should be to forget self in this aim prescribed for us by the exigencies of the times and accepted by us after consideration of all the pros and cons.

For the first time in the history of political agitation in this country under British rule, the goal of all our political effort has been so clearly laid down before us; and thank God that for that we are indebted to no other but one who is the flesh of our flesh and the bone of our bone—a chip of the old block. We are now no longer groping in the dark as to the final goal of our political ambition. Swaraj has now been, officially, so to say, and definitely set up as the polestar in the firmament of Indian nationalism, and there it shall stay and shine with ever-resplendent glory and splendour as the guiding star of our hopes and aspirations. So far well and good. The next question that now arises is how to reach that goal and how to realise that aim? Like practical men, who have every desire to go into the matter in a businesslike spirit, we should first of all make a complete survey of the difficulties in the way of our success and then take stock of our resources, so that we might successfully employ the latter to meet the former. Coming to our difficulties in my opinion the foremost place amongst them must be given to our want of faith in ourselves, to the scepticism that is the ruling doctrine of our life, to the habit of too close an analysis which paralyses both action and thought.

Unfortunately for us, though born in a country dominated by a religious atmosphere of great depth all round, we are wanting in "that power of faith and will which neither counts obstacles nor measures time." At present, we are nothing more than a set of doubting Thomases fond of analysis and entirely devoid of synthesis. Perhaps we are getting into a habit of destroying rather than that of building. We can calculate profits and losses to annas and pies, but we are devoid of that spirit of enterprise which can dare and at time play boldly. In a country whose history is brimful of instances of thousands of men and women having willingly and gladly sacrificed their all for the sake of honour and faith, we find that a century of Western domination has so changed the ruling impulses of life as to convert the people into a set of clay-puppets having no will or faith of their own. Thank God, the country has not lost all sense of spirituality. The gold is there. It requires the touch of a magician to find it out and to make it over to them whose it is by birthright. The true solution of the problem lies in appealing to the true instincts and tendencies of the Indian heart, mute just now, but revealed to us in the pages of our history. In the words of Mazzini, the first step towards this aim is "to make war against the existing idolatry of material interests and substitute for it the worship of the just and the true: and to convince the [Indians] that their sole path to reality is through sacrifice—constancy in sacrifice. The work before us is not only an endeavour to create a united nation but to make her great and powerful—worthy of her past glories and conscious of her future mission."

India is just now materialistic, believing in the benevolence of English Ministers or English Parliaments, seeking rather the amelioration of the condition of the classes than to constitute itself a nation. The country and its leaders rather fight shy of high principles, and are ready to accept any compromise, any offer of a post here or a post there, any tinkering with their rights, any mode of assistance and last but not the least "always ready to accept any man brought forward with a promise of relieving her immediate sufferings" as their *Messiah*. Our attitude towards the questions of the day is not determined by its inherent righteousness, but by the chance of its reception at the hands of the powers that be. We are not always actuated by truth and justice, but by expediency and tactics. Our object is to propitiate our foreign rulers, but not to inspire our people. We choose to live in a world of myth and fiction and not in a world of truth, faith and duty. We conceal our sentiments not because they are not true and just but because we cannot afford to offend those whom they might hurt. In trying to deceive others we often deceive ourselves. The result is that we are lacking in that power of faith which alone can make us men, able to create a nation and win liberty for the same.

"Our mortal disease is that unlimited confidence in every thing bearing the outward semblance of all calculation and tactics, that constant distrust of all enthusiasm, energy and simultaneous action—three things which sum up the whole science of revolution. We wait, study and follow circumstances ; we neither seek to dominate nor to create them. We honour with the name of prudence that which is, in action, merely mediocrity of intellect.

Our whole life from top to bottom smacks of fear, deadly fear of losing in the estimation of those whom we in our heart of hearts believe to be only usurpers ; fear of losing the sunshine of the smile of those whom we believe to be day and night engaged in the exploitation of our country and the spoliation of our people, fear of offending the false gods that have by fraud or force taken possession of our bodies aud souls fear of being shut up in a dungeon or prision house, as if the freedom that we enjoy, is not by its own nature, one to be abhorred, despised and hated,—a freedom by default or by sufferance. In my opinion the problem before us is in the main a religious problem—religious not in the sense of doctrines and dogmas—but religious in so far as to evoke the highest devotion and the greatest sacrifice from us. Our first want, then, is to rise our patriotism to the level of religion and to aspire to live or to die for it. We believe in religion for the sake of the truth in it which is to secure for our souls communion with God. There in the presence of our God we forget our tiny selves, the pettiness of our minds and rising above the same, drink from the pure fountain of bliss and love. In the same way, let the edifice of patriotism be raised on the solid rock of truth and justice. In worshipping truth and justice let us be honest and bold, regardless of worldly losses and gains. Let the people first learn to think honestly and boldly.

This will in course of time be followed by honest, bold and truthful words and the latter by honest, bold and inspiring deeds.

If we do this, the future of our country is in our hands. There is no power on earth that can stand between us and our country as there is no petty god that can ever come between the conscience of an honest, bold worshipper and his Almighty Maker. The first step of the political ladder, then, consists in our educating the people in a school of true politics, of our initiating them into a religion of true patriotism with a creed of Nationality, Liberty and Unity, to be believed and striven after with all the sincerity of heart and devotion, worthy of the oriental mind. Let us first renounce all kinds of self-interest and class-interest, in favour of a noble and universal patriotism embracing all the people and all the provinces of mother India, irrespective of creed, caste and colour. All talk of unity is futile unless we succeed in bringing about a unity of purpose in the minds of the people whom we desire to unite. An attempt to base this unity of purpose on material interests, might land us in interminable dissensions and endless controversies—in insuperable friction and unsurmountable irritation. But a sincere effort to give a higher and spiritual basis to our unity of purpose might save the situation and lead us safely to the haven of our hopes. That oneness of purpose is very happily summed up in the sacred salutation *Bande Mataram* and in the war-cry of 'Swaraj.'

Let us next proceed to examine the forces that are likely to oppose us in our propaganda. Here, again, the greatest danger is, in my opinion, from within and not from without.

To the Government there are only two paths that are open—a system of terror or a system of concessions. The latter possesses more possibilities of success than the former. A system of terror invariably recoils over the heads of those that resort to it, and I am confident that the British are sufficiently wise not to forget that there is a great deal of truth in what is so often quoted by European revolutionists that :—

" Blood calls for Blood, and the dagger of the conspirator is never so terrible as when sharpened on the tomb-stone of a martyr."

A system of small concessions, however, might be more effectual to stem the rising tide of nationality. Therein probably lies a greater danger to the rapid growth of the idea of nationality in the country than in a system of repression. Trivial changes in administrative machinery, the reform of the most crying Governmental abuses and a few more ineffectual concessions not involving any fundamental change in the principles of Government or in the constitution of the same, should not satisfy our people, unless the same are accompanied by a guarantee of fixed institutions, and a fundamental contract recognising a right, a power and a sovereignty in the people. That the opposition of the dominant race will be tremendous and terrible, I readily grant; but what I fear most is the opposition from within, the opposition of the classes enjoying the special patronage of the Government, the opposition of interest, the opposition of privilege, and last but not the least, the opposition of timidity and cowardice. The divine, whom I quoted in the opening lines of the paper, has in one of his essays on social amelioration drawn the following picture of the attitude of his countrymen towards the social evils existing in English society. He says :—

"The attitude of some—let us hope very few—is simply not to care at all to live in pleasure on the earth and be wanton ; to have hearts as fat as brawn and cold as ice, and hard as the nether mill-stone ; to heap up superfluous and often ill begotton wealth, to be hoarded in acquisition, squandered in luxury, or reserved for the building up of idle families. But to men, whose immense riches are squandered, in all but an insignificant fraction, on their own lust and their own aggrandisement comes the stern strong message of St. James, "your riches are corrupted, your garments are moth-eaten. Ye have lived delicately on the earth, and taken your pleasure. Ye have nourished your hearts in a day of slaughter." The attitude of others is that of a scornful pity, half cynical, half despairing. * * * * The attitude of others again is stolid acquiescence. They are weary of the whole thing ; sick of hearing anything about it. It annoys, them. Tell them of it and they shrug their shoulders with an impatient "what can we do !" Ask them for help, and they have "so many claims," that they practically give to none, Press the claims and they resent it as a personal insult. Suggest a plan and they will call it "Utopian." Describe a case of anguish and they will call you "sensational." Take part in a public effort and they will sneer at you as "self advertising." The one thing they believe in is selfish *laises* *faire.* Things will last their time and that is all they care about. They grow too indulgent and too selfish to care about anything but their own indulgences and their own ease."

Applying this to Indian society, I am afraid, the picture will have to be painted a great deal blacker. There are at any rate no traitors in English society. In our case the chief difficulty does not solely lie in the persistent and deliberate discouragement which is held out by a large section of the community to all efforts towards progress. Here it is not the scoffer and the cynic only that stand in the way of advance but even more dangerous are those who insist to be of you, and with you, but whose heart is not with you, and whose interests, as uuderstood by them, lie the other way. Although they are apt to betray themselves at every other step, they cover their shame by ridiculing the zealous and the earnest, by quietly and philosophically questioning their motives and by poisoning the minds of others against them. Their attitude undergoes no change whether the reform advocated is religious social or political. The first bores them as an affection of the brain; the second annoys them as tending towards puritanism and misanthrophy; the third frightens them. The beauty of the whole thing, however, lies in the fact that large number of them cannot help poking their noses almost everywhere. They enlist as members of societies whose proposed object is to preach religion. They display great interest in social reform so long as it does not interfere with what they call the joys of life. Maintaining an attitude of boldness and defiance to public opinion when the latter proposes to interfere in any way with the "pleasures of life," they are docile as lambs when their ladies and *biradari* (caste) people insist on the celebration of the marriages of their boys and girls at tender ages. As for political associations, these are their special hunting grounds. They have no objection to preside at public meetings or to move or second resolutions or to attend Conferences and Congresses, if it suits their convenience or is likely to be profitable, but all the same they will continue to revel in scoffing at and laughing down those who are serious and earnest about the matter. The general mass of the people are so ignorant of political ideas that it is impossible for them to understand or find out the real game which these gentlemen are playing. Consequently they are often cowed down and persuaded to let matters alone rather than make a bold stand for their rights.

The first necessity of the situation is, therefore, the coming forward of a number of whole-time workers in each province, devoted to the work of giving political education and imparting right ideas, irrespective and regardless of the scoffer and the cynic. Mr. Dadabhai Naoroji exhorts us to agitate, agitate and agitate. I say, Amen! but on the clear understanding that agitation is an educational duty which has to be performed regardless of success in the shape of concessions. Let the pupblic be accustomed to *agitate for the sake of agitation* and not in the hope of getting any immediate redress. That is, in my opinion, the only way to ward off disappointments and to prepare the people for more effective methods of political activity. Our esteemed countryman Mr. Tilak advises the people to make the work of administration on the present lines impossible by passive resistance. I say, that is only possible by training the people to a habit of suffering for principles, *i. e.*, to dare and to risk; and by infusing in them a spirit of defiance wherever a question of principle is involved. The way is to be shewn by personal example and not by precept alone. There is the old truth 'no risk, no gain.' The line of least resistance, of empty resolutions on paper, of simple resolutions, memorials, and not petitions backed up by anything which would place our earnestness beyond the shade of a doubt, is a line of action more worthy of women than of men. If I may be permitted to question the political leaders of the country, what irresistible proofs have they up to this time given of their earnestness for the political demand made by them? If the time was not and is not ripe for these proofs then why did they not follow the Japanese in making quiet preparations at home before coming out openly with fiery speeches and longwinded resclutions? If, however we have not wasted 22 years on political agitation and if the Swadeshi and Boycott are not lip-platitudes to be indulged in for the edification of our audiences, let us now take to it seriously and give incontestable proofs of our earnestness for political privileges.

Hitherto our work has lacked that system and solidity which are the outcome of well thought out and well organised plans. Hitherto the political movement has only been carried out by fits and starts. It has completely depended on the moments of leisure which gentlemen engaged in learned professions and business, could conveniently spare for the same. It has been a labour of love to them, but it has always occupied a secondary position in their thoughts. The country has so far failed to produce a class of men whose chief and prime business in life will be political agitation and political education. The chief and crying need of the national movement, in the coming forward of a class of earnest, sincere, able and devoted men, who will move about the country freely and preach the Gospel of freedom, both by word of mouth as well as by example—men who will win over the masses to the cause of Truth and Justice, by words of wisdom and lives of service. The non-existence of this class at the present moment, combined with other difficulties makes the national outlook very gloomy indeed, but the remedy to change the face of things lies in our own hands.

There is an all round awakening in the land, and if the awakening were to be properly utilised by the class of men I have spoken of above, I am sure that the dense gloom that prevails now, will soon be thinned by streaks of encouraging and cheering light, crowed by the dawn of hope and the sunrise of national birth. Most of our people are unnerved by the prevailing disunion and other vices which are the necessary outcome of a foreign domination. It is true that foreign domination is always brought on by disunion but once it has come in, it accentuates the same and adds to its volume and intensity, as without it, it loses the chief reason for its continuance. Some of our people are very angry (and at times rightly) at the narrow, sectarian, denominational spirit that is rampant in the land. In their eyes, it is the chief obstacle in the way of political independence and as a means to obtain the latter, they set about in all sincerity and earnestness to root out the former. All honour to their sentiments and to their impulses. But a calm consideration will show that the task is almost impossible. If the boon of Self-Government is to be denied to us so long as the people of this country do not give up denominationalism and do not take to one religion or no-religion, I am afraid there can be no hope for us. The problem before us is, to accept the facts before us as they are, and then to build up the edifice of nationality on them or in spite of them. I hope I shall not be misunderstood. I am not opposed to the cultivation of a spirit of catholicity amongst the followers of the different religions that are to be found in the country. By all means carry on your work in this direction as zealously as you can. I wish you all success. But I can not persuade myself to believe that it is possible to uproot denomiationalism from this land and for the matter of that, from any land. Our best efforts should then be directed to create a nation in spite of them. I am not quite sure, if it is desirable to do away with religion or with religious denominations altogether, even if it were possible to do so. All these differences in religion serve their own purpose in the general economy of the world, and there are a good many people whose views are entitled to the greatest respect from us, who are inclined to think that the world would be poorer and monotonous by the entire removal of these differences. Our readers are probably aware of the rebuke administered by Burke to the authors of the French Revolution in their efforts to enforce a universal equality. In his

"Reflections on the French Revolution," addressing the people of France, he questions the wisdom of the sweeping changes effected by them in their constitution in the following words:—

In your old States you possessed that variety of parts corresponding with the various descriptions of which your community was happily composed, you had all that opposition of interests, you had that action and counteraction which in the natural and in the political world from the reciprocal struggle of discordant powers, draws out the harmony of the universe."

I express no opinion upon the force of the anathemas hurled by Burke on the French Revolution, but I cannot help remarking that there is a great deal of truth in the general observation quoted above. The world is, no doubt, good and beautiful only with its diversity. The chief object of human yearning is, has been, and ought to be, to find harmony in diversity. Nations are built and unified by the differences that exist between the various classes of their population. The Apostle of Unity in order to succeed must find a common object to achieve and a common enemy to fight. All differences must be sunk in the presence of the latter and to achieve the former but not necessarily otherwise.

For as this and this only can be the common basis of nationality, I do not think there are insuperable difficulties in the way of Indian Unity, if the denominational and other differences are faced in that spirit

Another evil which often staggers us, is the illiteracy and ignorance of our people. Here again, while admitting the absolute necessity of educating the masses, I fail to see the soundness of the proposition, that universal education must precede any demand for self-government. In fact it is hopeless to expect anything like universal education without self-government. Over a century and a quarter of British rule has failed to educate more than 5 or 6 percent of the people of India, while Japan has been wholly educated within less than 40 years. The educational work is one of the most important of our national duties, but by no means should it be made a condition precedent to our demanding self-government. Here, too, the principal question is of men and money. Find out the former and the latter will be forthcoming. That is, therefore the chief thing, for the finding of which, the nation should put forth its best energy and talent.

Give us a dozen men in each province, exclusively devoted to the work of national regeneration, and the situation will at once assume a bright appearance and will promise the most hopeful results. Let us hope that the best talent and the best patriotism of the country are engaged in tapping the resources which are eventually to give us the desired class of men who shall be our national Sannyasis in the present crisis. It was probably said of times like these that " These are the times that try men's souls. The sunshine soldier and the sunshine patriot will, in this crisis, shrink from the service of their country; but he that stands to it now, deserves the thanks of man and woman. Tyranny like hell is not easily conquered; yet we have this consolation with us, that the harder the contest, the more glorious the triumph. What we obtain too cheaply, we esteem too lightly; it is dearness only that gives everything its value. Heaven knows how to set a proper price upon its goods; and it would have been strange indeed if so celestial an article as Freedom should not be highly rated."

LAJAPAT RAI

—o—

To His Government and Countrymen.

"THE POLITICAL SITUATION IN THE PUNJAB"

CAUSES OF DISCONTENTMENT IN THE PUNJAB'

Some people think that the situation in the Punjab has become very serious. The panic in official circles resulting in the arrest of 5 respectable citizens of Rawal pindi no doubt justifies that view. In my opinion, however, this panic has been artificially created by the Secret Police and the Government has simply played into the hands of its own agents. It is silly to reproach this or that man for having brought about this state of things to suggest that any one or two or three men in this province possess the power or influence to bring about this state of things is both stupid and absurd. It may be highly flattering to his vanity and in a sense complimentary also, but it cannot stand the test of close examination on the basis of actual facts. Discontent, no doubt, there is and a great deal of it. But this discontent has been brought about by Anglo-Indians themselves, and the causes of these may be thus summarised in chronological order.

(*a*) The letters and articles &c, that appeared in the Civil and Military Gazette sometime in July and August last year under the heading "Signs of the Times" &c.

(*b*) The prosecution of the *Punjabee*, coupled with the refusal of the Government to take similar action against the C. and M. Gazette.

(*c*) The Colonization Bill.

(*d*) The Land Alienation Act Amendment Bill.

(*e*) The increase of Canal rates on the Bari-Doab canal.

(*f*) The abnormal increase of Land Revenue in the Rawalpindi District.

(*g*) The appalling mortality from plague which has made the people sullen and labour scarce, and raised the wages abnormally.

Now the first 6 causes are directly attributable to Anglo-Indians. The last is a visitation of God. The first two might perhaps have been innocuous but for the four following. Joined however, they have increased the volume of discontent enormously. The sixth has played the most important part. The silent economic revolution caused by the same has acted terribly on the minds of men belonging to the lower strata of Government servants, and has very naturally brought about strikes such as would have been incredible a few years before. Under the circumstances can the Government honestly and conscientiously acquit its own officers of want of foresight and statesmanship in insisting on unpopular measures and passing them in the teeth of universal opposition, of disregarding the economic changes, and failing to recognise the claims of classes of Government servants to an increase in their salaries proportionate to the increase in the wages of private labourers? Had this been done in time with consideration, all discontent would have been quieted.

Agitators Responsible and Irresponsible

Are the agitators to be blamed for having pointed out the Government's mistakes and identified themselves with popular grievances? What have they done? They have enlisted the sympathies of the masses by standing for their grievances and agitating for the removal of the same. The Government had from time to time reproached them for standing alone, aloof from the masses and as, therefore, having no justification to speak in their name. Here was an opportunity for them to remove this reproach. Can any one honestly say that they have done wrong in utilising this opportunity? Should they have stood aloof from the people and refused to take up their cause and articulate the same? Had they done so they would have been unworthy of their education and guilty of treason to their own people. Why should they then be blamed for having espoused the popular cause? A year before they were incomprehensible to the masses. The masses did not and could not be expected to follow them in their cry for Self-Government. As for the demand for an increased employments of Indians in higher offices under Government, the people were not quite certain if that would immediately help them very much. They said that it made no difference in their lot whether they were governed by a Mister or a Lala or a Maulvi. The recent legislation, however, made them think differently. They found that the services rendered by them to the empire in the past had really counted for nothing and could not suspect that Government was treating them very badly up the class legislation indulged in by Government, so defiantly in the proud consciousness of their unlimited strength has affected class after class until there was hardly any class of population left which could honestly display any enthusiasm for the Government. We know that there is a class of Government hangers-on—their contractors, news vendors, title hunters, &c., whose leaders are always enthusiastic for the Government as it pays them so well to do so. But even they cannot honestly lay their hand on their hearts and say that they had no hand in the agitation over the Colonization Bill and the canal water rates resolution. The difference is this, that they acted behind the purdah, keeping appearances all right, while others acted boldly and openly. These unpopular measures gave an opportunity to some "young talkers" who utilised it to their heart's content. Their fearless speeches and their readiness to suffer for their convictions went straight to the people's hearts and attracted thousands to their meeting places. Now it is silly to assume that they had any responsible people at their back, for the simple reason that no thoughtful or responsible man could possibly bring himself to believe that the country was *at all* ready for a political cataclysm. The cry in the Punjab has always been for "organised work." No organisation could be started or perfected in the state in which the Province has been for the last nine months. The tree of organisation requires a cool atmosphere and undisturbed soil to take root and fructify. People have not rushed into print or in the public meetings to denounce youthful and impulsive speakers or writers, but they have all the same done their level best to influence them towards moderation and towards more permanent and solid ways of doing things such as might leave solid and lasting results behind. It is unfortunate that they did not succeed to the extent they wished, but even their failure has its own significance. If amateur orators and others whom nobody knew two or three months before, repulsed the advances of responsible leaders to control and guide them with impunity, if they have refused to listen to their advice, questioned their moral courage, and have at times denounced them as cowards and still have practically kept the field to themselves, that shows that they could depend upon the sympathies and appreciation of the people in general, ignoring those who wanted to control and guide them. They had some thing in them which appealed to the people and which brought them appreciation and encouragement.

REAL GRIEVANCES VIOCED BY THE AGITATORS.

It is again silly to suppose that their audiences consisted only or mainly of the juvenile population ; could any one in his senses maintain that meetings at Lyalpure Multan, Batala, Amritsar, and Delhi consisted of Students only ? Who attended the meetings at the local Bharata Mata office after the schools and colleges had been closed on account of the plague ? What is the total strength of the school population at Lahore or at Rawalpindi or at Delhi compared with the members that have been attending the meetings addressed by Sardar Ajit Singh and Syed Hyder Raza. The fact is, and it cannot honestly be ignored, that the propaganda carried on by these gentlemen has met with popular approval, it meets the fancy of the masses and their utterances find a ready and appreciative response from the thousands whom they address, and from tens of thousands, more who devour their speeches or writings as reported or published in the Vernacular press. The irresponsible writer in the Anglo-Indian journal may talk or write what pleases him, but the responsible authorities can no longer shut their eyes to the fact that Sardar Ajit singh and syed Hyder Raz really represent a solid bulk of public opinion which it will be madness to ignore or treat with contempt. I do not, however, believe that the state of things has come to such a pass as to justify the panic which appears to have got hold of Anglo-Indian circles in the Punjab. The discontent in the Punjab has not yet assumed proportions so as to lead people to overt acts of Violence. The stray acts of Violence hitherto in evidence represent the doings of the secret Police, or of *Gundas*, or of a few frenzied boys or perhaps of all these combined.

THE RIGHT PATH FOR THE GOVERNMENT.

But there is no denial that this may lead to further and greater disorders if nothing is done to remove the discontent that is at the bottom of it and to sooth the angered, outraged feelings of the people. Repressive measures might cow down the people for a time, but that they are bound to fail in the end, if it is intended to crush the spirit of the people thereby, is certain so long as people believe that their interests and those of the Government clash.

And so long as these two are in conflict, so long the popular feeling is sure to burst out from time to time, do what you may to crush or kill it by force. The thing is new just now. After over 50 years of peaceful Government, when the people have quite forgotten the troubles of a disordered state of society, and after they have taken to easy-going modes of life, it shocks them to hear of the arrests such as have taken place in Rawalpindi. It may unnerve them for the time and the political movement in the Punjab may be put down for some time to come. But as soon as the people recover their stunned senses and begin to think how insignificant are individual interests in the struggle for national rights, their sympathies for the first victims will change into homage for the cause and for those who were the first to suffer for the cause. Fear will give way to the desire for martyrdom and panic will disappear. This process will be facilitated and dishastened if these arrests become too common, as they are likely to be, in the present state of panic in official circles, but that these arrests will seal the fate of the national movement I decline to believe. The efforts of the Government at repression are only natural, the effect of these measures on the public mind will show how much real political life there is in the country and how far it can be relied on. It will give a fresh starting point to those who desire to devote their lines to this cause.' National evolution is bound to proceed on the lines of repulses, defeats, struggles, &c. None need despair. True wisdom as well as the spirit of resignation to the Divine Will teaches taking things as they come, drawing right conclusions therefrom, modifying ways and means in accordance therewith, and then proceeding steadily and surely.

CONGRESS ORGANISATION IN THE PUNJAB.

In accordance with the resolution passed at the last session of the Congress laying down certain rules of constitution it is necessary that the Punjab Congressemen should proceed to form a Provincial Congress Committee at once. The questions deserving consideration in connection therewith may be roughly stated as below :—

(1) Whether the Indian Association of Lahore should be converted into a Provincial Congress Committee for the Punjab, with such modifications in its constitution as may be found necessary or desirable or whether a separate Provincial Committee be organised which shall include the members or representatives from District Associations, and such other persons from Districts where the latter have not been organised as yet, who have ever attended a meeting of the Congress as delegates. This may not necessarily mean the exclusion of persons who may be otherwise qualified and also willing to become members.

(2) What should be the minimum subscription qualification (*a*) for ordinary members and (*b*) for members of the Executive Committee. I would suggest that all such persons as are prepared to pay Re. 1 per month for political work in the Punjab (including Re. 0-8-0 per month charged by the District Association) should be accepted as ordinary members of the Provincial Congress Committee. This will secure at least six Rupees a year

per member to the Provincial Committee and enable the latter to maintain an Office. The number of the Executive Committee should not be very large although it should be sufficiently large to allow of proper representation being given to the District Associations. One way of securing an effective committee is to fix a fairly high subscription qualification for the membership, say 5 rupees a month, with power to make a few exceptions in favour of deserving-men the total strength of the latter not to exceed 20 per cent of the former. I am very strongly of opinion that there is no use of talking of the want of political activity in the Punjab and throwing the odium of it on certain individuals unless there are at least some 20 people in the Province who are prepared to give time and money to this work.

(3) What to do of the Bradlaugh Hall. I am of opinion that such of the members of the Provincial Congress Committee as have paid Rs. 100 or are now prepared to pay Rs. 100 towards the construction of the Hall should form themselves into a society to rebuild and maintain the Hall. I understand that was the original intention of those who started the movement for a permanent public Hall in Lahore. Before I conclude I may add that these are only suggestions for consideration and discussion; personally I will accept any rules which are after discussion, agreed to by the majority.

I do not know what is the idea about the next meeting of the Punjab Provincial Conference. If it is likely to meet during the first six months of the year, the matter may be finally settled there. If otherwise, a special meeting of delegates of the Indian Association and of the several District Associations that have been formed or may be formed by that time, may be convened to settle this matter. The Punjab has all along been very keen about the constitution of the Congress. Now that a tentative constitution has been obtained it is absolutely necessary for the good name of the Province that we should show our readiness to act up to it and to profit by the same. I propose that the matter may be taken up for early discussion by the Indian Association of Lahore, and the District Associations that have been formed Subject to considerations of health and engagements already made. I am prepared to go to mufassil stations for organising District Associations whenever invited to do so by men who, in my opinion, are likely to do the thing successfully.

DESH BHAKTI.

Lala Lajpat Rai delivered a most impressive and eloquent lecture in Anaj Mandi, Aambla, before a large audience composed of men of all callings and professions in the course of which he said that it is but natural for every man to possess feelings of love ; but love is of two kinds, selfish, having the achievement of immediate gain in view, and unselfish—which impels us on to do works of public utility with more or less depending on the extent of the feelings of unselfishness selfless motives.

Selfish love cannot, however, make our minds peaceful or calm the inner cravings of man for blissfulness ; for the attainment of this end we must all needs do some selfless work. No country can prosper until her sons and daughters are imbued with a genuine sense of unselfish devotion towards her and ready to subordinate their personal interests for country's good.

The Japanese have recently shown to what lofty heights patriotic fervour can rise. A mother's stabbing herself in order to free her son from the burden of her maintenance so that he may go to war and die for her beloved country and the readiness of an overwhelmingly large number of sailors to drown themselves with ships in front of Port Arthur are instances which nothing short of a deep love for country's honor—much less lust for gold or glorification of vain self—can prompt. Even in European countries, with their long legend of national patriotism, such examples of sublime devotion are rare.

A degenerate country, like ours, badly needs for her service such selfless workers as neither wealth nor power could buy. We had a large number of them in our glorious past when our country's towering moral and physical capabilities had elevated it to the lofty pinnacle of prosperity and happiness.

Not long ago all our requirements were met with by articles of *deshi* manufacture. Woe, however, to our present situation of helpless dependence on foreigners, who drain away most part of the money earned by us with the sweat of our brow. And this drain is responsible for the oft-recurring famines and pestilence, which mainly victimise the poor owing to the unhealthy state of their habitations and their inability to get sufficient and wholesome food. Lord Curzon's government estimated that the Indian's average income then was Rs, 30 per annum or 2-8 a month. When this is the average there must be many who live on Rs. 1-8 or, even, Re. 1 a month. It is a mystery how a man can even parsimoniously feed and clothe himself for a month on this paltry income unless he half starves.

As a matter of fact there are seven crores of men who get only one meal in a day and there are many more who live on roots and barks of trees. About forty to fifty thousand are devoured by plague and other diseases every week. Any country having such a horrible and heart-rending tale of sorrow and devastation can never have a hopeful future. Europeans are living comfortably. The reason is that they are true to their country, following *Swadeshi* in its true essence. Plague and pestilence do not touch them because they live in commodious, well-ventilated houses in the healthiest parts of the towns. They carry most of our corn to their country—even when our own men are starving for want of food and famines are fiercely raging in the land—for maintaining an adequate supply of staple food for their own countrymen. Our raw products find their way to England in order to develop her trade in manufactured ariticles, which are brought back and sold in India at enormous profits. They do not scruple to provide lucrative employments for their own men in this contry and are always ready to do everything that is calculated to promote their people's welfare. This genuine regard for providing for the good of their whole community is the secret of their prosperiy and success all round.

Our countrymen sadly lack in that spirit of patriotism that characterises the citizens of every great and prosperous country in the world aud consequently there is no end to our troubles. Nothing short of true *desh bhakti*, which consists in sacrificing the hankering after pelf and power in favour of the unremunerative yet--important and divine--task of working for the welfare of our countrymen,—can save us from the death and destruction that is staring us in the face. Genuine and selfless devotion (*Bhakti*) for our *desh* ought to be the dharma, the noble mission of life, of every one of us and in the service of our country we should spare neither money nor life.

———o———

SCHOLARSRIPS FOR POLITICAL TRAINING.

LALA LAJPAT RAI'S LETTER

TO

The Editor, Punjabee.

Sir,--You are aware that in 1905 when I was deputed to go to England as a delegate from Punjab, Rs. 3000 were collected by public subscription towards the expenses of my trip. The expenses actually incurred having by far exceeded that amount, I, on my return. promised to repay the said amount by giving half of it in aid of the Foreign Education Fund of the D. A. V. College and by spending the other half in furtherence of the cause of political education in this province. The 1st mentioned promise has already been made good. The other remains yet to be fulfiled though I have never lost sight of the same and have been thinking of the best way to use it. At one time I proposed to organise a small Political

Council consisting of a limited number of members paying Rs. 50 as admission fee and Rs. 100 as annual subscription to start political work in this province on active educational lines. I intended to make over the amount to that council. The scheme was printed and circulated amongst a limited number of friends. It met with a fair amount of response in so far that over 15 gentlemen promised to join it on those terms. The idea was to have an office and a Library at Lahore in connection with the council. After a great deal of cogitation over the matter I have now decided to give up the idea of a separate political council (for the present at least) and resolved to utilise the money in my hands in providing for a training to a few Punjabi youths in methods of political work. I have so far decided to offer two scholarships of the value of Rs 50 per mensem each, to two masters of Arts or B.A. LL.B.'s of the Punjab University who promise to devote one year to the exclusive study of politics and political methods. It may be a presumption on my part to assume that I can guide even a novice in political studies but as at present advised I see no better course open to me. The terms of these scholarships are :--

(1) The scholarship shall run for a year.

(2) The candidate selected shall have to live at Lahore or travel to parts of India, at my discretion, his travelling expenses being borne by me.

(3) He shall not aim at a career in Government service and shall give a declaration to that effect.

(4) He shall prepare for no examination during the time he gets the scholarship.

(5) These scholarships are open to all Indians irresspective of caste, creed or colour.

(6) The scholarship will be held during good behaviour and may be discontinued on proof of misconduct or for want of diligence in studies.

(7) In case of qualified M. A.'s or B. A., L. L. B.'s not coming forward to take the scholarships one of these may be given to a distinguisned B. A., who has read up to the M. A. Standard, in English, History or Philosophy, or has passed the Intermediate in Law Examination of the Punjab University, and the other may be split into two or three, to be given to candidates of lesser qualifications.

(8) Applications shall be considered and elections made by a committee consisting of the followisng members of the Indian Association, Lahore :—

(a) The undersigned. (Lala Laiput Rai).

(b) Lala Shadi Lal, M. A., Bar-at-Law, Lahore.

(*c*) Lala Duni Chand, Bar-at-Law, Secretary, Indian Association, Lahore.

(*d*) Lala Mulkraj Bhalla.

(*e*) Sirdar Gurcharan Singh, B.A., Bar-at-Law, Lahore-

(9) Condition (6) shall not be enforced unless a majority of the above mentioned committee agree to do so.

(10) Rs. 1,500 will be deposited in the Punjab Cooperative Bank and the scholarships shall be payable on bills signed by the undersigned(Lala Lajput Rai).

(11) Applications shall be received up to the 15th of April and decision arrived at by the 1st of May. Ap-

plications should be addressed to the undersigned.

——o——

Alleged Seditious Speeches of Lala Lajpat Rai.

The Punjabee.

The following is the full text of Lala Lajpat Rai's speech delivered at the Anniversary of the Arya Samaj in November 1905, as published in the *Paisa Akhbar* from which the *Wafadar* made certain extracts.

Paisa Akhbar, December 12, 1905 (page 6).

We publish below the lecture delivered by Lala Lajpat Rai Sahib, Pleader, and renowned patriot, on the 26th November on the occasion of the anniversary of the Arya Samaj, Lahore, (College party) when a very large number of enthusiastic hearers was present:—

" Brethren,—Yon have come here as our guests and I am ashamed to find that we are unable to show the hospitality (of providing you sufficient accommodation here.) This poverty of ours is an index of the poverty of our country. However, there is no occasion for anyone to complain. We have been doing whatever is in our power, but there can be no help for that which is beyond our means, and we beg to be excused for it.

This morning I had begun by saying, that while I was in Europe I tried to find out a solution of the question, What is the secret of the progress of Europe? What are the causes which have raised the sun of prosperity of Europe to its zenith? How is it that, although the Europeans are few in number, yet they reign supreme in the whole world and nobody dare disobey their command? From the day on which I set my foot on European soil I began to ponder over this question. The fact is that he who has his eyes open can cleary see through such things as these. As soon as you set your foot on European soil, you begin to see things working in a way which itself suggests the solution of the question. He, who has his eyes open, can see that they (the Europeans) are more intelligent than ourselves. He sees that in their systems of education, in their arts and industries, and in their commerce there exists *organization* (*i. e.*, the quality of doing a thing systematically and continuously). Every man, then, is fond of organization, and nobody dare interfere with the law of organization. You find this law working not only in the navies, the armies and other Departments of Western Governments, but you find it also in their homes. The home of a European is typical of the marvellous system of organization that prevails in West, and from their very childhood they grow under its influence. There is not a single man who is not under (does not belong to) some sort of organization. In short, it is *organization* which rules supreme in Europe. But, gentlemen, the one thing that forms the backbone of *organization* is *education*. If any one wishes to see (an illustration) of the truth that knowledge is power and that even the elements, *i. e.*, air, fire, water and the oceans all recognise the Sway of man, let him go and see the ships, the machinery of the factories of Europe. There he will see how the stupendous power of nature has been enslaved to provide for the comforts of man. But the secret of all this power lies in the system of education which obtains there. All the nations of Europe are not equally great. Some of hese are of ordinary position, while others are highly advanced and powerful by virtue of the vastness of their empires and the infiuence they exercise over the world. The power and influence of the various nations of Europe depends upon their respective systems of education. The people of Switzerland do not busy themselves with taking away the liberty of any other nation. The system of education that obtains there (in Europe)developes the intelligent and makes man active and bold. In Europe, the prevalent notion about education is that it should make a man fit to meet his personal and national requirements, that, while, on the one hand, it should develop private virtue in him, it should, on the other, help in making him a true and honest lover of his country. The system that is followed there is such that it makes man fit and well equipped for all those requirements. It is necessary that a man be influenced by his surroundings. No one has the power to avoid the influence of his environments. Even plants and trees that grow in the jungle develop by absorbing the elements that are around them. Nothing in nature is free from the effect of the things that are about it, and development of each individual depends to a great extent upon his circumstances. European children are highly fortunate in that they are born of civilized parents, and, as such, are influenced, to a great degree, by that civilization. As soon as a child attains the school-going age, he, in a way, becomes free from the protection of his parents, and another power with vast and unbounded resources steps in to take upon itself the responsibility of bringing up the child. This power is the Government of the country. In cases, where parents are not in a position to satisfactorily discharge the duty of giving a proper education to their children, the Government takes this task upon itself, the fulfilment of which it considers the very object of its existence.

The Government there represents the people; it is the head of the nation and is composed of delegates chosen by the people. The state is responsible for the prosperity and protection of the nation. The Government takes upon itself the duty of seeing that no child grows up in ignorance and, therefore, legislates that education up to a certain age is compulsory for all children, whether male or female. In the education of their children, parents are relieved of the burden of providing them with books, pen, ink and fees. The children are not required to take these things with them to school, but they are supplied to them in school. The school authorities supply these things free of charge. Now they have gone a step further, in as much as poor students are supplied with good food on behalf of the school. Seeing that poor children are placed at a disadvantage compared to the children of the rich, and that mental work tells upon the physique of the former and consequently they cannot derive the fullest benefit from their education, it has been decided that those who cannot afford to get substantial food from their parents, are to be provided with it at the cost of the State. When this question came up for consideration before the Governments of the various self-governing countries of Europe, the French Government was the first to solve the difficulty and it laid down that the State should provide proper nourishment for those children whose parents cannot afford it. In England also the London County Council has introduced the same system in schools under its charge. There girls are taught cookery handicrafts, needlework and singing as part of the educational curriculum.

In connection with cookery they are taught Chemistry, and are told the ingredients and properties of various foods (and such details as the quantity of oxygen and hydrogen that go to make up a thing. In one room they receive theoretical instruction on the subject, in another arrangements are made for practical demonstration, where girls cook food with their own hands. The food thus prepared is given to those boys and girls who cannot themselves provide with it.

This would be sufficient to show how keenly the Europeans feel and realise the importance of education. We here (in India) wish to provide the cheapest form of education for our children, regardless of the fact whether the influence exercised by the institution is for good or for evil. And with all this we (Indians) want to imitate and rival those (the Europeans) who are the rulers of the world. In Europe no problem is considered of such paramount importance as the educational one. In India the function of a teacher ends when the school time is over, the relation of teacher and the taught also ending with it. But in very European country a large class of great thinkers is always busy in devising means for improving and perfecting the educational system of the nation. Some of the best intellects of the country are paid high salaries in order that they might go and study the educational system of every country and compare it with their own with a view to find out the defects of the latter and devise means for their removal. The results of such investigations are published in reports for the information of the people, they are discussed in public and conclusions are drawn therefrom. A large class (of experts) is always busy in thinking over educational matters and seeing that the country does not lag behind in any department of national advancement.

Here (in India) it is customary for the teacher to resort to the use of the cane as soon as the boy begins his alphabet. But in Europe the case is entirely different; there the children are given oral instruction for 2 or 3 years when they are instructed in drawing figures and entertaining exercises. They are taught the methods of bringing their hands and feet into play, such as walking, running, &c. After this, they are taught the alphabet. Drawing (*i. e.*, sketches and figures), singing, physical exercise are considered the essential points of elementary education. Boys brought up in these schools are never morose. No power can keep them back from the service to their country, the sense of and responsibility towards the nation. Neither can anything develop in them feelings of hatred towards their own nation. Through the teaching of music patriotism and love of the nation are impressed upon the mind of the children- They are taught colour painting as soon as they learn the elements of drawing, needle-work and cookery. The minds of the pupils are not unnecessarily burdened with useless information. They are told the names, colours and numbers of flower, which is intended to teach them the distinction of colours, their names and also Arithmetic. The teacher places various things upon the table and enquires from the puplis their names, colours and number. In Europe, children have not to read at home after school hours. We think, and it is no doubt true, that the minds of the children, here, are stinted in growth under unnecessary burden. In Europe the number of subjects taught in primary schools is not less than what it is here, but (the method of teaching there is such) that it does not burden the minds of the student. The result is that after an instruction of 5 or 7 years, the child can use his hands, feet and brain to good advantage and he is in a position to adopt any profession he likes. The grounding in education that he has received stands him in good stead everywhere. On the other hand, we, too, receive theoretical education in Geometry, but in practice we are unable to draw a straight line correctly. An Englishman, who begins his education with drawing, can draw good pictures with the least effort. In Europe, in one place, a teacher lectures theoretically (say) upon the art of making a table and the things required for it, and in another place the children are afforded the opportunity of translating theory into practice by direct manipulation. After receiving this sort of elementary education up to the 14th year, they have to decide how they are to live in the world. The arrangements for this purpose are wonderful indeed, some boys study for 5 hours and spend the rest of their time in earning their livelihood. Facilities for high education are provided for those who wish to earn in the day and study at night; even the best equipped educational institution in India does not possess the aparatus, which every night school of the

London County Council possesses. There (in England) absence of pecuniary support does not invariably mean the loss of higher education. Here, on the contrary, those who are intelligent but poor have, after a time, to give up their education and find out means for their livelihood, thus hampering their advancement in life. This involves individual as well as national loss, and the nation is deprived of the valuable services which he would have rendered to the nation by occupying, in his after life, an eminent position. In Europe steps have been taken to avert this national and individual loss. The education they receive is, moreover, intended to make the recipients honest, high-minded, religious and patriotic and capable of earning their livelihood by honourable and industrious means. Some of the officals, here, frequently remark that Indians do not acpuire education for its own sake, but as a means of earning livelihood; but if such a remark were made in Europe, people would ask in amazement, what on earth is the object of education, if it is not to make one better able to earn a living?

A great struggle for supremacy is going on in Europe, every nation is trying to march ahead of the rest. Every nation fears that if her educational system becomes defective and consequently its members are superseded by others in sending the cheapest and the best things to the markets of the world, she will lose her position in the field of commerce. The chief object of their education is to keep their people abreast of the others in Commerce and Industry. The competition of Germany and America is at present threatening to weaken the commercial ascendancy of England. It is certain that the educational system of Germany is comparatively much superior (to that of any other country in Europe) but after careful investigation great changes have been introduced into the educational system of England within the last 5 or 6 years. Now every school in England possesses a workshop for practical training. The English are seriously thinking that they may not be beaten by the Germans in the race of commerce.

Paisa Akhbar, 13th December, 1905, (page 6).

The object of educating a child is that in addition to being useful to himself and to the society, he should develop partiotic ideas, inferior to those of no other nation. Europeans in general and the English in particular are dovoted admirers of Liberty. They cannot tolerate a single word directed against it. They hate the word *Ruler*. Although they have got their own King and Parliament yet they do not look upon them as more than advisers, helpers and leaders in national advancement. A recently published book, "Struggle Against the Monarchy," forms a part of the scheme of studies for young boys, which is intended to show that the rights of privilege which the English enjoy have been obtained after manifold sacrifices. It has been stated above, music is an essential part of their elementary training. Boys and girls assemble in the halls of the schools to sing such songs as to impress upon their minds the importance of the fact that the child is the custodian of national interest.

Here in India physical training is considered a thing of minor importance, there it is a part of the instruction.

The bodily organs are devoloped by means of physical exercises in such a way that in times of emergency they may be able to be put to the best use in the service of the State. Europeans regard this world as a paradise (*i. e.*, a place worth living in), being the finest specimen of the workmanship of the Almighty Creator. They want to live in this world seeing that it is so fine, and they think it their duty to prolong their lives as far as they can, no matter how. We also daily pray for a life of hundred years, but we regard the world as a place of misery, hence we can achieve little. Unless we look upon this world as a place of bliss we can never be prepared to make any sacrifices for the attainment of happiness. So long as we do not consider the world as the abode of eternal happiness, our nation can make no progress. Europeans impress upon the minds of their children that the world is vast and is full of happiness, hence they teach them to be prepared for all sorts of struggles that they shall have to undergo in their onward march. They point to the vast world before them and direct them to go and achieve honours for themselves and for their nation.

In Europe no mother cares what her son will do in his life. They love their children (as well as we) but they themselves realise and make their sons realise that just as this world is infinite so their courage should be vast and boundless. It is our duty, therefore, to absorb this spirit from Europe. Besides this, there they have established schools for imparting technical education. Our rulers here are showing signs of impatience at the establishment of four or five Universities and the number of boys educated therein, but in the West there exists a University in every big town, and still the Government there are not impatient at all and are not busy devising means for reducing the numbers of students. On the contrary, their chief anxiety is to improve and perfect their educational systems and to remove whatever defects exist therein. The Universities there are authorised to impart education in all departments of learning and confer degrees in Banking, Commerce and the various branches of industrial and technical education. The question for us is how can we do anything for ourselves (*i.e.*, can we help ourselves in any way)? If you really wish that your industries may improve and you be not dependent for your necessaries upon foreign countries, then you should prepare your youngmen for (the task.) It is fortunate that there are a number of schools here, but they are not sufficiently efficient for the purpose. It is necessary for us to send our youngmen to foreign countries. The men of means among you should send their children to other countries for receiving industrial training. Instead of leaving large sums of money and large quantity of gold for your children at the time of death, it is better that you should give them education of the kind which might enable them to earn their living wherever they may happen to be. The vast world is before you. If there are not sufficient manufactories in India to provide (appointments) for those who return after a technical course in foreign countries, then why not go and earn a living in (the factories of) other contries? In America Arabs, Japanese, Chinese and Austrians labour during the day and receive education at night. They are not anxious to calculate what work they shall have to do on return to their own country. He who knows an art need not be anxious about the capital to work his schemes with. Indians who go outside think that on their return others should start factories for them. But a trained man should not complain on that score. When I think of the day when there will be colonies of Indians in all parts of the world who will not only pray for India and the Indians, but at times of need render them assistance, I feel immense pleasure. If there be settled in other countries 500 Indians trained in any art, they can at any particular time fully meet at a minute's notice all our requirements with respect to particular art. If the Indians spread themselves into the whole world and learn various arts and industries then what is the thing which they will not be able to achieve? (For instance) what an important thing ship building is for all nations? Now, if there be Indians who have learnt the art of ship-building in the great-making factories of the world, they can be helpful to India, to a great extent, in meeting her nautical requirements.

A number of factories exist in the Punjab, but they are not showing satisfactory progress. (The reason is) that those who work these factories do not posses sufficient skill and efficiency for the purpose. If the proprietors of these factories combine and send a number of young men to other countries for industrial training, on condition of the latter working in these factories on their return then both the factories and the student will be benefited. Such young men should not be married persons. If they do not object (think it below their dignity) to labour, then nothing can stand in the way cf receiving neccessary training. In America even an unskilled labourer who has not received any Special training in any particuiar art or industry, gets at least $ 1-50 or Rs. 4-8 as daily wages. If a number of youngmen gird up their loins to receive technical education in other countries and support themselves thereby labour and if there be an organisation formed here to find passage money and preliminary expenses for them and to render them other assistance whenever they are ill or out of appointment, a great deal can be done in this direction. The test of our progress, our advancement, our prosperity, aye, our very existence, is *education.* Twenty years ago the Arya Samaj put forward Swadeshi and National education as the two tests of advancement in the National struggle, and *now* you find Bengal demonstrating practically that the programme which the Arya Samaj adopted in this respect was the right one. The scheme of the Dayanand College, which was framed, after long and careful consideration of the needs of the nation, and taking into account the direction in which events were marching in India (has been shown) to be correct. The ideal of educa-cation put forward by the founders of the Dayanand College is the same which Europe has now adopted. Japan says that we cannot live so long as we do not appeal to our souls, so long as we do not keep in view our past greatness and do not draw the attention of the people to the grandeur of our ancient literature and civilisation. I do not wish to follow blindly ancient civilisation. I have pondered over the question and I have come to the conclusion that the ancient civilisation of India was superior to the modern civilisation of Europe and if I were asked to express my opinion (about the two) I would unhesitatingly give it in favour of the former. But, my friends, it is not in our power to save ourselves from the influenee of modern Western civilisation. Western civilisation is a gigantic force and we cannot protect ourselves from its advancing march. We can struggle against this civilization by modern weapons alone. Ancient weapons cnnnot check its progress in the least. It is absolutely essential that we should brave it with Western methods and Western means. We are only a portion of the world, we do not live beyond the globe, (and) as such cannot live without taking into account the forces that are working in the world. It is, therefore, only meet and proper for us that, while saving ourselves from the vices that prevail in the West, we should adopt Western virtues. In short, in this struggle with Western civilization we can hardly make any progress without adopting the means and methods that are adopted in the West.

The education of females depends upon the education of males. A nation can never be great until its mothers are great also. Our country does not now produce noble women like the mothers of Jaimal, Fatta, and other Rajputs. In these days, we do not suck the same sort of nourishing and invigorating milk from the breasts of our mothers as our ancestors did from theirs. The path of progress is straight, but so long as our country does not possess high-souled and patriotic mothers no advancement can be made. What can the sons of those mothers who do not allow their children to stir outside the four-walls of their houses do, as compared with the sons of those highminded ladies who are not afraid even of the roarings of the oceans ? In Europe, women possess both virtues and vices ; (but) so is the case here. If we wish to make any progress we should try to get rid of the vices and retain the virtues (that are in them) and make the greatness of women the test of our national advancement. Come! Let us all try and make the Dayanand Anglo-Vedic School a model for all other schools. Let this school possess well-equipped apparatus, and wellpaid teachers. Let us all come and help the cause of the Dayanand Collge because it is the custodian of our honour. This institution is the centre of all our national activities for (eductiaonal) advancement. It is the life and soul of our existence as a nation. The Dayanand College is also the head and heart of the Punjab. If the head and heart get weak or palsied how can the body be expected to exist for any length of time ? This College is your own property. It can satisfy all your requirements. Others have no hand in its conduct and cannot interfere with it in any way.

I was extremely pleased to learn in England that the number of new admissions in the College this year has been larger than it was last year. The students have in this way given a practical reply to those who are bent upon ruining the College. The (students) have thus shown that the latter cannot succeed in this matter. If national progress is proceeding on the right line nobody has the power to stop its advance. We value greatly University degrees, and we all are helping our young men to obtain these degrees. But if insurmountable difficulties are placed in your way, in qualifying yourselves for those degrees then you may give out this craving for these degrees. The Dayanand Anglo-Vedic College is a national institution. If it is a question between University degrees and national honour, you should give up the former for the latter. I wish that the world be filled with young students for the Punjab. There is no other Province in India which can beat the Punjab in determination and intelligence. Those who possess these qualities (determination and intelligence) will prosper everywhere. Young men! step forward, spread over France, Germany, Japan and Canada, you will then see how the powers of the material world quake before you. Those who now despise us and trample us under their feet will then respect us. The wide world is before you, the Aryan blood runs in your veins. None can stop your progress. You are the descendents of persons who imparted knowledge to the whole world. (Have you fallen so low now that you are unfit even to learn at the feet of others? *Those among us, who marry their children at an early age and thus stun their development by putting a heavy load (of family life) round their necks, ruin their children entirely. Keep your children free (from these trammels) and let Aryan young men soar upon their wings,* (*i. e.*, grow to the full height of their manhood.) *Do not cut off their wings and like featherless birds, cause them to be trampled under feet by others.*

Gentlemen! May I appeal to you in the name of nationality? Alas, where is nationality? This congeries of sects holding different views cannot but be altogether wanting in the sentiment of nationality. Our kith and kin have become our enemies, while others (non-Hindus) are our friends. Our own (kith and kin) are despised by us, while others are worshipped ! Would that in spite of internecine quarrels we could show a united front to the outer (non-Hindu) world ! We shall realize the true meaning of nationality when in the name of 'nationality' we shall become one to face the antagonist. We have entirely lost, the virtue of national self-respect. The nation gave birth to Rama Bai, and Rama Bai has been declaring in America that no girl of 13 or 14 years of age can boast of her chastity in India ! But are there not many even in this assembly who are warm admirers of the same Rama Bai ? Had we possessed any sense of national honour, would it be possible for us to be crushed under the heels of others or to be exposed to such calumnies ? How can national honour be said to exist where 70 millions of the nation's children are found starving and where girls are made over to outsiders (Christian Missionaries and Mahomedans) to save them from starvation !

Ye youth of the Panjabee ! There is one thing alone in the name of which I can appeal to you, and, that is, that during the last twenty years [referring to the foundation of the D. A. V. College in 1886] you have shown signs of life [by contributing to its success], and I appeal to you in the name of that very life ! Come, let us spurn away all worldly desires and stick to our word. We should not leave undone what we have once taken in hand. A wave of national advancement (in education) has arisen in another province [referring to the Bengal Association for the Advancement of Scientific and Industrial Education.] There money is pouring in, young men are coming forward. Youngmen, your blood is warm. The national tree requires your life blood for its watering. Heaven has written in letters of blood the history of the intellectual advancement of a nation , *i. e.*, it has been ordained that a country can advance intellectually only if its members practise the virtue of self-sacrifice. Your sacrifices will leave their mark in the history of the world. Concrete is required to strengthen the foundations of a building. Let us throw ourselves like concrete into the foundations of the national edifice. Let us forget ourselves in the interests of national progress. Ye student of the Punjab! students have written the history of the world in letters of gold. Old men can never accomplish what young men can do. Come, let us crown our national institutions with the spires of the edifices of our sacrifices, so that a time may come when we may also take our place among the nations of the world. If the young gird up their loins, our existence is insured and no body can destroy us.

THE COMING INDIAN NATIONAL CONGRESS-SOME SUGGESTIONS.

The date fixed for the celebration of the annual national festival of the educated Indians is drawing near and it is, I think, time to spend a few hours and devote a few thoughts to its programme, and see if there is any possibility of some serious business being gone through at the next meeting, along with the usual festivities. I purposely call it a festival, because as hitherto conducted it is at best only a festival—an occasion on which some educated Indians put on their best dresses, take a trip to one of the best cities in India, and after a year's hard struggle in life enjoy a few days holiday, and derive the greatest pleasure they can from seeing sights, hearing sights, meeting friends, making acquaintances, exchanging greetings, purchasing presents etc, in short, giving themselves up as completely as circumstances, to mirth and meirrment. Some of them enjoy all the fun at the cost of others. There are others who make name and add to their fames if they are already on the ladder, by uttering plausibly worded platitudes and well-disguised commonplaces in the shape of speeches. Even the last are losing their charm, as platitudes have become too common, and the commonplaces too apparent, to delude any longer people who are possessed of even ordinary intelligence and share a little at least, of common sense. I do not know if the Anglo-Indians are much to be blamed, if they judge the prosperity of British India, by the appearance and evidently rich surroundings of the Congress. The delegates mostly look well-to-do people who can spare enough money for taste, elegance and show. The decorations, receptions, furnishings, etc. are done on a scale which can hardly lend weight to our contention of being perhaps the poorest people on the face of the globe. These so-called political work done after all this fuss is of such a doubtful and ephemeral character as to raise serious doubts in the minds of even enthusiasts. Whether we are not frittering away our energies in trifles and, besides wasting away our own time and money, keeping the nation in delusion and under false hopes

I am not prepared to deny that as a festival alone the annual meeting is not without its value and should not therefore be altogether given up. Let me assure you, my brothren of the congress that by saying these unpleasant things, I mean no offence to any body. I am one of you, and all that I have said above applies to me with equal, perhaps greater force than to any body else. Nor do I mean there are no exceptions. There are honourable and good men amongst us who can be truly called patriots but their number is so small that I will prefer to make no exception. The truth is that till now, we have not realised the full significance of this "partriotism." We have been taking it easy, and never realised in our heart of hearts that patriotism is a cult requiring the most rigid and ascetic course of life from its devoties. It is only one degree lower than the absolute self-denial of a Sanyasi. What I am anxious for is to see, if it is not possible to achieve better and more laudable results and from this annual gathering of the best and most intelligent of the educated Indians. As at present conducted its principal defects are:—

(I) Its unwieldy size which precludes the very idea of serious work whether in shape of deliberations, discussion or action.

(2) The anxiety to speak in the name of all Indians, a good many of whom think otherwise, and repudiate all sympathy with it. This attempt at forced union is mostly at the bottom of the discontent which at present prevails even amongst those who have all along supported it, and who think that till now the congress

agitation has been a mere waste of energies, funds and opportunities.

(3) The want of sense of real responsibility amongst its members which results in total inactivity during the course of the year.

(4) The failure to afford the opportunity of comparing notes and exchanging views, by which the unity of the nation or at least of its principal components, may be really furthered and definite progress in this direction may lead to more exertion towards the same end.

This is mainly due to the mismanagement of the short time that is at the disposal of the delegates, owing to the lengthy programme of speeches and resolutions etc.

(5) Failure to take some practical steps to check the growing poverty of the country and to dispel ignorance which is still the crying need of India.

(6) Its unbounded but unreasonably mistaken confidence in its power to enforce the redress of the grievences, to extort political privilege by the passing of Resolutions and the making of speeches, which result in misleading the nation to place unjustifiable faith in the over-efficacy of the Congress agitation, and fails to impress upon them the necessity of a stupendous preparation attended with great sacrifices and mighty efforts before even one step can be gained in the ascent to political progress. The temple of freedom is not easily opened into those who claim admission into it by simply knocking at its gates. Mere aspiration is no guarantee of success. The intending worshipper or claimant for admission must show his mental by sacrifices and trials before he can obtain to the

states of a pilgrim, because the goddess of liberty is so jealous of its sanctity that it would admit none but tried of unquestionable sincerity, devotion and faith.

I will stop for the present and suggest remedies which in my opinion are calculated to remove the defects and which might be considered by Congressmen, before they meet at Calcutta, and then adopt or reject them with such modifications or alterations as to them seem desirable.

Under clause (1) :—I will suggest that the sitting of the general assembly be shortened as much as may be possible to do, at once. In no case should it exceed two days with a maximum sitting of 5 hours every day at the most. The programme might be something as follows :—

(*a*) Welcome by the chairman of the reception committee who will in it produce the president elect as the nominee of the Indian National Congress committee.

(*b*) Speech of the President.

(*c*) Omnibus resolution including all matters and subject upon which the Congress has, by the end of the preceeding year, pronounced definite views and upon which public opinion in this country is practically settled.

(*d*) Resolutions upon new subjects that have cropped up during the course of the year, on which the Indian Congress committee have recommended for inclusion in the Congress programme, and upon which there is a practical unanimity of opening between Indians of all classes, creeds, shades of opinion.

(*e*) Such other subjects recommended by the Indian Congress committee upon which there is a likelihood of a difference of opinion.

In the general assembly no speaker, whether the proposer or the supporter, should be allowed to exceed the limits of 10 or 15 minutes respectively except the chairman of the Reception Committee, the President or the proposer of the resolution or amendment falling under clasue (e).

This will leave the different committees, sub-committees and other special conferences, already organised or to be organised sufficient time to devote to serious work requiring discussion and deliberation; as, for example, the Indian Congress committee should every session devote at least some hours to the question of starting political organisation in places where there are none, and perfecting those where they already exist 2ndly, the education committee and 3rdly, the industrial committee. With the work of these two latter we will deal under clause (5). Under clause (2) I will suggest (a) total discontinuence of all such practices as are, if at all, adopted, encouraged or connived at to bring in such people to the congress as are otherwise either not eligible for its membership, or do not possess sufficient interest therein, or are of no use to it, except in increasing the number of delegates from a particular class. It should be the business and duty of every congressman to jealously maintain the honor, the dignity and the prestige of the congress, and nothing should be allowed or encouraged which has even the least semblance of being dishonourable, undignified, or likely to lower its reputation or to lessen its sense of self-respect.

(b) The number of subjects upon which there is any likelihood of a reasonable friction existing, or coming into existence, between members belonging to the different religious nationalities in India, ought to be reduced to a minimum, if there is still any room for the same, in the agenda paper of the general assembly, such subject being reserved for separate treatment by the inclusive organisations of these nationalities. This will lead to the necessity of a Hindu political or a semi-political congress or conference being organised, and the sooner it is done the better. As at present situated the absence of such an organisation places the Hindu at distinct disadvantage, and takes away from them, the chances of a united action or of a united expression of opinion upon matters, which affect the unity, prosperity the well-being and generally the interest of Hindu all over India. In order to leave no room for doubt as to the necessity for this step I will be more specific. In my opinion it should be the business of such a Hindu Congress or conference to support and take, as far as possible, such steps which might conduce to their unity and strength as a religious nationality, as for instance, the language question, the question of characters, the advisability of having common Text-books, the teaching of Sanskrit language and literature all over India, the taking of steps which might lead to the protection of Hindu orphans from the hands of the proselytising agencies of other denominations and if necessary to record a protest against those confidential circulars of the Government, which aim at the favouring of other communities to the loss of the Hindus. In my humble opinion it is futile to attempt at a chimerical and premature union of the various religious nationalities that are to be found in India, the principal of which are Hindus, the Mahomedans and the Christians. The wisest course will be to wait for a physical union and to aim at the same. This is impossible to achieve till these nationalities have had a free hand to strengthen themselves, and to exhaust all means by which they can do so at the cost of other or others. A physical union presupposes a common danger and a conviction that they cannot overcome it or meet it but by uniting and combining against a common foe. At present this conviction is wanting, and there is still lurking in the mind of at least one community, that they can crush out the other or the others. So long as one community looks the other down and talks of it with contempt, it is ridiculous, nay suicidal, for the latter to try to force a union and make advances which are liable to be misconstrued, as the outcome of fear or of expediency, or of treachery. I quite agree with a talented writer in the *Kayastha Samachar* that the springing up of so many castes or conferences against the Hindus is a menace to the development of the idea of Hindu nationality and might lead to harm. He has, I think, done a distinct service to the cause of Hindu nationality by giving public expressions to an idea, which has been causing a serious anxiety to many a lover of the idea of Hindu nationality or to many a Hindu Nationalist. It is time that the leaders and promoters of these conferences take notes of the warning so judiciously given—not to destroy the fabrics which they have constructed, but to so mould and guide them as to make them instrumental in the eventful construction and building up of a Hindu Nationality. Theirs should be the attempt to destroy the sub-castes, to bring about a fusion of the different sub-divisions in a caste and to eventually bring round Hinduism to its four original castes. There will be ample time then to think and talk of the evils of the caste system, and of modification in the latter, to suit the requirements of the times. Then the conferences can be used to spread education amongst the backward classes and to bring them to the level of the times, but their promoters ought to proceed very carefully, lest in their efforts to unite the sub-divisions of a caste they might be creating permanent schisms between the different main castes, and be creating barriers amongst them, impeding the fructification and the realization of Hindu nationality. It is therefore far immature and far before the time, to talk of intermarriages between the different castes of Hindus, as it is futile to think of bringing about a complete political union of Hindus and Mohamedans at once.

The Mohamedans think that the Hindus are physically inferior to them, and wanting in certain qualities —energy, pluck, boldness, fearlessness, stamina of character, capacity to command and ability to make a stand—which go to make a good, effective and capable administrator. But, in short, the Mohamedans think that they belong to a race of rulers, and their fellow-subjects, the Hindu, having been in slavery so long, cannot claim an equality with them in the scale of nations. Even the otherwise amiable Sir Syed talked of Hindus with contempt. The result is that every Mohamadan, be he a *julaha* or a *Penya* or the like, thinks that he can dominate over the Hindus and claim a superiority over them in the art of governing. The latter, on the other hand, retort, that, as a nation they have never displayed cowardliness, always proving equal to the occasion whenever necessity forced them to take up arms and assert their dignity as men, as is abundantly evident from the history of the Rajputs, the Sikhs and the Mahrattas, and that the physical inferiority of certain of their sections, even if admitted, is so much counter-balanced by their intellectual and moral superiority over their rivals that in this age of science of Art, they think they are sure to win the race and acquire qualification which alone can confer a political status in these days of learning and knowledge.

This is not the occasion to discuss how far these claims are well-founded, but it is a fact that a large class of educated Mohamedans keep aloof from the Hindus and suspect their organisations and agitations as likely to prejudice them in the race for progress and advancement. They think they have better chances of political prosperity as a separate nationality and in keeping aloof from the majority who are Hindus. There are a good many far-seeing men amongst them who can read the signs of the times and think that this game wont pay but the number, on the other hand, is preponderant, because in the case of the leaders especially and of other newly-educated young Mohamedans generally, personal benefit which follows this line of policy lends great weight to the other arguments and considerations by which their present political attitude aspires to be actuated. All welcome therefore to those who are prepared to foresee the future and join with the Hindus in the struggle for political rights. Let therefore there be a general assembly which can voice the joint aspirations of such Hindus, Mahomedans and Christians by all means, but let not this general assembly stand in the way of Hindu progress and in the name of a higher, though at present impracticable, impulse, lull them to sleep over their interests as such, make them forego the opportunities of furthering their own unity *inter se*, and neglect the placing of it on a firm, sound and unassailable basis. Once wisely led, no power in the world can stand in their way, retard their progress and stifle their aspirations. The Hindus have existed as a nation since times to which the memory of man runneth not, in weal or woe they have maintained their individual existence and have from time to time, given to the world lessons in religion and morality, which even to-day when the sun of European civilization is at its zenith, shine in the splendour of their purity and in the grandeur of their truth. Are they then to die as a nation in this twentieth century of the Bikram Era. True that just now we are in a very sad plight and if judged by the national vices that have crept into our society, and by their national weakness which are too numerous to be mentioned here, the last ray of hope often disappears and turns the most hopeful optimist into a disappointed pessimist. It is only in unity that the safety of the Hindu lies. No wise or prudent Hindu can therefore neglect the opportunities of seeking the safety. Let them once make up their mind to be a united nation and to continue as such. Let them once be inspired by a living faith in their future, and by a conviction that when God has willed the individuality of a nation and given it a mission to perform. He has at the same time given the people constituting that nation means, power, and capacity, by which they can successively resist all those forces which tend to disintegrate or disorganise them, and which trace their existence as a nation.

True that our selfishness and estrangement from national interests is simply indescribable. There have been and there are Hindus who have now and then sold the nation and its interests to the enemy, and aggrandised themselves at the cost of the former, still to a close and thoughtful observer who can feel the pulse of the nation and who has a mind and capacity to read the signs of the time, enough of life and vitality seems yet to be left in Hindustan, to enable the latter to respond to skillful treatment and kind and devoted nursing. Skill and devotion must therefore be put forth for this purpose by the whole Hindu community or at least by the thinking portion of it. It is on these grounds therefore that I suggest the formation of a Hindu congress or conference to meet annually at the place of the congress, and to discuss only such matters and devise such measures as are likely to further the cause of Hindu Unity and otherwise tend to the well-being and prosperity of the Hindus as such. Of course such an assembly should only consist of not a very large number of men, say 100 of the best and the most representative of Hindus. One word about the social conference. Indian social conference as at present constituted is no more a Hindu organization than the Congress. You might as well call the latter also a Hindu Congress. It is as powerless to do anything for the Hindus exclusively as the latter. In the anxiety to give it a national character the Mahomedans and Christians have been allowed to take part in its deliberations, and resolutions have been altered and weakened, nay rendered meaningless, in the attempt to make them acceptable to all. Here again Hindu interest, as such, have been sacrificed for a false idea of nationality and in the attempt to achieve it at once. For example, what on earth have the Christians and Mohamadans to do with the *Shuddhi* movement. The Shuddhi movement, which aims at the purification and readmission of all Hindu apostates is a purely Hindu movement, in which the Hindus alone are interested, the same may be said, of the resolution dealing with orphans. At the last conference both these resolutions had to be modified into vague generalities which deprived the proposition of much of their force and effect, and rendered them incapable of producing any impression either on the public or on the government. Then the conference is a gathering and an assembly of the advanced Hindus and does not represent the orthodox portion of the community who are still in an overwhelming majority over their English educated brothers. Then again, the conference, as at present constituted, cannot ventilate the grievances of the Hindus and is not in a position to speak for them. Hence the necessity of a general Hindu organisation with its provincial branches all over India. The functions and constitution of the provincial branches will be similar to those of the many Islamic anjumans already existing in the country without criticising the policy of the Government in the abstract, without passing resolutions on abstract political propositions, these Hindu organisations will confine themselves to concrete objects and tangible grievances. As such, the country will not be deprived of the valuable assistance which it can get from the co-operation of those Hindus who are in the employ of government and who in fact constitute the pick and the cream of the nation. I have been rather too long on this part of the subject but the importance of the point necessitated a full expression of my views. Thereupon clause (2) requires no further comments.

Under clause (3) :— I will suggest that only responsible and really working men should be selected as members of the Indian congress committee. Men whose interest in the movement is confined to annual visits ought not to find a place on this committee. One of the best methods of testing one's earnestness in a particular cause is to see if he is prepared to spend his money for the same. I will therefore repeat the proposal that was made at the last meeting of the congress at Lahore by one of the Punjabi delegates, and which was unceremoniously dismissed at the general meeting and ridiculed in the meeting of the subjects committee by two of our *revered* leaders that every member of the Indian Congress committee should be required to pay at least 5 Rs. a month towards the funds of the congress. The Provincial committees, moreover, ought to see that only such men are placed on this committee who take a real interest in the Political Reform Movement, and who are prepared to undergo some amount of sacrifice, in the cause of the country's political progress. Members who fail to attend even one meeting in the course of the year ought to be disqualified for re-election. Clause (4) does not require any further comment. The remedies suggested under clause (1) will remove this complaint.

Under clause (5) :—I will suggest, that the least that should be undertaken at once, is the employment of a paid officer whose business should be to go round and collect information on both these heads. I am glad to find that the Indian congress committee have decided to pass a Resolution whereby it is proposed to ask the Government to undertake an industrial survey of the country. This is a right move, no doubt, but the mere passing of the resolution does not advance us one inch in the cause which we have at heart. In my opinion we ought to be prepared to give a more substantial proof of our earnestness by voting a certain amount of money to be spent in the coming year, by ourselves on the object in question. One year's experience will give us sufficient ground to judge of the usefulness of the project and will strengthen our demand. I am afraid I have already exceeded the limits of an ordinary article and must stop here for the present.

LAJPAT RAI.

---o---

ARE THE DEPORTATIONS LEGAL ?

The following is published in *Justice*, London, from the pen of an Indian :—

LEGAL ASPECT.

In considering the legal aspect of the deportations I propose to discuss the question under two heads—

(1) Whether deportation is legal or illegal. In putting this part of the case before your readers I will assume the legality of the Regulation under which the two gentlemen are deported. I may say by the way, however, that the question whether the Regulation is *ultra vires* or not is undoubtedly a very important one and requires to be carefully considered, discussed and thoroughly threshed out. (2) If the deportation is illegal, whether there is any tribunal (*a*) in India or (*b*) in England, legally authorised to entertain, hear and finally determine an application if one is made on behalf of the sufferers.

As to (1) the second clause of Section 2 of the Regulation in question gives the form of the warrant, and the third clause enacts that the warrant of commitment shall be sufficient authority for the detention of any State prisoner in any fort, gaol, or other place within the "territory subject to the presidency of Fort William." Then we come to the Punjab Act II of 1872, which extends the application of this Regulation to the "Punjab," and if we read the Punjab in the place of the "territories subject to the presidency of Fort William," then the persons in the Punjab could be kept in confinement only in some place within the limits of the Punjab. This is the only possible interpretation of the Regulation and the Act read together, and consequently the detention of Messrs. Lajpat Rai and Ajit Singh outside the Punjab is clearly illegal.

The Regulation III of 1818 is, be it noted, repealed in part by Act XVI of 1874 amended by Act XII of 1891, and supplemented by Acts XIV of 1850 and III, of 1858

A drowning man, it is said, catches at a straw, and accordingly, the Government of India will, I am sure, try to rely on the last named Act (III of 1858) in justification of their action. Section 5 runs as follows.

"The Governor-General in Council may order the removal of any State prisoner confined under the provisions of any of the said regulations as amended and extended by this Act from any fortress or gaol or place in which he may be confined within either of the said Presidencies to any other fortress, gaol or place of confinement within the territories under the Government of India." I submit that neither the Act nor the particular section has any application to the present case for the following reasons :

(1) That the Act is only applicable to cases of persons belonging to a place within the Presidencies of Bengal, Madras, or Bombay, to none of which, either of the two gentlemen belongs, and (2) that the section in question empowers the Governor-General in Council the removal of a State prisoner who is in the first instance confined in any fort, gaol or place of confinement within the territories under the Government of India. The section gives no power to the Governor-General in Council to confine, in the first instance, a person dealt with under the said Regulation in any place outside the three Presidencies.

For these reasons and apart from the question of the inherent illegality of the Regulation itself as well as apart from the question of the insufficiency of the grounds on which the powers given by the Regulation are to be exercised, I hold that the detention of these two gentlemen is *ab initio* illegal. Let us now turn our attention to the second question.

(a) As regards courts in India the position is this; the Supreme Court was invested with jurisdiction to issue writs of habeas corpus by charter of the year 1774. The jurisdiction was of a very limited character and was allowed only in cases where a person within the local limits of the ordinary jurisdiction of the Court, or a British European subject without those limits, alleged wrongful confinement.

Under the old Criminal Procedure Code (1872), this writ was issued by the High Courts of Calcutta, Madras and Bombay: Section 82 of that code having empowered them to do so. But such powers now no longer obtain. Section 82 is replaced by section 491 (1) of the Code of Criminal Procedure of 1882 which provides that the three High Courts of Calcutta, Madras and Bombay may, whether they think it, issue, not the writ of habeas corpus itself, but directions in the nature of such writ. I may be permitted to set out in full the whole section in view of the fact that some of the English newspapers are very fond of indulging in isolated phrases and commenting on them (at least as regards matters Indian).

CHAPTER XXXVII.

Directions in the nature of the Habeas Corpus.

Section 491 (1): Any of the High Courts of Judicature at Fort William, Madras and Bombay may, whenever it thinks fit, direct powers to issue directions in the nature of habeas corpus.

(*a*) That a person within the limits of its ordinary

original civil jurisdiction be brought up before the court to be dealt with according to law ;

(*b*) That a person illegally or improperly detained in public or private custody be set at liberty ;

(*c*) That a prisoner detained in any gaol situated within such limits be brought before the court to be there examined as a witness in any matter pending, or to be inquired into in such court ;

(*d*) That a prisoner detained as aforesaid be brought before a court martial or any commissioners acting under the authority of any commission from the Governor-General in Council for trial or to be examined touching any matter before pending such court martial or commissioners respectively.

(*e*) That a prisoner within such limits be removed from one custody to another for the purpose of trial: and,

(f) That the body of the defendant be brought in on the sherif's return of *cepi-corpus* to a writ of attachment ;

(2) Each of the said high courts may from time to time make rules to regulate the procedure in cases under this section.

(3) Nothing in this section applies to persons detained under the Bengal State Prisoners Regulation II of 1819, Bombay Regulation XXV, of 1827, or the State Prisoners Act 1850, or State Prisoners Act 1858.

The section is clear. Under its provisions (I) no writ of habeas corpus properly so-called can be issued; (2) even the directions in the nature of habeas corpus are allowed to be issued only in cases of persons within the ordinary original civil jurisdiction of the particular high court, but (3) the most significant part of the section is put at the end and it expressely excepts the Regulation III of 1818 under which the deportation has been ordered: and (4) the section does not apply to the Punjab whence the two gentlemen were taken, nor to places where they are kept in confinement. Thus no courts in India have any authority to hear any application to enlarge these gentlemen.

As regards courts in England the fundamental principle of the English constitution denoted by the various phrases "right of personel security" "liberty of persons" "liberty of the subject" which is the essential part of the common law of England and which is defined and declared though in no sense originated by Magna Charta and a number of statutes affirming that enactment, is effectively protected by the common law writ of habeas corpus I will make a passing reference to two of these statutes.

(1) Habeas Corpus Act 1678. It is entitled "An Act for the better securing of liberty of the subject and for the prevention of imprisonment beyond the seas.

(2) Habeas Corpus 1816 which is entitled "An Act for more effectually securing the liberty of the subject" Under this Act amongst other things, judges are empowered to examine and determine the truth of the facts set forth in the return and in all cases of doubt to bail the prisoner I mention this particularly, as I am, whilst writing this, put in mind of the most evasive and annoying way in which Mr. Morley has been answering the questious put to him by Sir Henry Cotton and other

members of the House regarding his information as to the alleged connection of Lala Lajpat Rai with Ajit Singh of the so-called seditious speeches and I wonder if the matter is at all brought before the court empowered to examine and determine the truth of the facts whether it will not be "injudicious" and "entirely adverse to public interest" for Mr. Morley to open his heart there.

After this Act and in the year 1861, in the matter of John Anderson, a very important decision was given by the Court of Queen's Bench. In that case a writ of habeas corpus was issued to a gaoler in Upper Canada. In the course of the judgment the court said :—

"We are quite sensible that it may be felt to be inconsistent with that higher degree of Colonial independence, both legislative and judicial, which has happily been carried into effect in modern times ; at the same time it is observed that in establishing local legislation and local judicial authority the Legislature has not gone so far as expressly to abrogate any jurisdiction which the courts in Westminster Hall might possess with reference to the issuing of a writ of habeas corpus into any part of Her Majesty's dominions. The writ of habeas corpus has been issued even into dominions of the Crown in which there were local judicatures and local legislatures. Hence we feel that nothing short of legislative enactment depriving this court of such a jurisdiction would warrant us in omitting to exercise it when we are called upon to do so for the protection of the personal liberty of the subject." This led to the passing of the Statute 25 and 26 Vict., chap. 20. This Statute has partially restricted the common law jurisdiction vested in Courts of issuing this prerogative writ of habeas corpus, which is supposed to issue on the part of the King, and which, therefore, runs into any part of the King's dominions. The title to the statute is "Act respecting the issue of writs of habeas cropus out of England into Her Majesty's possessions abroad" The sections run :—

(1) No writ of habeas corpus shall issue out of England by the authority of any judge or Court of Justice herein into any colony or foreign dominion of the Crown where Her Majesty has a lawfully-established Court or Courts having authority to grant and issue the said writ and to ensure the due execution thereof throughout such colony or dominion.

(2) Provided that nothing in this Act contained shall affect or interfere with any right of appeal to Her Majesty in Council now by law existing.

In construing this statute you will excuse me if I take you back to my observations in the first part of this letter wherein I have made it clear that there is no court in British India authorised to grant and issue the writ of habeas corpus (as it is understood in this country) and to ensure the due execution thereof: that section 161 of the present Criminal Procedure Code allows the issue of the directions in the nature of habeas corpus by the High Courts of Calcutta, Madras, and Bombay: that this limited jurisdiction is again further restricted by the section to cases of persons within the ordinary civil jurisdiction of the respective high courts that even this limited and restricted jurisdiction did not and does not obtain either in the Punjab or in Burma the two places with which we are at present concerned and lastly that proviso at the end of the section takes away in one breath what the section gives in another by enacting that persons detained under Regulation III of 1818 have no right to appeal under this section.

In this state of the law I have no doubt that the prerogative writ of habeas corpus in vogue in England still runs in all parts of British India for the reasons given above, with much more force in the Punjab and in Burma.

I may add, in conclusion, that any one has a right to move the proper tribunal in England for the issue of such a writ and venture therefore to express the hope that my countrymen will give the question their most serious attention and careful consideration and organise a campaign to take the necessary steps to regain the liberty of the two gentlemen so ruthlessly taken away by the monstrously illegal and inhuman action on the part of the despotic and irresponsible Government which knows no constitution, recognises no limits to its powers and no apology to offer for any thing that it does.

VANDE MATARAM.

---o---